· *Gentlemen and Freeholders* ·

Early America

History, Context, Culture

Jack P. Greene and J. R. Pole
Series Editors

Gentlemen

and

Freeholders

*Electoral Politics in
Colonial Virginia*

John Gilman Kolp

The Johns Hopkins University Press
Baltimore and London

© 1998 The Johns Hopkins University Press
All rights reserved. Published 1998
Printed in the United States of America
on acid-free paper
9 8 7 6 5 4 3 2 1

The Johns Hopkins University Press
2715 North Charles Street
Baltimore, Maryland 21218-4363
The Johns Hopkins Press Ltd., London
www.press.jhu.edu

Library of Congress Cataloging-in-Publication Data
will be found at the end of this book.
A catalog record for this book is available
from the British Library.

ISBN 0-8018-5843-7

For the family
Liesl, Marc, Mark, Ande,
Ian, Johnathan, and
especially Ruth

Contents

Preface and
Acknowledgments

This book seeks to understand the process of selecting representatives to the Virginia House of Burgesses—"the flame of burgessing," as one contemporary called it—and the hundreds of citizens in each of Virginia's political communities who took part. The actors in this eighteenth-century drama include candidates and voters, incumbents and challengers, justices and vestrymen, big planters and small farmers, landowners and tenants, and the enfranchised and disfranchised.

While this cast of characters operated within a broadly defined political culture and a specific body of electoral law, each performance of the electoral play had a different plot and a different ending. Every county and borough of the Old Dominion offered a unique stage and a unique backdrop defined by local personalities and problems and shared regional, provincial, and imperial influences. Specific regions within the colony amplified certain features of the political culture and deemphasized others. New counties moved through developmental cycles that combined patterns inherited from older regions with the geographic and demographic features of the new area. Long-established communities experienced less dramatic change, but nonetheless their political cultures also reflected evolving local issues as well as occasional outside influences.

A thorough understanding of this dynamic and diverse political culture necessitates a two-pronged attack, one at the provincial level and one at the local level. Part 1 examines the entire set of legal, procedural, demographic, and behavioral parameters within which Virginians elected members of the House of Burgesses. The goals here are comprehensive and comparative. The first two chapters suggest how the development and application of colonial law governing elections allowed a wide range of campaign practices and procedures to evolve, while unique demographic, settlement, and economic patterns combined with these laws to produce local electorates of widely varying size and composition. The third chapter investigates comparatively how the intersection of these electorates with local, regional, provincial, and imperial developments resulted in a dynamic political culture in which electoral competition was uniform neither over time nor space.

Part 2 exposes the actual workings of this varied political culture through detailed case studies of four local political communities. These communities should not be thought of as representative, in the normative use of that term, but rather they speak to the different ways candidates, voters, and local issues and problems meshed over an extended time period in four very different places. The case studies proceed geographically from east to west and chronological from oldest to newest: Accomack and Lancaster became separate counties in the middle of the seventeenth century, while Fairfax and Halifax emerged in the mid-eighteenth century. Each community also allows us to study a unique set of geographic, economic, and demographic circumstances within which local elites and voters responded to developing local political concerns and provincial and imperial developments. The search for responsible authority and local governance in Accomack, the long-standing parish divisions of Lancaster, the developing political consensus in Fairfax, and the unabating contentiousness of Halifax all speak to the variety of political communities possible within the single political culture of colonial Virginia.

This study sputtered to life nearly twenty years ago as a doctoral dissertation at the University of Iowa, and I incurred many debts in that formative stage. Initial encouragement came from Lynne Withey, Marc Baer, Peter Taylor, and Andrew Federer, who shared with me their ideas on early modern history, political communities, social structure, and electoral analysis. A dissertation research grant from the National Science Foundation (SES 83-11781) provided needed funds for travel, photoduplication, and technical support at a crucial stage in the project. Linda K. Kerber and the late Sydney V. James guided the dissertation to completion and helped to improve it immeasurably.

Richard Beeman and Norman Risjord read the completed thesis and encouraged me to pursue publication. Robert Brugger of Johns Hopkins University Press first suggested building a book around the dissertation and has been exceptionally patient as I slowly expanded, revised, edited, and reedited the resulting manuscript. An early anonymous reviewer also saw the kernel of something better within an immature manuscript and suggested numerous ways it could be improved. Although the suggestion that I undertake a fourth case study added nearly two years to the project, the resulting chapter on Accomack offers a final and crucial example of the workings of local politics and colonial neighborhoods. Comments received at a colloquium at the Institute of Early American History and Culture in 1991 sparked important revisions to chapter 7; suggestions by John Hemphill II were particularly important. Continuing encouragement from Linda Kerber has been especially appreciated.

A series of grants from the U.S. Naval Academy Research Council allowed me to devote several entire summers to these additions and revisions. I have benefited enormously from my affiliation with the USNA History Department, where an incredibly stimulating teaching and research environment encourages specialists to share knowledge and ideas. The department's works-in-progress seminars and specific comments by colleagues William Roberts, Mary DeCredico, and Thomas Brennan have also been of great help.

The staffs of the Virginia Historical Society, the Virginia State Library, the University of Virginia Library, the Research Center of the Colonial Williamsburg Foundation, the Huntington Library, the Latter Day Saints Genealogical Library, the Iowa State Historical Society, the University of Iowa Library, and the Nimitz Library of the U.S. Naval Academy were exceptionally helpful.

Ultimately, this project would have been impossible without the extraordinary support of Ruth Kolp. Her willingness to act as a research associate in archives and libraries doubled the productivity of numerous trips to the Old Dominion, and her continual encouragement has kept the project from faltering.

Parts of the introduction and chapter 3 appeared previously in "The Dynamics of Electoral Competition in Pre-Revolutionary Virginia," *William and Mary Quarterly*, 3d series, 44 (1992): 652–74, and are used here with permission.

A Pole of Freeholders for Electing of Burgesses in Essex County Taken by Thomas Boulware for Simon Miller Gent Sheriff of said County the 1st Day of Decr. 1755

Candidate	Candidate	Candidate	Candidate
Capt. James Garnett	Mr. John Upsham	Col. Wm. Daingerfields	Col. Francis Smith
Willm. Boulware	1 Willm. Boulware	1 William Covington	1 William Covington 1
Joseph Crop	2 Joseph Crop	2 Greensby Evans	2 Greensby Evans 2
Saml. Hopkins	3 Saml. Hopkins	3 Joseph Sanders	3 Joseph Sanders 3
Francis Waring	4 John Waring	4 John Brizendine	4 John Brizendine 4
James Colquitt	5 James Colquitt	5 John Tayloe	5 John Tayloe 5
James Rennolds	6 James Rennolds	6 Leonard Hill	6 Leonard Hill 6
Richard Holt	7 Richard Holt	7 William Beverly	7 William Beverly 7
John Powell	8 Henry Ball	8 James Medly Senr.	8 James Medly Senr. 8
Henry Ball	9 James Clark	9 Edward Beamer	9 Edward Beamer 9
William Brooke	10 Isaac Gatewood	10 Augustin Owen	10 Augustin Owen 10
James Gray	11 Henry Woolbanks	11 William Lowry	11 William Lowry 11
James Clark	12 Mark Ball	12 Francis Waring	12 John Lowry 12
Isaac Gatewood	13 John Covington	13 Willm. Montague	13 Willm. Montague 13
Henry Woolbanks	14 James Upsham	14 Thos. Howerton	14 Thos. Howerton 14
Mark Ball	15 John Smither	15 John Booton	15 John Booton 15
John Covington	16 John Motley	16 William Brooke	16 William Beal 16
James Upsham	17 John Dix	17 James Gray	17 Paul Micou 17
John Smither	18 Abner Ball	18 William Beal	18 Richard Tayler 18

Essex County Pollbook, 1755

Essex County Deed Book 27 (Richmond: Virginia State Library)

· *Gentlemen and Freeholders* ·

Introduction

Gentlemen and Freeholders

One hundred years ago, a New England historian discovered in the records of colonial Virginia a peculiar set of documents called *pollbooks*.[1] Frequently found in county deed and record books and occasionally in private papers, pollbooks report the voting behavior of individual adult white male freeholders in elections for the provincial legislative assembly, the House of Burgesses. They not only include a listing by name of all persons voting for each candidate but also the total votes often appear at the bottom followed by the signatures of the county sheriff and clerk attesting to the document's accuracy and authenticity. Concentrated in the fifty-year period before the American Revolution, these surviving colonial pollbooks have long puzzled historians, for it has never been perfectly clear what they reveal about the political culture of this critical era in Virginia's and America's past.

To those writing a century ago, these lengthy voting lists documented democratic practices and representative institutions many decades before Jefferson and Madison extolled the virtues of republican government. As late-nineteenth-century historians scanned column after column of names taken down in the 1740s or 1750s, it became clear to them that "the people of Virginia and not the people of Massachusetts or New England are entitled to the credit of establishing true Republican methods of thought and manners in the United States."[2] The tobacco plantation of the Chesapeake, not the much-revered New England village, was the birthplace of American democracy.

Yet as tantalizing, appealing, and truly American as this interpretation seemed at the time, most twentieth-century historians

have found it difficult to square such evidence of popular sovereignty—these pollbooks—with the traditional interpretation of
southern gentry culture. Wealthy planters with their stately homes,
fine clothes, handsome coaches, slave quarters, and genuine belief
in rule by "Gentlemen of Ability and Fortune" appeared an unlikely group to place political power and their own political fortunes entirely in the hands of several hundred ordinary farmers.[3] After all,
these gentlemen won nearly every election and seemed to pass their
seats in the House of Burgesses from father to son and from brother
to brother. Clearly, the voters mattered little. Or did they? Somehow, a system of broad popular participation, as evidenced by these
pollbooks, upheld and directly supported the long-standing hege-
mony of the Virginia gentry. Gentlemen ruled over common freeholders, while freeholders kept gentlemen in office. How did it
work?

Our search for answers begins in the capital of Williamsburg,
where the legal, structural, and cultural definitions of politics took
shape, but it soon wanders into the countryside, where a broad set
of provincial parameters confronted ever-changing local conditions
and traditions. Here, along the rivers, creeks, and tidal inlets, com-
plicated patterns of association spiraled outward from family to kinship group to neighborhood to precinct to parish and, finally, to
county. Although the social and economic importance of these "cir-
cles" has been amply demonstrated, the political role of these rural
"webs of association" remains obscure.[4] Pollbooks and a variety of
other documents open up to us this distant rural Chesapeake world.
They improve our understanding of the political dimensions of
neighborhood, parish, and county and the critical role that elections
often played in the public culture of Britain's most populous North
American colony during the middle decades of the eighteenth century.

These critical years from the late 1720s to the 1770s represent the
end point of a long maturation process for Virginia's political system. As the House of Burgesses gradually came to dominate provincial politics, elections to that body took on increased meaning.
Those members of the gentry instilled with a sense of duty, responsibility, or obligation, as well as those who sought the power and
prestige of office, found the local electoral arena the key to political
service and advancement. With the rules of engagement firmly in
place by the 1730s, elections in each locale came to represent the

unique intersection of local personalities and problems with shared provincial developments and crises. Surveying this electoral system at midcentury offers an important window into this mature but diverse and dynamic colonial political culture.

At the same time, however, these decades also witnessed the unraveling of the provincial order. Beginning with the Board of Trade's careful scrutiny of the revised Virginia law code in the late 1740s and culminating in the actual break with Britain in 1776, a series of provincial and imperial crises buffeted the Old Dominion, affecting not only politics in Williamsburg but also indirectly influencing political decisions and outcomes in Virginia's numerous electoral districts. The Pistole Fee controversy, the loan office proposal, and the Parsons' Cause of the 1750s altered the political climate in some locales, but the French and Indian War and the deepening imperial confrontation thereafter modified electoral activities nearly everywhere. The angry dissolutions of the House of Burgesses resulting from its stand against the Stamp, Townshend, and Boston Port Acts as well as the coming and going of several governors sent the provincial electoral system into a tailspin. Tracing provincial and especially local responses to these dramatic events provides another perspective on how Anglo-Virginians—common freeholders and gentlemen—navigated the road to independence.

Previous attempts to understand the workings of Virginia's local political culture have produced portraits of a stable, consistent, and uniform system, defined alternatively as aristocratic, oligarchic, democratic, or ritualistic. Patron/client relationships grounded in coercive power or reciprocity dominate oligarchic explanations, while aristocratic depictions focus on the hierarchical nature of early modern society and the concept of deference.[5] Electioneering and voting become a mere facade in ritualistic models and contrast sharply with democratic portraits that posit a budding republican culture with a strong representational and electoral ethos. Each model has found favor among colonial historians.

Progressive historians, who dominated much of the scholarship in the early decades of the twentieth century, saw most relationships among men in terms of conflict and coercion. Elections, therefore, were contests between aristocratic candidates from the upper levels of society and voters who had just enough land to qualify for the franchise. "At elections held in the open air in county towns, slaveowning barons . . . easily cowed all but the bravest freeholding farmers and named their own men for public office." These lower orders formed a "restive democracy" held at bay during the colonial period by substantial limitations on the franchise and through social and economic pressure from above. In this view, the gentry so overwhelmed the average planter with raw social, economic, and political power that freeholders simply voted as directed.[6]

In the late 1950s and early 1960s, careful and detailed research into eighteenth-century county records turned this earlier view on its head and declared the small farmer the winner. Using a wealth of data on the voting behavior and socioeconomic status of both candidates and electors, historians found a society less economically differentiated than earlier studies portrayed. Widespread landownership gave a majority of the adult white male population the franchise and provided an electorate substantially broader than that of Massachusetts, for example, or the mother country, England. Moreover, wealthy candidates could not always count on the support of the poorest of planters, and on occasion, the most prominent gentleman in the county went down to defeat at the polls. With clear proof that so many men owned land and voted, arguments for an aristocratically dominated electoral system seemed tenuous. Instead, one historian concluded, Virginians of the prerevolutionary period experienced nothing less than the operation at the local level of "what now passes in this country as middle-class, representative democracy."[7]

While some historians found a broad-based electorate making rational choices between candidates, others discovered a system in which *deference* defined the relationships between freeholders and gentry and elections that served social rather than political purposes. Elections represented one of several important social "occasions" that reinforced the deferential relationships between upper and lower strata. The small planter accorded deference in the simple daily greetings extended to his wealthy neighbor and at election time similarly offered his vote as a gesture of goodwill toward that same gentleman. Treats—in the form of food and drink—were less a means of buying votes than an obligation on the part of the gentry to show munificence to voters. This behavior by candidates in turn reinforced the notion that the gentry deserved the deference they received. Deference was the cornerstone of social relations, at least in the older parts of Virginia before the Revolution.[8]

Historians also offer a more cynical view of the deference model, seeing elections as nothing more than "a hilarious county reunion" in which "the rivalry between backers of different candidates was often of the sporting kind, like that of football teams, excited but inconsequential." Widespread treating fostered drunkenness and rowdy behavior on the part of the voters and further reinforced the social, not political, importance of the event. This ignoble and circumscribed role for the electorate seemed natural in a society in which small men deferred all important tasks and decisions to their betters. Voters "willingly acknowledged the leadership and authority of the gentry," and elections served no other purpose than to please the banal instincts of the population.[9]

Others, however, see purpose and meaning in the carnival-like atmosphere and argue that the actual voting process served an important ritualistic function for Virginia and other early modern Anglo-American societies. In this view, the festive nature of elections highlights the notion that the contest itself mattered more than the outcome. As long as voters in Virginia and elsewhere could "participate in the charade and act out the fiction of their own power," the "half-comic battle was a mode of consent to government that filled a deeper popular need than the selection of one candidate over another." The only choice made by the voters was whether or not to participate, because issues remained unimportant, and only personality traits occasionally distinguished one candidate from another.[10]

For several generations of undergraduates, graduate students, and scholars, the most evocative portrait of this political culture has come from historian Charles Sydnor and offers a very different view—one that includes a serious, positive, and crucial role for both the elite and the electorate. "Gentlemen of long-tailed families" with appropriate wealth in land and slaves did indeed dominate local politics with their service as justices of the county court, parish vestrymen, sheriffs, county clerks, and militia officers. Those with the greatest talents became "gentlemen acceptable to ordinary men" by winning election to the House of Burgesses through a process that often involved "swilling the planters with bumbo" and suffering the "tumults and riots" of the "vulgar herd." Candidates could afford the expense of an election and could and did use their social and economic influence to point voters in the desired direction. Voters, for their part, usually followed the advice of the leading gentlemen of the county but, ultimately, provided a kind of check on the autocratic tendencies of the planter oligarchy. Most important, during the prerevolutionary era voters were a critical part of a process "that sifted through the whole population, discarding most men while selecting for political preferment those few who are now called the great generation of Virginia."[11]

At least one of the reasons for historians' contrasting views of this political culture is the kind of evidence used. A wealth of information from a variety of sources survives for this period, and choosing among the material can lead to dramatically different conclusions about this society. The correspondence and diaries of prominent members of the gentry point unmistakably to a hierarchical, oligarchic society, in which a few men from a few families controlled the social, economic, and political arrangements in each community and, therefore, had little to fear from a broad-based electorate. Descriptions in the House of Burgesses journals of controverted elections, especially suspected irregular and illegal practices, on the other hand, suggest that candidates expended considerable effort to achieve election and that freeholders often sold their votes for a bowl of punch. Conversely, the fact that there are hundreds of freeholders listed in pollbooks surviving from closely fought elections elevates the political role of the electorate and places a democratic, not oligarchic, aura over the political system.

Although they read different political, social, and cultural messages from these elections, most historians agree that the electoral system was static, consistent, and uniform. As expressed by Charles Sydnor and others, the dominant interpretation is of a common set of electoral conventions and behaviors operative across the counties and regions of Virginia from about 1725 to about 1815. Because the legal framework for elections changed little after 1735 and remained unaffected by the Revolution, historians assume that the behavior of candidates and voters changed little as well. Evidence from elections in 1728, 1768, and 1799, for example, became part of a composite portrait spanning nearly a century.[12]

The static image of local electoral politics also stems from the long-held view that peace, harmony, and serenity had settled on the colony's political system by about 1725. The ending of the controversial years of Governor Alexander Spotswood (1710–22), the short but tactful term of Governor Hugh Drysdale (1722–26), and the arrival of Governor William Gooch (1727–49), who further calmed the political waters, ushered in a long period of apparent tranquillity, at least at the provincial level. This "friendly intercourse" between governor and gentry coupled with the withdrawal of the governor from electoral politics seemingly signaled the arrival of a local political culture reflective of the harmonious provincial scene.[13] Before 1725, voters responded to disputes between local elites and governors by assuming an "aggressive and participatory" posture toward the electoral process. When these controversies subsided, many historians argue, political tensions lessened and electoral intensity steadily declined for the entire period up to the Revolution.[14]

Despite wide acceptance of a model of stability and harmony, this static portrait may mask significant developments, important changes, and substantial diversity. The period 1722–49, for example, might represent nothing more than an abnormally peaceful interlude between the political turmoil of the preceding two decades and the provincial and imperial problems that developed after 1755.[15] The Tobacco Inspection Act of the early 1730s and the Two-Penny Act, the Parsons' Cause, and the war with France of the 1750s and early 1760s clearly heightened political debate for brief periods, but the impact of these events on the local electoral scene remains obscure. Political discourse certainly increased in Williamsburg and in the counties as the crisis with Britain deepened, but whether election battles subsided or multiplied as the dispute intensified is uncertain.[16]

Most students of Virginia's political culture have also assumed uniformity and consistency in electoral practices across local political communities; evidence from Accomack County on the Eastern Shore, trans-Allegheny Augusta, Tidewater Richmond County, and Piedmont Hanover blend into a single snapshot of the entire colony. Because the same electoral rules applied to every constituency, the game of politics is thought to have been played everywhere the same.[17]

Historians posit some differences between the "staid Tidewater plantation counties" and those turbulent counties on the other side of the Blue Ridge, or they argue that "the stable, hierarchical political culture which most historians have associated with the entire colony of Virginia may in fact have typified only the more settled and orderly societies of the Tidewater and Northern Neck."[18] According to this latter theory, Virginia's central Southside tried to replicate the traditional gentry culture of the older counties but nev-

er could shed its rough frontier edge throughout the prerevolutionary period. In earlier decades, most of Virginia's counties successfully made the transition from disorderly frontier societies to stable
communities, but just when the Southside reached maturity, coun-
terforces—first evangelical religion and then the Revolution itself—
"permanently impede[d] that transition toward traditional, hierarchical social arrangements." The roughness of these societies may
have carried over into the political arena, as both candidates and voters behaved in a manner considerably different from that of their
counterparts in the older, eastern sections.[19]

Furthermore, some believe that the Great Awakening had a pro-
found impact upon the general social behavior of the lower orders of
society, particularly in places like the Southside, where the Baptists
found the most converts. Evangelicalism altered the perception that
small men had of big men, and deference and all it implied declined
as the central force holding communities together. The character of
elections changed, therefore, and at least by the 1770s and 1780s
lesser men won contests that emphasized issues rather than abilities.[20]

Confining sources of diversity entirely to the Southside, however, may divert our attention away from other factors leading to instability, including the spread of local governmental institutions—
parish vestries and county courts—to all newly settled regions
of Virginia. At the time of the 1728 general election, Virginia had
thirty-one electoral constituencies: twenty-eight counties, one college, and two boroughs. Over the next fifty years, settlement pushed
westward across the Piedmont, over the Blue Ridge, and into the
Great Valley and beyond. Virginia's white population increased
from about 75,000 to almost 300,000.[21] Western sections of original
counties became new counties, and those in turn lost their frontier
parts to the same process. By the eve of the Revolution, the number
of electoral districts had grown to sixty-five, with thirty-three new
counties and one new borough. Forty-five constituencies either
came into being or lost territory between 1728 and 1775, some split-
ting two, three, or four times. When a county divided, the old and
new sections experienced some period of adjustment: authorities in
the reduced older section no longer shared power with leaders in the
new county, and those leaders in turn often rose in stature with the
departure of the long-established elite from the more-settled older
section. Gentlemen who had once joined forces to send one of their

number to Williamsburg could now come to blows over representation in the smaller unit. Voters, too, faced a reduced or altered set of leaders from which to choose. These local political adjustments came quickly to some counties and slowly or not all to others, adding potential volatility to the local electoral scene.

Ultimately, the failure of historians to appreciate fully the wide-ranging behaviors possible within a single colony has hindered construction of a dynamic model of Virginia's local political culture. Gentry domination of elective office, near-hereditary seats in the House of Burgesses, uncontested elections, and voter apathy coexisted with highly competitive elections, long and costly campaigns, excessive eating and drinking by candidates and freeholders alike, and voter independence at the polls.

To understand how such divergent actions and attitudes fit into a coherent whole, we must recognize that no Virginia community exhibited all of these attributes at the same moment, and therefore we must begin to pay attention to the "when" and "where" of our evidence. It does matter that the data survive from 1735 and not from 1769 and that it originated in Halifax County and not Lancaster County. Few of Virginia's political communities remained politically static during the half century before the Revolution, but rather each responded uniquely to a combination of local, regional, provincial, and imperial influences. At various times, those influences produced regular, highly competitive, elections; at other times, the competition occurred only intermittently; and in some periods, the voters played no direct role in the selection of representatives.

Part I

Provincial Patterns

1

The Political Culture of Elections

Ladies and gentlemen, to-night you'll see
A bard delighting in satiric glee;
In merry scenes his biting tale unfold,
And high to Folly's eye the mirror hold:

Here eager candidates shall call for votes,
And brawling voters louder stretch their throats:
Here may you view, in groups diverting, join'd
The poor and wealthy rabble of mankind;

The state of things was such, in former times,
Ere wicked kings were punish'd for their crimes:
When strove the candidates to gain their seats
Most heartily, with drinking bouts, and treats.

These few verses from the prologue to Robert Munford's prerevolutionary drama, *The Candidates*, set the stage for the three-act play that followed.[1] In this satire from "Virginia's first and only comic son," the playwright offers a full cast of characters from an eighteenth-century election: a highly respected and incumbent legislator, Mr. Worthy, who has already decided as the play opens that he will not stand for reelection; his fellow incumbent, Mr. Wou'dbe, who is "well enough in his neighbourhood" that he will run again; Sir John Toddy, a candidate who drinks with the freeholders and has promised, if elected, to reduce the tax on rum; Mr. Strutabout and Mr. Smallhopes, who suffered defeat in the last election and will try again in this one; and a few servants and four freeholders and their wives.

The opening scene of the play finds Sir John Toddy at the home of Mr. Wou'dbe, soliciting his support in the upcoming election. Although Wou'dbe refuses, rumors spread through the county that Toddy and Wou'dbe have "joined interest." Later, at a barbecue, the freeholders and their wives discuss the merits of the candidates, Toddy continues to canvas for votes, Wou'dbe makes it clear that he does not support Toddy, candidate Strutabout promises the voters he "shall be able to do every thing you have requested," Smallhopes challenges Wou'dbe to a fight, and several of the freeholders and their wives get roaring drunk. Near the end of the day, Mr. Worthy notifies the freeholders that he will "stand a poll" again to ward off the efforts of the "scoundrels who opposed us in the last election." With Worthy back in the race, Toddy withdraws, and Wou'dbe feels "the pulse of all the leading men, and find they beat still" for Worthy and Wou'dbe. On election day, the voters reelect Worthy and Wou'dbe without a formal poll.

The Candidates offers a tantalizing portrait of eighteenth-century elections. Its scenes and dialogue speak directly to the candidate selection process, the joining together of interests to form a slate, the use of food and drink and campaign promises to influence the voters, the rowdy nature of eighteenth-century elections, the apparent nearly automatic reelection of incumbents, and the ultimate wisdom of the electorate in selecting "the ablest, according to the writ."[2] The play's characters and details stand out in sharp relief after two centuries, but the broad message conveyed about Virginia's local political culture is less clear.[3]

On the one hand, the drama provides a picture of a highly deferential society, in which wealthy gentlemen, like the play's Mr. Worthy, exercised political power that "was, in effect, hereditary and was accepted by all classes of Virginians as partaking of something akin to divine right." Yet it emphasizes the democratic nature of the society, as well, and "shows how dependent the candidate was on the people."[4] Moreover, the satire suggests that small men supported big men because the two groups shared a number of common problems.[5] Munford's writings may also offer a description not of the political culture of the entire colony but of the excessive "contentiousness and disorderliness" existing primarily in the Virginia Southside.[6]

We do know that, before writing *The Candidates*, Robert Munford witnessed local politics as a youth in Tidewater Essex County and as a young man in Southside Prince George and Lunenburg Counties, saw local and colonial government in action as a young law student in Williamsburg, participated as a successful candidate in four elections in Mecklenburg County, and heard a variety of testimony concerning electoral irregularities and controversies as a member of the House of Burgesses.[7] Whatever Munford's intentions in writing the play, his experiences no doubt taught him that local politics in general and electoral politics in particular came in a variety of forms.

Munford's play opens one important door to this eighteenth-century world, but it is not the only entrance available. The developing legal and cultural definitions of candidate qualifications help us understand what Virginians sought in their representatives. Petitions presented to the House of Burgesses complaining of election irregularities and the subsequent testimony gathered in investigating these complaints provide considerable evidence concerning competitive and controversial elections. Private correspondence, diaries, personal account books, and newspapers note both the unusual and the mundane. By contrasting the activities of county leaders, candidates, voters, election officials, and the population at large in different locales, we begin to see the commonplace as well as the exceptional in local electoral politics.

BURGESS QUALIFICATIONS

Formal qualifications for those seeking election to the House of Burgesses began to emerge in the seventeenth century. As early as 1655, candidates had to be "persons of knowne integrity and of good conversation and of age one and twenty years."[8] In 1705, the House debated a new election law that included a provision limiting burgesses to the county in which they resided, but this stipulation disappeared in the final law, which only stated that the person had to be a freeholder in the county.[9] A few candidates without the appropriate freehold sometimes asked a member of the local gentry to "spare a Legal Title for a short time," but most of those who seriously sought office already possessed the necessary property.[10] Throughout the eighteenth century, men could and did represent constituencies where they owned land but did not reside.

The House questioned the qualifications of burgesses only rarely.

In Lancaster County in 1748, a losing candidate challenged Peter Conway's election because he did not appear to hold proper title to his freehold. Upon further investigation, however, Conway demonstrated that he had held, paid quitrents on, and received rents from two hundred acres for eight years, even though the deed to the land from his father seemed somewhat irregular.[11] On the other hand, after the first election in Halifax County, the House declared George Currie unfit because the three hundred acres he had acquired the year before had not been properly owned by the man from whom he had made the purchase.[12] A few years later, in the same county, Abraham Maury exclaimed with certainty that newly elected Nathaniel Terry "will not be allow'd to take a seat in the house, where none but gentlemen of character ought to be admitted."[13] Although no one challenged Terry's election, he may have had a few ungentlemanly traits: in the 1769 election he tried to beat the sheriff with a cane.[14]

The House declared two other individuals unfit for service: William Clinch of Surry and Robert Doak of Fincastle. Doak's disqualification occurred because at the time he ran for election he had knowledge of his forthcoming commission as county surveyor.[15] The House expelled Clinch in 1757 because he tried to get out of a debt he owed by locking his creditor in a small room and threatening him with a gun. Although the House would not tolerate such behavior, it did not seem to concern the voters of Surry, who elected him again in 1758. The burgesses, however, remained intolerant of a convicted extortionist in their midst and expelled Clinch again in September 1758.[16] Other than the basic freehold requirement and an accepted mode of behavior, the only additional restrictions imposed on representatives related to those individuals who also held offices of profit under Crown appointment.

During the seventeenth century, the House had shown little concern for burgesses who also served other governmental functions. However, when several early-eighteenth-century governors effectively utilized their appointive powers to gain greater influence over members of the House, the burgesses objected. The House passed several general "place bills" in 1705 and 1715, and in 1718 it approved a bill to specifically exclude county clerks. None of these reached the statute books because of the governor's veto. By the late 1720s, however, the antagonism between the governor and the

House had subsided to the point that the House could again consider appropriate restrictions on its membership.[17]

County sheriffs had complete control over the conduct of elections, and when in 1730 the House became aware that several of its members also served in that capacity, it appointed a committee to look into the matter. Finding no precedents, the committee brought in a bill to disable sheriffs and all holders of offices of profit from serving in the House. The bill eventually passed the House and was signed by the governor. In the act's final form, sheriffs could not sit in the House under any circumstances, but holders of all other offices could run for reelection immediately after receiving such appointments.[18]

The office of tobacco inspector had similar problems. In 1714, Governor Spotswood appointed twenty-five burgesses to inspection posts and in so doing gained nearly complete control over the House.[19] Although shortly thereafter the governor's scheme backfired in a general election in which most of the inspectors lost their seats, nonetheless the potential power of these patronage positions remained. In 1730, the burgesses added an amendment to a tobacco bill excluding inspectors, but they eventually voted it down, thirty to twenty-five.[20] However, the matter came to a head during the 1735 election, when several inspectors openly tried to influence voters through their power to accept or refuse planter's crops.[21] Shortly after these abuses came to light, the burgesses disabled tobacco inspectors from sitting in the House.[22]

On sixty-nine occasions between 1728 and 1775, members of the House of Burgesses accepted offices of profit, resigned their seats, and stood for reelection as specified by law. In a third of these cases the burgess received an appointment as county sheriff. Designations as county coroner accounted for another 20 percent of the elections. Tobacco inspector, county clerk, and county surveyor represented another fourth of the appointments. Incumbents continued serving in only 17 percent of the cases, although there is no evidence of defeat for those who sought to retain their seats. Generally speaking, persons did not attempt to hold both administrative and legislative offices at the same time, although many—other than sheriffs—could have done so legally. Once he had served his term in the appointive office, however, a politician often tried to regain his seat in the next available election.

A TALE OF TWO CAMPAIGNS

Although burgess qualifications remained unchanged after 1736, the approach taken by successful candidates to the election process rarely achieved such stability. These often dramatic differences between one year's campaign and the next or between one constituency and another come to light through two diaries, kept during the summer of 1769, and provide an additional window into the local political culture of eighteenth-century Virginia.

Circumstances surrounding the House of Burgesses elections of September 1769 made it an atypical but illuminating political event. The colony had held general elections just nine months earlier, in November 1768, but prorogations by Governor Botetourt kept the burgesses away from Williamsburg until May 8, 1769.[23] The governor dissolved the assembly only nine days later after the House passed several resolutions related to the developing crisis with Britain, including one proclaiming the rights of the inhabitants of Virginia to petition their king for redress of grievances.[24] The governor did not immediately call for new elections, but anyone could have guessed that he would probably issue election writs before the end of summer. On August 8, the Governor-in-Council authorized writs bearing the date of August 14, returnable by September 28.[25]

When the governor dissolved the assembly on May 17, 1769, the two burgesses for Richmond County were John Woodbridge and Thomas Glascock. The sixty-three-year-old Woodbridge had served on the Richmond county court for many years and had been a burgess from the county since 1735. Although he considered dropping out of colonial politics in 1765, he continued to run for reelection and presumably would do so again in 1769.[26] We know little of the second incumbent, Glascock. He first entered county politics in 1768, defeating the county's other long-term representative, Landon Carter; one of the tobacco warehouses in the county also bore his family name.[27] When the burgesses returned home from Williamsburg in late May 1769, Woodbridge's reelection seemed assured; only Glascock appeared the least vulnerable.

Two things changed this seemingly tranquil electoral scene: John Woodbridge died in June,[28] and a young, wealthy politician from another county took up residence in Richmond. The new resident was Francis Lightfoot Lee, aged thirty-five, who had served as burgess from Loudoun County for the prior eleven years. His marriage to Rebecca Tayloe of the county and their subsequent settlement at Menokin prompted his move to Richmond County.[29] Lee's father-in-law, John Tayloe, wanted to help his new son-in-law continue his legislative career and apparently expended considerable effort over the summer to that end.[30]

Robert Wormeley Carter entered the race as the third candidate. His father, Landon, had served the county from 1752 to 1768, when he lost to Glascock. The elder Carter could have tried to regain his seat in 1769, but a combination of his age (sixty) and his disenchantment with politics probably led to the decision that brought the son into the electoral arena.[31] We do not know how Francis L. Lee and Thomas Glascock spent the summer of 1769, but Robert W. Carter used a good bit of it to conduct his election campaign.

Well before the governor issued the writ on August 14, Carter had concerned himself with the election. From July 10 to July 14 he was away from home and "among the Freeholders." On July 15, he "went down to a muster at Reids old Feild," where he "saw a good many Freeholders." He "returned from Farnham" in the southeast part of the county on July 29 and "treated both Capt. Peacheys & Griffin's [militia] companies at the Church," purchasing more than twenty gallons of rum for the occasion from Will Miskell. Before early August, his campaigning took him on a "Rout in the upper parts" of the county. He spent at least seven pounds on election activities before the campaign ended. On September 22, 1769, he reported in his diary, presumably with great satisfaction, that "this day came on the Election. I was returned first by a Majority of 9 Votes; Colo. F. L. Lee also returned."[32] The final pollbook showed a slightly different result: Carter 179 votes, Lee 173, and Glascock with a respectable but distant 105.[33]

About ninety miles northwest of Richmond, in Fairfax County, electoral activities during the summer of 1769 differed considerably. Here, the two burgesses in the 1769 session were John West and George Washington. West had been active in the militia from 1744 to 1765; had been a merchant, a justice of the peace, and a vestryman; and except for a brief break from 1758 to 1761 had served as burgess from the county since 1754.[34] The younger of the two representatives, Washington, had also been principally a military officer but now actively ran his inherited estate, Mount Vernon. He had served as a burgess for Frederick County from 1758 to 1765, but in the latter year he took advantage of an opening and changed his service to his home county of Fairfax. He was also a justice of the peace and a member of the parish vestry.[35] There are only a few surviving records of Colonel John West's activities, so we do not know whether he actively campaigned during the summer of 1769. We do, however, possess a reasonably detailed account of Washington's activities during this period, and there is little or no hint of the type of electioneering engaged in by Robert W. Carter of Richmond County.

Immediately after the dissolution of the assembly on May 17, Washington met with the majority of the burgesses at Raleigh Tavern in Williamsburg, and there he took the lead in developing a nonimportation association to protest the latest parliamentary actions against the colonies.[36] On May 20, he started for home, arriving there on May 22. During his first month at home, he was away from Mount Vernon a good deal of the time at a variety of public functions. He attended a race at Cameron on May 26, a barbecue at Alexandria the following day, and the baptism of Bryan Fairfax's son on May 31. Washington dutifully appeared at a funeral in Alexandria on June 2, attended church and a baptism a week later, and performed his duties as a justice at the meeting of the county court from June 19 to June 23.[37] During these numerous public appearances, Washington probably promoted the nonimportation association; he probably did not directly solicit votes for a future—and as yet unspecified—election.[38]

These four weeks of rather substantial public activity preceded a two-month period in which Washington had little contact with the voters of Fairfax County. Instead, he devoted his time to business and family affairs. With the exception of one day at church and three at court, he stayed at home, overseeing field work and conducting other business during the entire month of July. On July 31, Washington and his family left for Warm Springs (now Berkeley Springs, W. Va.), in Frederick County, where they hoped the waters would help restore the health of his stepdaughter, Patsy Custis. While there, Washington tended to some business matters but mainly socialized with friends at the springs and with acquaintances in nearby sections of Frederick.[39]

During Washington's stay at the springs, the governor issued election writs, and presumably someone brought this news to Washington toward the end of August. The Washington party left for home on September 9, arriving at Mount Vernon three days later. On September 14, Washington made his first real public appearance in more than two months when he "went to Alexandria to the Election of Burgesses for Fairfax & was chosen together with Colo. West without a Poll, their being no opposition."[40]

THE ELECTORAL SEASON

Although the electoral season of 1769 lasted four months, the nature of parliamentary government held out the possibility that Virginia campaigns could last anywhere from a few weeks to nearly a year. In every case, the season began with the dissolution of the assembly by the governor. If an immediate crisis precipitated the dissolution, as it did in 1755, 1765, 1769, and 1774, the election process began with the termination of the assembly and ended with the completion of new elections. The electoral season was just over a month in length in 1765 and 1774 and six to seven weeks long in 1755. On the other hand, a predictable dissolution, such as those following the death of the king or the appointment of a new governor, often lengthened the election process considerably. The Hanover County contests of 1752 and 1764 demonstrate the variety of activities possible during these electoral seasons.

On December 12, 1751, the new governor, Robert Dinwiddie, dissolved the assembly and immediately issued writs for new elections to occur in January 1752.[41] Although this formally meant a four-to-five-week electoral season, in some counties it began much earlier. In May 1749, the governor, Sir William Gooch, prorogued the assembly then left for England for health reasons, turning the daily operation of the government over to the Council, a twelve-member advisory board appointed by the Crown, with seats often held for life. Active participants in Virginia politics probably guessed Gooch would not return and, therefore, that the appointment of a new governor and the resulting new elections would occur within the next year or so. Although Gooch did not die until December 1751, a successor had been named the previous July 4. The new governor arrived in Virginia in November 1751, but news of his appointment probably reached Virginia some months earlier.[42]

Even before Dinwiddie became the new governor, campaigning for the anticipated general election had begun in Hanover County. One reason for the early activity may have been some important interests to be cultivated by any candidate in this county, chief among them the large population of dissenters. The people of Hanover had responded in significant numbers to the "New Side" preachers, who first appeared in Virginia in 1743. Over the following few years, more preachers traversed the county, converts erected meetinghouses, and permanent ministers with Presbyterian affiliation became firmly established.[43] These dissenters paid parish taxes to support the Anglican establishment, like everyone else, but they also supported their own ministers and churches. When rumors flew that the parish might be divided, dissenters strongly opposed the division, since it benefited only Anglicans while increasing the taxes of all planters. The potential division became an important issue in the campaign and embroiled all three candidates in controversy following the election.

In late December 1751, John Chiswell, incumbent candidate and burgess since 1741, got involved in a discussion with a voter and dissenter named Morris. Morris said he would not vote for Chiswell unless he received assurance that Chiswell, if elected, would oppose the division of the county and parish. Chiswell claimed he had always opposed such a plan and immediately stated his position in a formal document that circulated throughout the county. A week or so later, "one of the Principal Men among the Dissenters" told another candidate, John Syme, about Chiswell's written declaration. Not to be outdone, Syme executed a similar document just four days before the election and had it "published" at the meeting of the dissenters the following day. Morris also asked the third candidate, Henry Robinson, to state his position on the issue, but Robinson responded by saying that "it was not a fair Question." Clearly, two of the candidates thought the issue of enough import to publicly state their positions, and there is some evidence that voters responded to those statements.[44]

Another reason for the early electoral activity in Hanover County concerned twenty-five-year incumbent William Meriwether, who may have already announced that he would not seek reelection. With such knowledge, political hopefuls had every reason to start the electoral season early. In fact, John Syme, a young planter just beginning his career in local politics, initiated the Hanover campaign of 1751–52. In July 1751, Syme employed a Mr. Hicks to "solicit Freeholders" on his behalf and gave him money "to be laid out in treating them with Liquor." Well before the governor issued the writ, probably in November, Syme again paid for treats for a group of freeholders and after the writ arrived in the county (late December or early January) provided several more general "Treats" with one or more of the candidates present. Just three days before the election, Hicks gave out three gallons of rum to freeholders at a "Mare shot." Finally, on the eve of the election a number of voters "who lived remote from the Court-house" stayed the night with—and were entertained by—a Mr. Higginson, another friend of John Syme.[45] John Syme and John Chiswell won the election; Henry Robinson lost.

Robinson, however, petitioned the House of Burgesses, charging Syme and Chiswell with unspecified election irregularities. The Committee of Privileges and Elections, which examined all such petitions, conducted a thorough investigation, including extensive interviews with many witnesses, and concluded that Syme and Chiswell were "not duly elected to serve as Burgesses in this present General Assembly for the County of Hanover." The chief campaign activity that offended the House was not the entertainment of voters with liquor but the written promises issued by both candidates, which violated a 1705 law. The assembly ordered these promises to "be immediately torn, and thrown under the Table." The House requested a writ for a new election, and sometime in April 1752 the voters of Hanover selected Robinson and Chiswell.[46]

Twelve years later another lengthy election campaign occurred in Hanover County, but the cast of characters and the issues differed markedly. Some time after the close of the 1763 session of the House of Burgesses, probably in September or October, incumbent burgess Nathaniel Dandridge accepted the office of county coroner. The election law passed in 1730 mandated a new election whenever any member of the House accepted an office of profit. The officeholder could run for reelection, but the voters had to approve such an arrangement formally. With the House out of session until January 12, 1764, Hanover residents waited several months for the required by-election. The long-anticipated writ appeared on the January 13, and in early February the sheriff held the election.[47] However, like the 1752 contest, the electoral season was much longer than the brief period following the issue of the writ.

As the incumbent, Dandridge could legally run for reelection, but he added a great deal of confusion to the electoral climate in the fall of 1763 by providing no clear indication of his intentions. He either let it be known that he would not run again or remained ambivalent on the matter. As a result, two other candidates mounted intensive campaigns for the seat, and a third individual apparently gave serious thought to entering the contest.

Shortly after Dandridge's appointment as coroner, again probably in September or October 1763, James Littlepage began his own campaign for the seat.[48] He initiated his quest for office by first writing to John Boswell, a justice of the peace, inquiring about his chances for election in Boswell's part of the county. Boswell replied that Littlepage's chances were good "if he would go up amongst them" sometime in the near future. At about the same time, Littlepage also had a conversation with Dandridge, who according to one source advised Littlepage to "set up as a Candidate."

These incidents apparently gave Littlepage enough encouragement to announce his candidacy for the seat on or just before November 12, 1763. He immediately wrote to a number of freeholders in different parts of the county. He asked William Hughes Sr. for his "Vote and Interest"; to William Hawes he announced that Dandridge would not run again, that "I shall be obliged to you for your Interest," and that he would do everything in his power to repeal the present tobacco inspection law.[49] Littlepage also wrote to several other freeholders explaining his position on the tobacco law and promising "if they would send him Burgess" he would get the law repealed. This letter may have had some impact, for although Littlepage "had at first very little Interest in that Neighborhood," after hearing of "his Promises to be of so much Service to them," many probably voted for him. On election day, however, Littlepage publicly declared "that he did not look upon any of the Promises he had made to the People as binding on him, and that they were all void."

Letter writing composed only one of Littlepage's many campaign activities. Following advice received earlier, he did travel to the part of the county where John Boswell lived and "rode about with him among the People." A number of the freeholders objected to the twenty-five-mile journey to the courthouse on election day in the cold weather. Littlepage assured them that all could stay at his house the night before the election, a distance of only five miles from the place of voting. In mid-November, Littlepage also visited several of the houses of worship in the county: one day he went to "the lower Meeting House of the Dissenters" and on the November 20 scheduled a stop at the church attended by Hughes and Hawes.

Littlepage's chances of being elected dimmed in early January with the entry into the race of two additional candidates and the rumor that a third would soon declare as well. By the first of the year, Samuel Overton, justice of the peace since 1757, had entered the race. In addition, Nathaniel Dandridge, who apparently stayed out of the contest in November and December, suddenly reentered in mid-January. Furthermore, Patrick Henry's recent success and considerable notoriety in the defense of the Two-Penny Act in Hanover Court encouraged the young lawyer to offer his services to the freeholders. On January 14, Overton and Littlepage toyed with the possibility of telling Dandridge that they would "decline standing a Poll if he would pay them the Expenses" they had incurred thus far. They never approached Dandridge with the proposition, but instead Littlepage agreed to pay all of Overton's expense in this race and in a previous election if he would drop out of the contest. Overton did drop out, Henry decided not to run, and on election day Littlepage opposed the incumbent, Dandridge.

Treating occupied an important place in the 1764 Hanover election, as it had in 1752. On January 12, 1764, Littlepage presided at a treat given for the freeholders. On the following day, Samuel Overton arranged to have four gallons of rum distributed at Jacob Huntley's house. When the liquor began to run low, Littlepage ordered two more gallons in Overton's name. Finally, on election day, Littlepage employed Paul Tilman "to prepare his Entertainment" but ordered him to give no liquor to voters until "after the closing [of] the Poll."[50]

James Littlepage won the by-election, and despite a formal protest to the House by Dandridge, the burgesses found nothing wrong with Littlepage's activities during the campaign. If his conduct appeared abnormal, it was at least not outside the bounds of behavior thought proper by the House.

ELEMENTS OF THE CAMPAIGN

The Hanover elections of 1752 and 1764 as well as the contrasting campaigns of Robert W. Carter and George Washington in the summer of 1769 reveal much about how men became candidates, the kinds of activities that took place during the campaign, what occurred on election day, and the types of candidate and voter behavior considered appropriate. Viewed together, these descriptions suggest a set of elements common to eighteenth-century elections, including a candidate nomination process, the use of something the early modern world called *interest*, the treating of voters with food and drink, and the crucial role of the county sheriff in conducting the election. Examining each element in turn gives further definition to the broad political culture and suggests the remarkable variation possible at individual electoral contests.

Nominations

The process of identifying candidates, or what today we call nominations, occurred in two ways: incumbents automatically became candidates for reelection unless they specifically stated otherwise; and new candidates either announced their own candidacy or, as in the case of James Littlepage of Hanover, first sought the opinions of several prominent gentlemen in the county and then made the announcement. Like Littlepage, most candidates found it politically wise to check with local leaders before entering an election contest.

In 1755, young George Washington asked his half brother Augustine to "come at Colo. Fairfax's Intentions" and those of a number of other important members of the Fairfax County gentry to see if there might be a place for him in the upcoming election. As it turned out, there was not, so Washington concentrated his efforts in nearby Frederick and did not seek election from his home county for another ten years.[51] Similarly, Dr. Theodorick Bland Jr. wrote to John Randolph Sr. in September 1771 offering a "proposal," as he called it, to run in the elections scheduled for November. He asked that Randolph take up the matter with "Colo. Nash, Mr. Peter Johnson, Mr. Greenhill, Mr. Scott and any other of the heads of that County" he thought appropriate. If they approved of this proposition, Bland would "wait on them before the Election." Bland not only sought the approval of the leaders of Prince Edward County but also asked Randolph to "spare a Legal Title for a short time to a few acres of your low grounds" so that he could meet "the necessary qualifications in a freehold."[52] Although incumbents Scott and Greenhill suggested earlier that they would not seek reelection, Greenhill and Peter Legrand, former burgess and sheriff, ran and won. The answer to Bland's letter does not survive, but "the heads of the county" no doubt advised him not to run, and probably he did not do so.

County leaders did not always wait for candidates to approach them but might have asked a particular individual to run for office. "Some people fond of novelty . . . set up two boys" to oppose Edmund Pendleton and his young colleague James Taylor in the Caroline County election of 1774.[53] The "boys" lost when the freeholders reelected Taylor and Pendleton. The same process occurred in Spotsylvania nearly a year before the 1771 general election. "Immediately upon my Return home," Mann Page Jr. wrote to his brother, "I was induced by the persuasion of the Gentlemen in the Neighborhood, to declare myself a Candidate for the County."[54] Page ran a distant second in the election but edged out ten-year-incumbent Benjamin Grymes for a seat in the assembly. Support from the "Gentlemen in the Neighborhood" may have decided the contest.

Of equal concern to county leaders was the disposition of vacant seats. When Lord Dunmore dissolved the assembly on May 26, 1774, incumbents John West and George Washington represented Fairfax County—West had served the county since 1754, Washington since 1765. A few weeks later, Dunmore reluctantly issued writs for new elections, and on Sunday, June 26, West announced that he would not seek reelection. During the week that followed, Charles Broadwater announced his candidacy for the vacant seat, Bryan Fairfax debated whether to run, and Washington busied himself trying to get Fairfax to make "an open declaration" concerning his intentions or "to press Colonel Mason to take a poll." Washington tried to convince Fairfax to enter the race by noting that "the country never stood more in need of men of abilities and liberal sentiments than now" and that "Major Broadwater, though a good man, might do as well in the discharge of his domestic concerns, as in the capacity of a legislator."[55]

On a few occasions, broader segments of the population participated in the nomination process. For example, following the dissolution of the assembly on May 17, 1769, the *Virginia Gazette* reported from Norfolk that

> on the return of Col. Joseph Hutchings from Williamsburg, he was waited on by a number of the principal inhabitants of this borough, to testify their intire approbation of his conduct in the late Assembly; and having requested him to accompany them to a tavern, where he was genteelly and elegantly entertained by them, they unanimously assured him, that if he would serve again, they were fully determined to elect him their representative, without suffering him to be at Any expense.[56]

Hutchings won the September election, and it seems evident that this same type of enthusiasm appeared among the voters in the Elizabeth City election of the same year and in the 1774 elections in Williamsburg and Prince George County.[57]

Interest

One of the key ingredients in eighteenth-century elections, both during the nomination process and in the successful execution of the campaign, was the development, use, and application of something called *interest*. An important and frequently used term in local political discourse, the word took on a number of meanings related to electioneering. To campaign for someone was *to make interest* on their behalf. The word meant *support* when a candidate's agents got persons to sign a document in Westmoreland in 1728 to see "what Interest he should have at a new Election."[58] It implied *influence* in New Kent in 1771 when Richard Adams declared that he would "devote all the Interest I have in the County" for one of the candidates.[59] It also conveyed both meanings, as in the testimony taken by the House of Burgesses in the controverted Lunenburg election of 1758: "Mr. Marrable wrote a Letter to Mr. David Caldwell, a Man of Great Interest in the County, strongly soliciting his Interest" in the forthcoming election.[60]

The word might indicate a candidate's *cause* in the election: William Jordan was "an open Abettor of the Interest of Mr. Flautleroy" in Richmond in 1741; an agent "treated in the Interest of Mr. Marrable" in Lunenburg in 1755; and there were "more Persons there in the Interest" of Henry Robinson in Hanover in 1752.[61] Several candidates could also "join in Interest," as they did in King George County in 1735.[62] Interest was the political bond that held equals and unequals together for a sometimes brief but common cause, and it was a key element in Virginia's local political culture especially at the neighborhood level.

Treating

When Hanover County candidates John Syme and James Littlepage gave food and drink to gatherings of freeholders in 1751 and 1764, respectively, they participated in an activity often imagined as the cornerstone of Virginia's colonial electoral system. Clearly, *treats* or *entertainments* played a prominent role in this culture. At some elections, candidates gauged, maintained, or strengthened their interest by providing liquor in various forms and occasionally other food and drink, but the extent of the practice is more difficult to measure.[63] Evidence of treating exists for only twenty-nine elections held between 1728 and 1775, but while this represents only a fraction of the total contests held, the temporal and spatial distribution of these elections along with an analysis of the legal aspects of treating confirms the pervasive nature of the practice.

We know that voters accepted treats in at least one constituency in every general election from 1735 to 1774, with the exception of 1748, and in the by-elections of 1734 and 1764. Treating occurred in seventeen counties located in the Northern Neck, Southside, Eastern Shore, Tidewater, Piedmont, and Shenandoah Valley. It took place more frequently in Piedmont than in Tidewater; the Southside had a lower incidence of the practice than the Northern Neck section of the Piedmont. Virginians condoned, or at least tolerated, treating as one of the many elements of an electoral campaign. Voters in some counties expected treats, and candidates for their part had to be prepared, logistically as well as financially, to provide beverages and food at specific points in the campaign.

Although Virginians accepted treating as part of their political culture, most understood that it could be practiced on either side of the law. A 1705 act declared treating illegal during certain stages in elections: it strictly forbade anyone "to give or allow any money, meat, drink, provision, present, reward, or entertainment . . . in order to be elected . . . to serve in the General Assembly . . . after the test, or issuing out or ordering of the writ or writs of election."[64] The law permitted treating before the local sheriff received the writ and after the election ended but not between the time the writ arrived and the time the polls closed on election day. Several examples from each of these stages in the election campaign serve to illustrate both the legal and extralegal aspects of this practice.

The Hanover elections included treating groups of freeholders very early in the campaign; this phenomenon occurred in other constituencies as well. Following the death of a burgess in Accomack and before the House requested a writ for a by-election, a prospective candidate, Edmund Scarburgh, gave "strong Liquors to the People . . . once at a Race, and the other Time at a Muster."[65] Although these activities were entirely within the law, some politicians did not approve of either candidates or voters who participated in them. Theodorick Bland Sr. noted with disdain that "Our friend, Mr. Banister, has been very much ingaged ever since the dissolution of the assembly, in swilling the planters with bumbo, and I dare say, from the present prospect, will be elected a burgess, at least he has this satisfaction, that every man of the least distinction in the county is in his interest."[66] Occasionally, even candidates found campaigning and treating unpleasant. Mann Page Jr. noted in despair that intense electioneering was "the most disagreeable Business I ever engaged in. My whole time is spent in courting a set of People who have not sense to distinguish any thing but the Size of a Bowl. Toddy supplies the place of merit with them & they have had too plentiful a Dose of that already for me to hope for success."[67] Although distasteful to some candidates, the law clearly allowed treating at this stage in the election process.

The most intensive campaigning occurred during the three-week period between the issuing of the writ and the election, making it difficult for both candidates and voters to refrain from excesses. In trying to stay within the law, Matthew Marrable of Lunenburg had his agent excuse him from a promised treat to a company of militia on the day the governor issued writs "because if he should treat it would vacate his Election" but to maintain his interest with the group "to tell them he would handsomely treat them after the Election was over."[68] Likewise, when several persons approached Nathaniel Dandridge "to prevail upon him to consent to their treating the Freeholders . . . until the Day of Election . . . he absolutely refused to do so."[69] Finally, on a few occasions, legally apolitical members of the community—the candidate's wife and black slaves—offered treats to voters and in so doing may have shielded the candidate from impropiety.[70] Candidates could show their generosity to voters just before the election as long as the candidate did not "procure any Votes thereby" or otherwise extract promises from the electors. Factors that determined the legality of such a treat included questions about who ordered the refreshments, whether the candidate knew of it, who hosted the function, who paid for it, and whether those providing the fare solicited votes for a specific candidate.[71]

Most treating occurred on election day. The prospect of receiving food and drink probably helped attract voters to the courthouse for the election and no doubt kept them there through what was sometimes an all-day affair. Candidates or their agents might arrive early in the morning to ready the treat for distribution as soon as the election concluded, or a tavern near the courthouse might serve as the venue from which treats, liquor in particular, flowed. However, candidates could not serve liquor until the polls closed, and this made restraint particularly difficult in close races. Sometimes the candidate initiated the impropriety, but frequently the voters encouraged breaches of the law. In one instance, a candidate specifically requested that an ordinary keeper give anyone liquor who wanted it on election day, agreeing to pay for everything served.[72] In another case, a candidate ordered "strong Liquor to be brought in a Cart, near the Court-house Door, where many People drank thereof, whilst the Polls of the Election were taking."[73] Problems also ensued when an occasional voter appeared and declared "he was ready to vote for any one who would give him a Dram."[74] During one Prince George County election, voters began helping themselves to an unattended hogshead of punch placed about one hundred yards from the door of the courthouse. Friends of the candidate providing the punch recorked the hogshead so that the punch could be served, as intended, after the election.[75]

Many colonial Virginia elections included treating, and the majority of such activities fell within the law. Thomas Jefferson paid two individuals, one a possible running mate, "for bringing up rum" and "in treating for me" in his first election to the House of Burgesses in 1768.[76] In 1769, he bought more than five pound's worth of cakes on election day, presumably as part of a treat for the freeholders of Albemarle County, and settled an account nine days later for "bumbo" that someone probably served on his behalf.[77] In a similar way, William Cabell of Amherst gave liquor to voters in both the 1768 and 1771 elections. In the latter, he "sent up 120 gals. of Cyder and 110 Gallons of Bumbo to the Election by Wm. Joplin's wagon." Apparently, both men treated after the polls closed.[78]

George Washington also regularly treated the voters in both of the counties he represented. In the 1774 Fairfax election, Nicholas Cresswell reported that "the Candidates gave the populace a Hogshead of Toddy (what we call Punch in England). In the evening the returned Member gave a ball to the Freeholders and Gentlemen of the town."[79] Although Washington gave balls in 1768 and 1771 as well, there is little evidence that such activities occurred elsewhere. The town of Alexandria provided unique opportunities for

more lavish entertainments than were possible at the normal crossroads courthouse.[80]

Among the twenty-nine elections with some evidence of treating, twelve contained only legal incidents, twelve had only illegal
incidents, and five had both legal and illegal incidents. Illegal treating occurred at a slightly higher rate in the Piedmont than in the
Tidewater, with the Northern Neck again having the greatest incidence of such illegalities. Examples of legal treating also prevailed
in Piedmont and Shenandoah Valley counties, with only 30 percent
being from elections in the Tidewater. The practice was not restricted to particular sections of the colony or to particular points in
time, but treating did occur more often when the incumbent lost and
less so when the incumbent won. Treats appeared in elections won
by candidates who either had not served in the assembly previously or who had sought reelection after a break in service. The competitive nature of the election and the aggressive posture of the candidates determined how much or how little the practice dominated
the electoral process.

The Role of the Sheriff

The task of keeping treating under control and the general management of all other aspects of the election process fell to the county sheriff. He set the date and time of the election, scrutinized the
qualifications of voters, determined the method of voting, and
curbed the restive crowds who spent the day at the courthouse. The
sheriff controlled all formal aspects of the electoral process and thus
substantially influenced the outcome of the contest. The power and
prestige of the office were great, but so were the responsibilities.
Candidates and voters scrutinized his every move, issuing more
complaints against him than against any other election participant.
Several examples, again from petitions brought before the House of
Burgesses, illustrate both the power and the problems of the office.

On October 12, 1771, the new governor, Lord Dunmore, dissolved
the assembly elected in 1769 and shortly thereafter issued writs for
a new general election.[81] On November 4, the sheriff of Henrico,
George Cox, received the election writ for his county. Since by law
he could not hold the election for at least twenty days,[82] he selected November 29. Again, as the law specified, he sent notice of the
upcoming election to all of the churches, and the following Sunday

each house of worship in the county made the announcement. But only after he had thus set the election date in the specified manner and had properly ordered the writ read in the parish churches, Cox realized that he could not conduct the election that day. His commission as sheriff expired just before the election, and the new sheriff would not take office until after that date. Hoping to ensure a proper election for this county, Cox, on November 17, changed the date of the election to December 6 and again had notices sent to the churches. Cox's commission expired, and Nathaniel Wilkinson became the new sheriff on December 2, conducting the election "in a fair and usual Manner" on December 6.[83]

Five candidates ran in the election: incumbents Richard Adams and Richard Randolph and challengers Peter Randolph, Samuel DuVal, and a Mr. Prosser. Adams had a considerable majority of the votes, but Richard Randolph edged out DuVal by only two votes. DuVal thought that a reexamination of the pollbook might give him the few votes he needed to win, so he petitioned the House to have the poll checked. Richard Randolph, however, "not carrying to enter into that dispute" (or perhaps fearing a recount), launched a petition of his own to have the election set aside "for want of form."[84] The House of Burgesses decided that the election had been conducted irregularly: less than twenty days had elapsed between the time the sheriff appointed the new date and the actual election, and the new sheriff may have engaged in official business related to the election before being sworn into office.[85] The House invalidated the first election and requested a writ for a new election, which the sheriff held on March 10, 1772. However, "the Freeholders not approving of Col. Randolph's conduct" in the matter of the petition elected Adams and DuVal instead.[86]

Two years earlier, in Fauquier County, the sheriff had used his office to further his own candidacy. When the governor dissolved the short-lived assembly in May 1769, it seemed likely that Fauquier's two incumbents would seek reelection: James Scott had been elected for the first time just seven months earlier, and Thomas Harrison had served since 1761. In June 1769, Thomas Marshall, whose commission as county sheriff expired at the end of the summer, announced his candidacy for the forthcoming general election. On August 14, the governor promulgated writs for new elections; Marshall, as sheriff, received them in Fauquier on August 23. Although confident that he had a strong majority among county residents, Marshall questioned the support of some seventy additional voters who lived in adjacent counties but met the freehold requirements in Fauquier. He knew that nearby Stafford was to hold its election on September 18, so he selected that day for Fauquier also—hoping, presumably, to discourage Stafford residents from casting votes in his county as well. William Eustace became the new sheriff on September 2 and conducted the Fauquier election on the September 18.[87]

The former sheriff, Thomas Marshall, received 329 votes, while the incumbents, Scott and Harrison, received 273 and 196, respectively. Displeased with his loss and with the conduct of Marshall as sheriff, Harrison petitioned the House to have the election thrown out. Upon investigation, however, the House concluded that only about twenty persons from Stafford missed the opportunity to vote in Fauquier, not nearly enough to change the outcome. Further, it did not appear to the burgesses "that any undue Practices were used by Mr. Marshall, in his Office as Sheriff, in order to influence Votes in the said Election."[88]

An example from Westmoreland County in 1728 further illustrates the sheriff's election duties. Here, a defeated candidate accused the county sheriff, Augustine Washington, "of acting partially & unfairly, in determining the Election." Although the House exonerated the sheriff of any wrongdoing and declared the petition a "false, forged, pretended Complaint," testimony taken in the case demonstrates nonetheless the authority and responsibilities of the sheriff.[89]

At about twelve o'clock on election day, the sheriff read the writ signaling the start of the election. One of the incumbent candidates, George Escridge, asked that all those present divide themselves into two groups: those who supported Escridge and the other incumbent, Thomas Lee, and those who supported Thomas Barnes, the third candidate. The voters separated into two groups, with Lee and Escridge having perhaps four times Barnes' number. Virginia law provided that either freeholders or candidates could demand a written poll at any time, but at this stage no one made such a request. At about one o'clock, the sheriff asked Barnes what he intended to do, and Barnes responded that while he had no hope of winning the election, he wanted to wait until about two o'clock to decide on his course of action. The sheriff then warned him that if he waited another hour it would be too late to conduct a written poll and that the election would have to be determined by "View." Finally, around two o'clock the sheriff told Barnes that the January weather made many freeholders uneasy and that a number wanted to go home. Another general division of the voters in the courtyard produced approximately the same results as before, and the sheriff proclaimed Lee and Escridge "duly chosen Burgesses for the County of Westmoreland." Barnes now demanded a formal poll, but the sheriff considered the election at an end.[90]

CONCLUSION

While Robert Munford's *The Candidates* offers important insights into the local political culture of colonial Virginia, we would severely restrict our view of that distant world if we looked no farther than this melodrama. A more complete picture emerges when we consult a variety of sources. This enlarged portrait incorporates a broad set of behaviors involving candidate nomination, campaigning, and treating, which constituted the general political cultural baggage available to any candidate seeking election to the House of Burgesses. Local customs and practices dictated to some extent how and when candidates employed these processes; more important, the particular circumstances of each individual election in each constituency played a far greater role in determining how these elements came into play.

2

The Colonial Electorate

On July 17, 1765, William Robinson journeyed from his modest hundred-acre farm to a small set of buildings clustered around the courthouse at the center of Lancaster County. There, he found many men he knew among the hundred or so milling about the dusty crossroads. To one side, he saw Colonel James Ball, justice and vestryman, who owned Bewdley, a two-thousand-acre riverfront plantation not far from William's humble farm; to the other side stood John Pope, a tenant of one of William's wealthier neighbors. More familiar to him were his cousin Giles Robinson and his neighbor Samuel Newsome. Although his hundred acres seemed tiny when compared with the vast holdings of Colonel Ball, Robinson nonetheless knew that he fared much better than the four Cundiff men who chatted nearby and eked out a meager living on their fifty-acre plots. Despite the wide variation in economic circumstance, all were assembled at the courthouse on this hot July day for a single purpose: to elect two burgesses to the colonial assembly.

When Robinson arrived, nearly a hundred men had already announced their vote to the sheriff and clerks sitting behind the long table on the courthouse green. Although the reelection of incumbents Charles Carter and Richard Mitchell could not be taken for granted, at this point in the polling it did appear that the "old Burgesses" would certainly be returned with little opposition. Mitchell's success at this point in the contest probably pleased Robinson: he had voted for him in the previous election, and he had supported Mitchell's father several times in the 1740s. On the other hand, challenger Richard Ball's showing probably disappointed William, for both Ball and Mitchell were gentlemen from his neighborhood, and they all attended St. Mary's White Chapel. The other incumbent, Charles Carter, lived in the lower precinct, Christ Church, and while Robinson no doubt had great respect and admiration for members of the great Carter family, he had closer ties to gentlemen from his own neighborhood.

Robinson probably chatted with neighbors and relatives for some time before deciding to vote. As he approached the official table, however, he must have heard Merryman Payne proclaim his vote for Carter and Mitchell. Next came William Chilton and then John Pope: both announced for Carter and Mitchell, as well. Samuel Newsome followed, and he too declared for the incumbents. Now William Robinson's turn came, and despite the pressures from previous voters, he offered his support to Mitchell and Richard Ball. Voting continued in a similar manner for the remainder of the afternoon, making it clear that the "old Burgesses" would be sent again to Williamsburg. Finally, the sheriff closed the poll and declared the election results: Mitchell 167, Carter 141, and Ball 21.[1]

Half of the adult white males in the county made the journey to the courthouse on that July day, substantially fewer than had done so in the general election just four years earlier but considerably more than had voted in several previous contests. Among the 171 who voted that day, most owned the land they farmed, but about 20 percent held no permanent title to their properties. About a dozen had never voted before but were now over twenty-one years of age, owners or leasers of the requisite acres, and members of an appropriate Protestant religious group, so they could join the majority of the white men in the county who felt "the flame of burgessing" every three years or so.[2]

This Lancaster County election scene, or some variation thereof, had occurred hundreds of times in the counties and boroughs of Virginia during the last fifty years of the colonial period. Beginning in the seventeenth century, the House of Burgesses had developed and refined a set of laws that governed the right to vote in these constituencies. The number of persons meeting such requirements depended upon landholding and demographic patterns in the individual communities, and the proportion of the electorate actually exercising the rights of citizen subjects[3] varied according to local political practices and procedures as well as the personal circumstances of individual freeholders.

FRANCHISE LAW

The government is a royal one: the legislature consisting of a governor appointed by the king; a council of twelve persons, under the
same nomination; and a house of burgesses, or representatives, of a
hundred and eight or ten members, elected by the people; two for
each county, and one for each of the following places, viz., the College of William and Mary, Jamestown, Norfolkborough, and
Williamsburg.[4]

The English traveler Andrew Burnaby had little trouble constructing this description of Virginia's system of government. Each element—governor, council, and representative assembly—had its
counterpart in the British constitution's king, lords, and commons.
Similarly, Burnaby found familiar features in the process of electing
members to the colony's legislative body. The designation of electoral constituencies, the basic franchise requirements, voting procedures, and electioneering had much in common with England. Yet
despite these similarities, election law on this side of the Atlantic
gradually came to represent Virginia's own particular perceptions
and needs.

In 1760, when Andrew Burnaby described Virginia's political system, the multinational House of Commons included members
elected from England, Scotland, and Wales. Of the 489 members
from England, 80 came from the forty counties, 405 came from the
203 boroughs, and 2 each came from the universities of Oxford and
Cambridge. Although similar in kind, Virginia's system of representation had considerably fewer total members, as befitted the age
and the population of the colonial society. As Burnaby noted, Virginia had the same three types of constituencies: counties, boroughs, and collegiate. At the accession of George II in 1727, Virginia's House of Burgesses included fifty-six members elected from
twenty-eight counties, but because few towns had developed, only
the boroughs of Jamestown and Williamsburg sent representatives
as well. Moreover, Virginia had its university representation in the
form of a single member from the College of William and Mary.[5]

In England, the large number of borough seats and the uneven distribution of those seats across the countryside meant that certain
sections and certain counties in particular had a disproportionately
large influence in the House of Commons. To the contrary, because

representation in the House of Burgesses centered on county constituencies, a more even distribution of seats prevailed in the Old Dominion. Only Virginia's James City County seemed overrepresented in 1727, with its normal county representation plus all of the borough and collegiate members as well. Yet even these five seats paled in comparison to the English county of Cornwall, whose combined county and borough electorates sent forty-four members to the House of Commons.[6]

English county constituencies also varied widely in size: the county of Rutland had approximately 600 voters, while Yorkshire recorded more than 15,000 in the 1741 election. The borough electorate also varied considerably, from as few as the 7 enfranchised house lots in Old Sarum to the 9,000 voters in the City of Westminster.[7] Less dramatic differences prevailed in Virginia: the average county constituency was approximately 350 voters (the smallest, about 125; the largest, 1,200). Williamsburg had perhaps 75 to 100 voters, while the president and faculty elected the burgess from the college. The colony's seventeenth-century capital, Jamestown, was much in decline in the eighteenth century and beginning to look a good deal like the rotten boroughs Americans of the revolutionary generation saw as symbols of ministerial corruption.[8]

Growth and change in electoral districts also distinguished Virginia from the mother country. After 1673 virtually no change occurred in the House of Commons until the Reform Act of 1832,[9] while in Virginia the House of Burgesses continued to increase in size throughout the period. In 1660 there were seventeen constituencies, twenty-seven in 1715, thirty-one in 1728, thirty-nine in 1741, fifty-four in 1755, fifty-eight in 1761, and sixty-five on the eve of the American Revolution.[10] The westward movement of population produced continuous pressure on the House of Burgesses from residents of these new areas to provide appropriate access to local governmental institutions. The House established new counties on a fairly regular basis, and each of the new units sent two representatives to the colonial assembly.

Although seemingly quite different from that of England, the franchise under which eighteenth-century Virginians conducted elections derived from the same set of principles. The English county franchise—established in 1430—gave the vote to freeholders whose land produced an income of at least forty shillings per year. Although the requirement eventually allowed those with leaseholds for lives, annuities, mortgages, and so on to vote in county elections, the franchise reflected the belief that only those with a long-term stake in society should participate in the selection of representatives.[11]

Virginia began with no specific franchise and gradually developed a set of requirements based upon the stake-in-society concept. We do not know precisely who voted in Virginia in the 1620s and 1630s, but by 1646—and probably before—all freemen could participate in the election of burgesses.[12] In 1655, the House restricted the franchise to "all house keepers whether freeholders, lease holders, or otherwise tenants" but with the provision "that this word house keepers . . . extend no further than to one person in a family."[13] A year later, however, the assembly (reflecting perhaps the leveling spirit of the English Commonwealth) decided it was "something hard and unagreeable to reason that any persons shall pay equall taxes and yet have no votes in elections" and repealed that part of the earlier act restricting the franchise to housekeepers.[14]

In 1670, for the first time, the law included property requirements as part of the county franchise: only freeholders and housekeepers subject to levies could vote.[15] These regulations, in turn, disappeared during Bacon's Rebellion in 1676 but became law again when the next assembly repealed everything passed by Bacon's Assembly.[16] With the reestablishment of the freehold requirement, Virginia's franchise rested solidly on the possession of property until well into the nineteenth century. Most of the legislation after 1680 sought only to clarify earlier acts.

In 1684, tenants with life leases became freeholders, and for the first time the law clearly stated that a person could vote in any county in which he possessed a freehold. In 1705, a further definition of the term *freeholder* included "every person who hath an estate real for his own life or the life of another or any estate of any greater dignity," thus clarifying what types of tenants could participate in elections. The amount of property remained unspecified in these early laws, and presumably a freehold or life lease on just a few acres made the holder a member of the electorate.[17]

As early as the 1735 election, if not before, individuals obtained small parcels of land for the sole purpose of enlarging the pool of potential voters. In York County, for example, the sheriff apparently executed nineteen such leases subsequent to the election, and in

King George County one of the candidates and his associates did the same.[18] Immediately following the resolution of the disputed York election, the House of Burgesses instructed the Committee of Privileges and Elections to prepare a bill "to prevent making fraudulent Freeholds."[19] The resulting law specified that a freehold must include either one hundred acres of unimproved land or twenty-five acres with a house and that the holder had to possess such property for at least one year before an election.[20] In 1762 and 1769, the House attempted to reduce the number of unimproved acres to fifty and to shorten the possession time of such property, but neither act received approval in England, and the 1736 law governed election procedures for the remainder of the colonial period.[21]

While the 1736 law and its predecessors gave definition to the freehold requirement, additional regulations restricted the franchise by sex, race, age, and religion. The law did not specifically exclude women from voting until 1699, although it seems unlikely many had participated previously, following the custom of the time in England. The 1699 act and a 1705 act denied the vote to those not of age, which generally meant under twenty-one. Specific disfranchisement of free Negroes, mulattos, and Indians occurred in 1723, although probably few such persons voted before this date. Presumably, during the seventeenth century only Anglicans could vote, but following the spirit of the English Toleration Act of 1688, Virginia formally gave one group of dissenters, the Quakers, the vote in 1699.[22]

Virginia had neither a large number of chartered boroughs nor the variety of borough franchises that existed in England. In the home country, no uniform franchise prevailed, and strictly speaking each borough charter defined voting requirements. This resulted in at least five different types of borough: (1) inhabitant, where almost any adult male resident could vote, (2) scot and lot, where those paying a particular tax could vote, (3) freemen, where all freemen could vote, (4) corporate, where only members of the borough corporation could vote, and (5) burgage, where only those owning certain pieces of property could vote.[23] In Virginia, requirements for county voters living in unincorporated towns mirrored those in the three chartered boroughs.[24] Voters had to own a lot and house or visible property worth fifty pounds a year or serve a five-year apprenticeship in the town or borough.[25] The apprenticeship and house-and-lot requirements gave the vote to most members of the artisan class and provided a franchise very similar to that of the freemen boroughs of England.

Despite refinements and a good deal of specificity in the franchise law, disputes over voter qualifications continuously arose. Of the sixty-nine election-related petitions presented to the House from 1728 to 1775, more dealt with voter qualifications than with any other irregularity. Furthermore, every general election after the passage of the 1736 law included at least one petition challenging the freehold status of voters; after the 1761 election, for example, the House conducted such investigations in five separate counties. Although these petitions came in equal numbers from the Tidewater and Piedmont regions of the colony, a higher rate of petitioning came from the latter. Southside counties such as Amelia, Brunswick, Prince Edward, Lunenburg, Mecklenburg, Halifax, and Prince George accounted for a significant number of these as well.

Investigations of franchise irregularities began when both the petitioner (usually a losing candidate) and the winner prepared a list of all persons whose votes they questioned. A quorum of the county Commission of the Peace then examined the questionable voters and forwarded the resulting depositions to the House Committee of Privileges and Elections. This process might remove the names of some voters from the election pollbook. An examination of the 1761 Prince William pollbook revealed, for example, that several persons having one hundred acres or more "had no Right to vote" because they had not properly executed their leases in court or could show no actual deed for the property; those who had had their deeds executed and recorded "had a good Right to vote." The House disqualified another voter because he had only ninety-three acres and no evidence of a house or improvements of any kind. Ultimately, the committee decided that while illegal voters appeared on both the original winner's and the petitioner's pollbooks, the petitioner still did not have enough legal votes to change the outcome.[26] However, such scrutiny could go the other way.

In the investigation into the 1771 Lunenburg election, the original pollbook showed that Thomas Pettus had defeated Henry Blagrave 192 to 179. After careful examination of many voters, the House determined that Pettus had 27 illegal voters and Blagrave 15. Pettus still appeared to be the victor, with a vote of 165 to 164, until the committee discovered that 2 of Blagrave's votes had gone unrecorded. Blagrave won by a single vote, and the House ordered "that the Clerk do amend the Return for the County of Lunenburg, by rasing out the Name of Thomas Pettus, and inserting the Name of Henry Blagrave, instead thereof."[27]

THE ELECTORATE

The freeholders who voted for Pettus and Blagrave were part of a demographic boom that increased Virginia's population fivefold, from about 100,000 to 500,000 during the final half century of the colonial period. A considerable part of that growth occurred within the black population due to substantial importations of new slaves directly from Africa before 1740 and, thereafter, to a natural increase within the existing slave population. In 1725, black slaves totaled about 28,000, or 28 percent of the population, but by 1775 they had grown to more than seven times that number (200,000) and represented 40 percent of all Virginians. Immigration and natural increase affected the white population as well, quadrupling it during the same fifty-year period, from 72,000 to 291,000.[28]

Virginians claiming the right to vote constituted at most 15 percent of this white population. White males over twenty-one years of age formed the pool of potential electors, but a somewhat smaller group was actually eligible to vote. Although the 1736 statute conferred political citizenship on freeholders who owned one hundred acres of unimproved land or twenty-five acres of improved land, by law and practice freehold status came to encompass more than outright ownership of property and meant that both actual owners and holders of life leases could vote. Short-term tenants or tenants-at-will as well as those adult white males with no legal attachments to the land remained disfranchised (see figure 2.1).[29]

Adult white male landowners represented the permanent core of the colonial electorate, but the proportion of this population achieving such status varied substantially across Virginia's counties (see table 2.1). Only about one-quarter of the white men in Fairfax County owned the land they tilled, while nearly three-quarters of their cousins farther west in Berkeley County attained such titles to their property.

Because land availability fell and prices normally rose as settlement progressed, some counties presented greater opportunity for

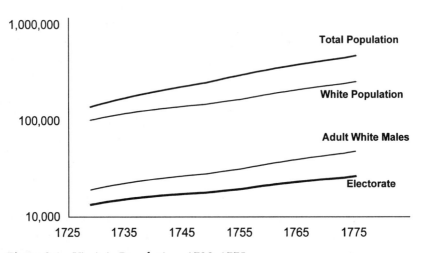

Figure 2.1   Virginia Population, 1729–1775
The vertical, or population, axis is a logarithmic scale.

landownership—and thus political participation—during the initial period of settlement (Lunenburg, Amelia, Prince William, and possibly Berkeley, for example). On the other hand, ownership opportunities in the extremely large frontier county of Frederick apparently increased only slightly over time, while they remained remarkably stable in Fairfax. Even the long-settled Tidewater region witnessed considerable variation, with low ownership rates in Norfolk (35%) and substantially higher ones in Lancaster, James City, Northumberland, and Richmond (40–65%). All in all, perhaps one-half of Virginia's adult white males enjoyed the franchise through direct ownership of property.[30]

Long-term leases, not outright ownership, enfranchised a minority of the colonial electorate. The longevity of these leases gave tenants the necessary attachment to property—the stake in society—that Anglo-Americans equated with full political subjecthood. Without this protracted commitment to property and, in theory, the economic and political independence that came with it, citizenship did not exist, as one Prince William County tenant-at-will with 660 acres discovered in 1761.[31] Throughout Virginia, however, enfranchised life leaseholders participated in elections on an equal footing with landowners. Indeed, before 1736 men became long-term tenants before elections specifically for the purpose of enlarging the

Table 2.1
Composition of the Virginia Electorate, by County

Region, County, and Year	Adult White Males	As % of Adult White Males		
		Landowners	Eligible Tenants	Electorate
Northern Neck				
Berkeley				
1772	780	70		70+
Dunmore				
1774	1,245	39		39+
Fairfax				
1744–48	688	24	42	66
1761	694	23	26	49
1765–68	847	20	25	45
1770	780	23	12	35
Fauquier				
1770	999	35		35+
Frederick				
1758	1,900	38	15	53
1761	2,156	34	15	49
1764	2,399	46		46+
Lancaster				
1750	392	57	20	77
1773	410	62	19	81
Loudoun				
1761	779	20	c.25	45
1769	1,213	24	c.15	39
Northumberland				
1758–59	751	48		48+
Prince William				
1754	1,035	42		42+
1760	464	59		59+
1773	753	36		36+
Richmond				
1744	513	65		65+
1770	586	41		41+
Southside				
Amelia				
1749	831	76		76+
1768	1,243	55		55+
Charlotte				
1764	365	67		67+

continued

Table 2.1
Continued

Region, County, and Year	Adult White Males	As % of Adult White Males		
		Landowners	Eligible Tenants	Electorate
Halifax				
1764–65	1,438			85
1768–69	940			74
Lunenburg				
1750	712	78		78+
1769	523	61		61+
Mecklenburg				
1764	1,113	60		60+
Appalachian				
Augusta				
1760	2,155	52		52+
Tidewater				
Accomack				
1738	979	48	20	68
1748	1,118	43	20	63
1755	1,130	42	22	64
1768	1,396	33	18	51
James City				
1768	325	58		58+
Norfolk				
1771	1,441	35		35+

Source: List of Officers in Virginia in 1729, PRO CO5, 1322:127–29; List of Tithables Taken 1750, Chalmers Collection, New York Public library; List of Tithables in the Dominion of Virgina 1755, PRO CO5, 1338:364; List of Tithables Taken 1773, reprinted in *Virgina Magazine of History and Biography* 28 (1920), 81–82; U.S. Bureau of the Census, *Heads of Families at the first Census of the United States Taken in the Year 1790: Virginia* (Washington, D. C.: U.S. Government Printing Office, 1907), 9–10; Evarts B. Greene and Virginia D. Harrington, *American Population before the Federal Census of 1790* (New York: Columbia University Press, 1932), Allan Kulikoff, *Tobacco and Slaves: The Development of Southern Cultures in the Chesapeake, 1680–1800* (Chapel Hill: University of North Carolina Press, 1986), 135, 154, 156; Albert H. Tillson Jr., *Gentry and Common Folk: Political Culture on a Virginia Frontier, 1740–1789* (Lexington: University Press of Kentucky, 1991), 13; Robert E. Brown and B. Katherine Brown, *Virginia, 1705–1782: Democracy or Aristocracy?* (East Lansing: Michigan State University Press, 1963), 13–14, 143, 145; Fairfax Rentals, 1761, 1764, 1770; Richmond Rentals, 1744, 1770; Northumberland Rentals, 1758–59; Lancaster Rentals, 1748, 1750: Huntington Library; Lanchester Rentals, 1773, Virginia Historical Society; Ralph T. Whitelaw, *Virginia's Eastern Shore: A History of Northampton and Accomack Counties*, 2 vol. (Richmond: Virginia Historical Society, 1951).

Note: Eligible tenants are persons who participated in elections of the period but never appeared on lists of landowners. These figures are a conservative estimate.

pool of potential voters. Thereafter, the law forbade such practices by specifying the size, conditions, and length of tenure of properties, but petitions related to these matters continued to plague the House of Burgesses for the remainder of the colonial period, and they involved the intricacies of leaseholding as much as landholding.[32]

While the extent and circumstances of leaseholding have received little attention from historians, limited evidence suggests that tenants played a vital role in Virginia's rural communities.[33] In frontier areas, tenants often received leases for several lives at nominal rates on condition that they make improvements to the land; landlords clearly enhanced their properties through such arrangements, while low rental fees benefited those initiating careers as farmers and planters. Yet the general decline in opportunity that restricted landownership in some areas in the late colonial period also affected tenancy contracts; as population increased, land availability fell, and land prices increased, resulting in shorter leases, higher rents, and fewer tenants.[34] In Fairfax County, for example, these conditions produced a slight decline in landownership in the 1760s but a dramatic reduction in long-term tenancy (see table 2.1). Similarly, the Eastern Shore county of Accomack witnessed a gradual decrease in opportunity for ownership from about one-half to about one-third but only a slight decline in the proportion of tenants eligible to vote. On the other hand, long-settled Lancaster County experienced almost no change in tenancy in the last years of the colonial period, while by the 1760s mountainous Frederick mirrored marshy Accomack. While information on eligible tenants remains limited and sketchy, it may be that 20 percent of Virginia's adult white males entered the electorate through some kind of long-term leasehold arrangement.

Although some historians claim that 85 percent of Virginia's adult white males attained freehold status in the eighteenth century, such estimates substantially overstate reality for most locations and mask considerable diversity among the counties and regions of the Old Dominion.[35] It is probable that such levels existed in some long-settled Tidewater counties like Lancaster (see figure 2.2) and in newly formed Berkeley in the 1770s or in Southside Amelia or Lunenburg about 1750 or in Halifax (see figure 2.3), but it seems highly unlikely that such patterns were widespread. The Fairfax (figure 2.4), Dunmore, Norfolk, Prince William, Fauquier, and Loudoun electorates, for example, may have been just above a third of the

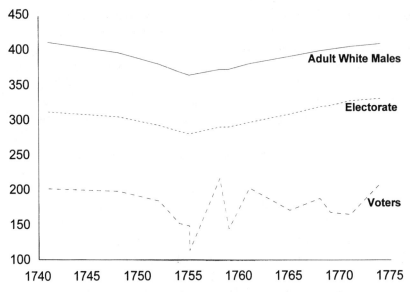

Figure 2.2   Lancaster County, Eligible and Actual Voters, 1741–1774

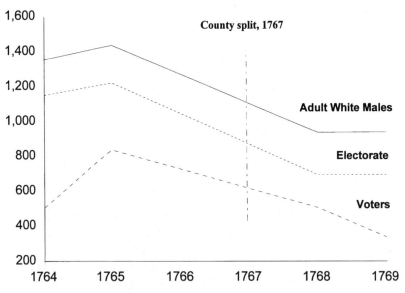

Figure 2.3   Halifax County, Eligible and Actual Voters, 1764–1769

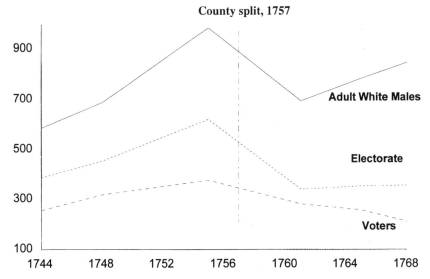

Figure 2.4   Fairfax County, Eligible and Actual Voters, 1744–1768

adult white male population by the 1770s, while somewhat more than half became enfranchised in Frederick (figure 2.5), Augusta, Accomack (figure 2.6), Amelia and James City.[36] While the level of enfranchisement declined nearly everywhere in the closing decades of the colonial era due primarily to a steadily increasing population coupled with stable or declining opportunities for ownership and long-term tenancy, approximately two-thirds of Virginia's adult white males attained freehold status in the eighteenth century. Those residing in the Southside and in the oldest Tidewater counties had, in general, the greatest opportunities to participate in the political life of their communities.

VOTER TURNOUT

While a majority of Virginia's adult white men claimed freehold status in the eighteenth century, a smaller number regularly exercised the rights and responsibilities of that privilege. Conditions controlling voter participation included such mundane factors as the time of year, weather, distance to the courthouse, and condition of the

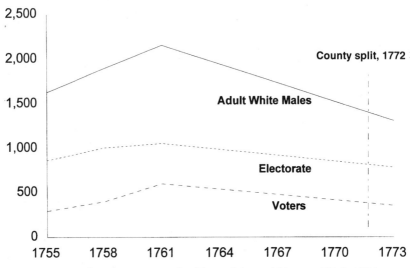

Figure 2.5   Frederick County, Eligible and Actual Voters, 1755–1773

roads, as well as election frequency, circumstances relating to the dissolution of the previous assembly, local controversies and issues, competition among county leaders, and voter perceptions of the importance or closeness of contests.[37] The blending of these and other factors produced voter turnout rates ranging from 14 percent of

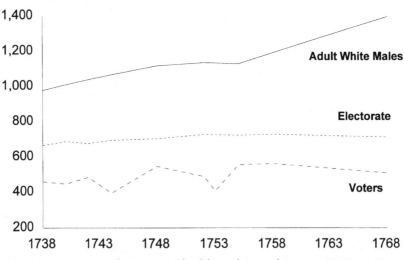

Figure 2.6   Accomack County, Eligible and Actual Voters, 1738–1768

the adult white males in a 1770 by-election held in Essex County to 76 percent in the 1735 general election in nearby Richmond County. Eighty percent of the elections had turnout levels between 31 and 52 percent; average turnout among white men during the late colonial period was 43 percent.[38]

Because the electorate never constituted the full adult white male population, actual turnout among those eligible reached substantially higher levels. Although our ability to count the exact number enfranchised is limited, rough estimates nonetheless suggest that, on average, two-thirds of the electorate turned out to vote. Such rates rarely remained constant, however: over time, turnout fell among adult white males, while it increased among the more narrowly defined electorate. As landholding and tenancy opportunities stabilized or declined slightly in many Virginia counties, fewer white men, proportionally speaking, were eligible to vote, but those in this narrowing group exercised their franchise at the same or at higher levels. Specifically, the elections of the 1740s drew about 60 percent of eligible men to the hustings, while in the 1760s more than 65 percent—and in some cases nearly 75 percent—cast votes (see figure 2.7).

Fairfax and Accomack Counties illustrate this trend. During its first decade of growth, the large and partially frontier county of Fairfax offered ownership and tenancy opportunities that allowed the electorate to grow alongside the booming white population, but after the county divided in 1757 the now smaller and more heavily settled Tidewater region provided not only fewer, but also decreasing, chances for freehold status (see figure 2.4). Although this constricted electorate helped Fairfax County achieve political consensus by the final decade of the colonial period, local controversies still had the power to spark "the flame of burgessing." For the 1765 contest involving new candidate George Washington and a fierce debate over parish boundaries (see chap. 6), nearly 73 percent of eligible voters turned out. Similarly, the number of freeholders in Accomack County remained nearly constant from 1740 to 1770, while the adult white male population grew steadily, and election turnout increased only slightly (see figure 2.6).

Richmond County provides a variation on this theme. The adult white male population increased steadily from the 1730s to the 1770s, while landownership—and probably tenancy opportunities—decreased. Within this initially expanding and then steadily

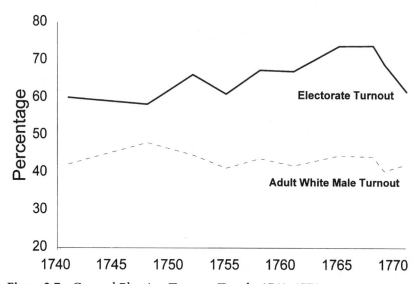

Figure 2.7   General Election Turnout Trends, 1741–1771

Figure includes only seventy-nine general elections; data points average from six to eleven individual elections.

contracting electorate, turnout fluctuated according to provincial and local influences (see figure 2.8). In 1735, more than 90 percent of the eligible freeholders assembled at the county courthouse to reject one incumbent and raise two new men to burgess status, at least partially as a result of the continuing debate over the Tobacco Inspection Act of 1730.[39] On the other hand, the fewest voters appeared and the lowest turnout occurred in the county in 1755, when Governor Robert Dinwiddie sent the House packing after it passed a public credit bill he intensely disliked. Richmond freeholders overwhelmingly returned incumbents Landon Carter and John Woodbridge over challenger Robert Mitchell, sending, in part, a not-too-subtle message that they approved of their burgesses' actions in the previous assembly.[40] In four elections after 1755, the number of voters barely changed, fluctuating between 225 and 235, but the slowly shrinking electorate increased turnout rates from 59 to 70 percent.

Few freeholders permanently stayed away from the election process, resulting over time in an active electorate that encompassed nearly everyone who was eligible. For example, the active

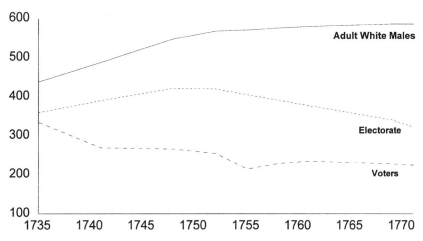

Figure 2.8   Richmond County, Eligible and Actual Voters, 1735–1771

electorate of Lancaster County was considerably larger than the 199 men who voted in 1748 or the 185 who voted in 1752; 269 individuals cast votes in the two elections (see table 2.2). While each of these elections brought out more than 60 percent of the electorate, more than 90 percent of the eligible voters participated in one of the two elections. Even in Frederick County, which exhibited one of the lowest election turnout rates of the period, nearly 80 percent of freeholders voted at least once in the three contests held between 1755 and 1761. In Fairfax, Halifax, and Accomack, similar patterns prevailed. Clearly, in many counties the electoral process ignored few and included nearly all enfranchised citizens.

While more than 80 percent of Virginia's freeholders apparently took part in the process of electing members to the House of Burgesses, the regularity of that participation varied enormously. In Halifax, for example, the frequent voter was a rarity, and the irregular or occasional voter dominated elections (see table 2.3). Of those eligible, only 4 percent participated in all four Halifax elections of the 1760s and only 8 percent in three of the four. Broadly speaking, freeholders went to the polls three of the eight elections available to them, or 38 percent of the time. Given the frequency with which elections occurred in Halifax, these Southside freeholders exercised their franchise once in every four and one-half years, although they

Table 2.2
Multiple-Election Turnout, by County

County and Years	Electorate	Electorate as % of Adult White Males	Electorate Turnout (%)
Lancaster			
1748–52	269	71	92
1758–61	293	77	99
1765–69	272	68	85
1768–71	270	67	82
Frederick			
1755–61	833	39	79
Fairfax			
1744–48	448	65	98
1765–68	338	40	95
Halifax			
1764–65	1,113	77	91
1768–69	644	69	92
Accomack			
1755–58	732	61	83

had the opportunity to vote approximately every twenty-one months.

The citizen subjects of Fairfax's early years exhibited similar patterns, with 71 percent voting just once in the three elections between 1744 and 1755. However, as populations stabilized and the physical size of counties shrank, the frequent voters' importance in the electoral process increased. Such trends are just barely visible in Halifax and Fairfax (see table 2.3) but are readily apparent in long-settled counties like Accomack and, especially, Lancaster. Here, the frequent voter dominated activities at election time, with 60 percent voting more than once in any three successive contests. Put simply, a Lancaster County resident attaining freehold status in 1741 had an opportunity to go to the polls on fourteen occasions between that date and the opening shots of the American Revolution, and on average, he did so in eleven (nearly 80%) of those contests.[41]

Only a handful of men in Lancaster held freehold status for these thirty-five years, but nonetheless the majority voted with similar frequency. Like William Robinson, introduced at the beginning of

Table 2.3
Multiple-Election Participation, by County

County and Years	Voted Once (%)	Voted Twice (%)	Voted Three Times (%)
Lancaster			
1758–61	39	29	32
1768–71	41	26	34
Frederick			
1755–61	59	26	15
Fairfax			
1744–55	71	20	9
1761–68	54	28	18
Halifax			
1764–65	79	21	
1768–69	69	31	
Accomack			
1755–58	47	53	

this chapter, the average Lancaster freeholder arrived at the court-house on election day already a veteran of two or three contests, and he would participate in several more before ill health, death, or a change in his land tenure removed him from the electorate. As the owner of the land he cultivated, he spent, on average, more than fourteen years as an eligible voter, while as a tenant his intersection with the electoral process lasted only four years. Similarly, landowners in Fairfax County were far more likely to fill the ranks of the frequent, long-term voter than those without permanent title to their properties. In the elections of 1744, 1748, and 1755, 18 percent of those who voted just once, 46 percent of those who voted twice, and 66 percent of those voting in all three elections were landowners.

Geography, local officeholding, wealth, and longevity in the community also affected the frequency with which freeholders participated in the electoral process. In Halifax, for example, individuals living in the more settled eastern portions of the county, where distance to the courthouse was much less, participated to a greater extent than those living in more remote sections of the county.[42] In Fairfax, those who undertook various community responsibilities remained active members of the electorate, even as turnout gener-

Table 2.4
Participation and Wealth, by County

County and Years	No. of Times Voted					County Average	N
	0	1	2	3	4		
Average Acres Owned							
Accomack							
1755–58	258	293	271			273	524
Halifax							
1764–65	968	577	400			634	380
1768–69	1,033	662	507			764	179
Fairfax							
1765–68	981	594	1,064			905	181
Frederick							
1755–61	414	487	491	517		454	738
Lancaster							
1752–55	275	180	272	218	189	241	223
1768–71	225	273	353	199		251	253
Average Slaves Owned							
Halifax							
1764–65	3.3	2.6	1.6			2.6	79
1768–69	3.8	3.2	2.3			3.1	67
Fairfax							
1744–55	1.2	1.6	1.9	1.5		1.4	659

ally declined. Although justices turned out for the 1744 election at a rate well below that of the eligible male population, turnout rose to 81 percent in 1755 and to 100 percent in 1765. Turnout among vestrymen hovered near 80 percent for most of the period, while participation among the eligible population was nearly always below that level (see chap. 6).

In some of Virginia's communities, an increasing "stake in society" heightened interest in local elections, as in Frederick County, where nonvoting landowners held fewer acres, on average, than those participating regularly (see table 2.4). Moreover, those absent from electoral activity in Fairfax County in the 1740s and 1750s, in Accomack County in the 1750s, and in Lancaster County in the 1760s and 1770s were also toward the lower end of the economic scale in their respective communities. On the other hand, in frontier counties like Halifax, where the size of landholdings remained large, those with the most land and slaves voted the least. Here, land speculators and out-of-county residents controlled many of the largest holdings and apparently cared little for local issues or local elections, preferring instead to immerse themselves in the political systems of older Piedmont or Tidewater counties (see chap. 7).

Although the relationship between economic status and electoral participation depended upon a myriad of local variables, including size of holdings, availability of land, population mobility, and settlement patterns, there is a sense that the franchise held real value in many communities and that those toward the economic bottom of the electorate held the rights and responsibilities of freeholder in greater esteem than those better positioned. In Lancaster, Accomack, early Fairfax, and Halifax Counties, those with the highest participation rates held average or below average wealth in land or slaves (see table 2.4). Furthermore, large landowners rarely dominated the voting process at single elections: in Lancaster, those with holdings below the median (150 acres) turned out for elections to a greater extent than those at higher levels. Similarly, tenants may have held their often brief membership in the electorate in much higher regard than those holding property outright. In every contest in which comparisons can be made, tenants in Lancaster County

Table 2.5
Electorate, Turnout, and Tenure, Lancaster County, 1748–1774 (%)

Election Year	Electorate		Turnout	
	Landowners	Tenants	Landowners	Tenants
1748	72	28	71	92
1752	58	42	68	93
1754 (by)	59	41	62	77
1755 (by)	52	48	42	48
1755	52	48	56	60
1768	75	25	69	87
1769	80	20	64	77
1771	78	22	60	82
1774	73	27		

participated to a greater extent than landowners. Although they constituted only one-fifth of the electorate, they often made up near-ly half of those voting at single elections (see table 2.5).

The right to vote, according to a recent study of Chesapeake so-ciety "separated white men into two groups, freeholders welcome to participate in political discourse and men too poor or unsettled to be full members of civil society."[43] For the former, citizen subject-hood meant stability and longevity on the land either through out-right ownership or through a life leasehold. In some locales, freehold opportunities remained widespread and open throughout the late colonial period, but in a number of places original land acquisition patterns and subsequent demographic trends substantially restrict-ed entry into the local polity. It should come as no surprise, there-fore, that being a full member of their own small political commu-nity meant a great deal to adult white males in many of Virginia's eighteenth-century county constituencies. Even when the size of their farms or the term of their tenures just barely qualified them for membership, they took full advantage of that status and voted as of-ten as they could.

voters took all day. The election could be so lopsided that the outcome became obvious almost immediately after polling started, but
occasionally the results remained in doubt until the very last freeholder announced his preferences. Incumbents usually won reelection, but a significant minority went down to defeat. Some contests
attracted almost a thousand voters, others barely a hundred. Turnout could include nearly every eligible adult white male in the county or as few as a sixth of them. In some locales, rivalry among candidates became so intense and the election so controversial that the
House of Burgesses in Williamsburg, rather than the local sheriff and
the freeholders, decided the outcome. Clearly, some elections were
highly competitive, others less so, and some not at all.

A variety of factors contributed to this remarkable diversity in
electoral competitiveness. Local conditions at specific elections had
the greatest influence, but the age of the constituencies, the conditions of their founding, and the political cultures of the broad regions
they inhabited all played important roles as well. Moreover, gradual, colonywide, institutional change, coupled with irregular and
temporary responses to particular provincial and imperial events,
shifted competition first one way and then the other.

COMPETITION

Electoral competition in its simplest form meant rivalry among candidates and choice for voters.[3] Competitive elections witnessed candidates striving for office and voters selecting between these rivals
on election day. Specifically, a competitive election occurred when
there was more than one candidate per seat, an incumbent lost, a formal or informal poll of the voters became necessary to determine
the outcome, or the House received a petition challenging the results. In contrast, noncompetitive elections included those in which
the incumbents won and there is no other evidence of competitive
activity or no poll occurred because there was only one candidate
running for each seat.

In county elections, two seats were open at each general election.
Candidates contested only one seat in most by-elections and in all
elections in the three boroughs and the College of William and Mary.
In the absence of long-standing parties or factions, the number of
candidates running in any of these elections depended upon the am-

3

The Dynamics of Electoral Competition

In September 1727, William Gooch arrived in Williamsburg to assume his duties as the new governor of Virginia. Following custom, he dissolved the sitting House of Burgesses and on December 14 ordered writs for new elections.[1] From this first set of contests under Gooch until the last by-election conducted just before Governor John Murray, Earl of Dunmore, left Williamsburg in June 1775, 882 constituency-level elections occurred in the counties and boroughs of Virginia.

At the time of Gooch's first election, Virginia had thirty-one electoral constituencies. Except for Spotsylvania County, all were within the Tidewater plain. Over the next fifty years, the House of Burgesses created new counties as settlement pushed westward across the Piedmont and over the Blue Ridge. By the eve of the Revolution, the number of electoral districts had risen to sixty-five. Constituencies that existed in 1728 participated in thirteen general elections before the colonial era ended; several newer counties participated only in the 1774 election. By-elections were also a regular part of electoral activity in most locales, averaging nearly three per constituency.[2] Some counties held as many as twenty-two elections (both general and by-elections) between 1728 and 1775, while one—Berkeley, formed in 1772—held only two.

The competitive nature of the 882 elections examined here varied enormously. In some contests, up to seven serious candidates vied for the two available seats, while in others no one opposed the incumbents. Sometimes, the sheriff determined the outcome in a matter of minutes, simply taking a quick head count, or "view," of the assembled freeholders. In other cases, the formal polling of the bitions and aspirations of the local elite at election time.[4] On average, three persons ran for every two seats, although almost 40 percent of the contests included two or more candidates for every seat. Variation in the number of candidates running in particular contests charts the rising and falling satisfaction with incumbents, the developing or diminishing rivalry among the local elite, and the availability of interested challengers. The more candidates running, the greater the level of competition.

A highly competitive electoral environment is also apparent in contests in which an incumbent went down to defeat. Although an incumbent lost in only 11 percent of the elections, even that level indicates a certain lack of solidarity among the local elite that a challenge could be mounted and a lack of loyalty among the freeholders that they would support one candidate at one point in time and a different candidate at a succeeding election.[5] In nine out of ten contests, however, incumbents either did not run or ran and won. While the reelection (or nondefeat) of an incumbent does not necessarily mean that the election lacked competition, it does suggest a less competitive contest.

Petitions to the House of Burgesses for redress of electoral grievances further demonstrate competition. The majority of election petitions came from losing candidates challenging the legitimacy of votes for the winner. The House journals indicate that on several occasions no more than a dozen votes separated winner from loser; thus, it is easy to understand the appeal for a recount. If the petitioner won his appeal, the House declared him the winner, and he immediately obtained a seat.[6] If he demonstrated that the winner or the sheriff had engaged in some kind of illegal activity, he could try his luck in a new election.[7] Sixty-nine contests, or 8 percent of those in the final fifty years of the colonial period, resulted in such petitions.

Elections with more than one candidate per seat were clearly competitive, but the level of such competition varied substantially. Contests in which a single challenger took only a few votes away from a sitting incumbent exhibited a good deal less competition than elections in which the winner squeaked out a victory over four or more rivals. Similarly, elections that attracted a large proportion of the electorate were probably more competitive than those in which many fewer voters appeared. In these predominately two-member districts, losing candidates garnered as much as 60 percent of the votes cast or as little as 6 percent. On average, the losers received just 33 percent of the votes. The higher the percentage of the vote received by a single loser or group of losers, the greater the intensity of the rivalry among candidates, the less likely the outcome was a foregone conclusion, and the more competitive the election.

Finally, turnout rates paralleled the rise and fall of voter interest in the election outcome. When the outcome appeared predictable or unimportant, voter turnout decreased; when the outcome seemed uncertain or voters perceived something of importance at stake, turnout increased.

All in all, 35 percent of the elections held between 1728 and 1775 were competitive.[8] In the remaining two-thirds, no real contest took place, and the freeholders who assembled on election day either played no political role or at most only affirmed the candidates running unopposed. Since noncompetitive elections were often the norm, it is possible that the selection of representatives relied much less on electoral choice than has previously been believed.

TRENDS

Although choice may have been absent from many—perhaps even most—eighteenth-century elections, competition was hardly uniform and varied substantially both over time and between counties. The final fifty years of the colonial period, in fact, witnessed a sharp decline in the number of competitive elections, dropping from more than 65 percent in 1728, 1735, and 1741 to less than 40 percent in the decade just before the American Revolution (see figure 3.1). Only 9 percent of the contests sparked competition in 1774, suggesting that the immediate prerevolutionary era provided much less opportunity for the venting of public sentiment at the polls than earlier periods had.[9] Decreased tensions between local elites and governors after 1725 partially explain this decline in electoral intensity, but provincial and imperial developments had a significant impact as well.

Although elections between 1728 and 1741 probably contained some of the "aggressive and participatory" residue from the pre-1725 era, heightened competition in the 1735 election reflected a new provincial controversy with local ramifications. The continuing debate over the Tobacco Inspection Act of 1730 apparently pro-

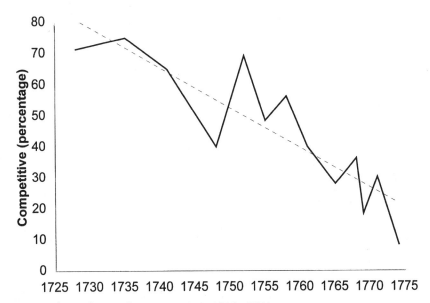

Figure 3.1 Electoral Competition, 1728–1774
The trend line was determined using simple linear regression.

duced the increased level of competition. Because the law favored the higher quality leaf produced by large planters, small planters rioted in 1732, burned tobacco warehouses, and sent dozens of petitions to the House asking for repeal. When the House refused to bend to public pressure and renewed the act in 1734, protesters took out their frustrations in the electoral arena and turned out many of the act's original supporters (see figure 3.2).[10] Following the election, large numbers of defeated candidates rushed petitions to the House asking that the results be overturned (see figure 3.3).[11]

The 1741 and 1748 general elections were the last of the colonial era called to comply with the British practice of holding elections at least once in seven years.[12] Although the 1741 contest took place in a sea of political tranquillity, Governor Gooch's use of the seven-year rule in 1748 also allowed him to end more than a year of incessant bickering over the possible relocation of the burned capitol. If the relocation issue affected the campaign, it did so only negatively, as the level of competition dropped precipitously, and nearly 60 percent of the burgesses returned to continue the squabble over rebuilding the capitol (see figures 3.1 and 3.2).[13]

Figure 3.2   Defeat of Incumbents, 1728–1774

The trend line was determined using simple linear regression.

After 1750, general elections occurred for two reasons: a change in imperial administration (the death of the monarch or the arrival of a new governor) or the governor's belief that the burgesses had overstepped their powers.[14] In 1752, 1758, 1768, and 1771, newly appointed governors dissolved sitting assemblies and issued writs for new elections; in 1761, Governor Francis Fauquier did the same at the accession of George III.[15] Although provincial administrators issued writs approximately a month in advance, which resulted in a relatively short official electoral season, a change in the governorship was often known or anticipated up to a year before the actual election. In such cases, potential challengers had ample time and opportunity to cultivate carefully the interests of the local elite and to campaign extensively among the freeholders. These lengthy campaign seasons produced, not surprisingly, higher levels of competition and fewer returning incumbents (figure 3.1). In addition, electoral intensity received a boost in some counties in 1758 from Indian troubles associated with the Seven Years' War, while in 1768 continuing fallout from the Parsons' Cause probably stirred the political waters in some locales.[16]

Figure 3.3 Petitions to House by Defeated Candidates, 1728–1774

The trend line was determined using simple linear regression.

Elections called because of the governor's displeasure with the activities of the assembly often produced an entirely different set of responses. In 1755, Governor Robert Dinwiddie sent the House home after it passed a public credit bill to establish a loan office and issue £200,000 in paper money.[17] The elections that immediately followed witnessed considerably less competition than the general election just three years earlier. A relatively short (six-week) electoral season coupled with voter support for the burgesses' activities in the previous session brought a slight upswing in freeholder participation (see figure 2.7) and returned more than 60 percent of the incumbents, while fewer than 15 percent suffered defeat (see figure 3.2).

The developing imperial crisis following the French and Indian War decreased electoral competition even more dramatically. As a succession of governors angrily dissolved assemblies for passing the Stamp Act Resolves in 1765 and for opposing the Townshend Acts in 1769 and the Boston Port Act in 1774, a kind of patriotic solidarity developed among the gentry and small planters in many of Virginia's constituencies. In some communities, enthusiastic crowds greeted members returning home from these dissolved assemblies and pledged unanimous support for the burgesses' strong stand against British authorities. Such unanimity allowed a number of incumbents to run unopposed; George Washington's only uncontested election occurred in 1769, for example. Solidarity discouraged opposition to incumbents, as reflected in a low candidate-per-seat ratio in 1765, 1769, and 1774, the small numbers of incumbents defeated in 1765 and 1774, and the smaller number of petitions challenging the election results in 1765, 1769, and 1774. The diminished competition among candidates produced either lower levels of turnout among the voters in 1769 or a dramatic thrashing of the challengers at the polls in 1765.

The deepening imperial crisis and the more frequent dissolutions of the House that resulted from it combined with constant changes in administration to produce five general elections in the final ten years of the colonial period. In contrast, elections between 1728 and 1752 were on the average more than six years apart. The shorter intervals between contests in the immediate prerevolutionary decade only accelerated the decrease in competitiveness. Fewer new candidates had the time to mount a serious challenge to sitting burgesses, and thus fewer incumbents suffered defeat at the polls. Voter interest, at least in moderately competitive contests, remained high but served to affirm, not reject, incumbents who stood their ground against Britain (see figures 2.7 and 3.1 through 3.3).

Local electoral patterns clearly responded to provincial and imperial events. The Tobacco Inspection Acts of the early 1730s, events of the 1750s, and the worsening crisis with Britain after 1765 all had an impact on electoral activity. This is not to say that candidates debated such issues in any formal sense or that freeholders spent much time thinking about events outside their local communities. Local problems and personalities dominated most contests, but provincial and imperial issues helped set the tone of elections at certain times and in some constituencies. Outside events discouraged or encouraged incumbents and potential challengers, and voter enthusiasm for electoral participation rose and fell under similar influences. Because fluctuations in competitiveness correlate closely with provincial and imperial developments, elections to the House of Burgesses seem more than the ritualistic and issueless events they are often portrayed to be.[18]

CONSTITUENCY PATTERNS

The broad institutional decline in electoral competitiveness during the final half century of the colonial period affected individual constituencies in a variety of ways. Many mirrored the colonywide pattern of decline and witnessed highly competitive contests in the 1730s and 1740s and limited competition in the 1760s and 1770s. In other constituencies, contests remained vigorous through the final election in 1774, while a number of districts saw little or no competition during most of the eighteenth century. Parochial concerns often overshadowed provincial and imperial issues, producing at times localized patterns entirely at odds with colonywide trends.

Declining Competition

Westmoreland and Prince William typify the handful of Tidewater counties that mirrored the broader trend: a highly charged electoral environment through 1761 and a noncompetitive atmosphere thereafter. In Westmoreland's 1728 general election and 1734 by-election, for example, losing candidates petitioned the House, demanding that the initial results be overturned. In the former, Sheriff Augustine Washington determined the outcome by view instead of by a formal poll, while in the latter a Maryland resident, three mulattos, and a voter with a questionable life lease had participated in the contest.[19] Although no incumbents suffered defeat in these or subsequent elections, three or four candidates normally battled in moderately close contests during the 1740s and 1750s. Even members of the prominent Lee family had trouble being elected: Richard Lee, Esq., lost in the elections of 1752, 1754, and 1755. However, when Richard Henry Lee outpolled William Bernard in a 1757 by-election, Westmoreland took the first step toward a consensual political environment. Only another challenge by Bernard in 1761 disturbed the developing quietude, and Richard Henry Lee and cousin Richard Lee, Esq., monopolized Westmoreland representation for the remainder of the colonial period.[20]

The history of electoral activity in Prince William County followed a similar pattern. In four elections between 1732 and 1741, three incumbents suffered defeat, two of the elections resulted in petitions before the House of Burgesses, coercion of voters through threats of physical violence reportedly occurred at one contest, and

the House declared another election void because one candidate inappropriately used his office of tobacco inspector to influence the
electors.[21] Although the 1748 election occurred with little fanfare,
the 1752 contest saw the return of the earlier contentiousness, including a near riot, disruption of the polling, and an assault on the
sheriff. In 1755, one of the leaders of the riot, Henry Peyton, ran and
lost but later successfully demonstrated that winner Henry Lee had
illegally treated voters. The two antagonists then both won in 1758
but had to withstand a feeble assertion that they had received votes
from disqualified freeholders. Finally, in 1761 Peyton lost second
place to Lee by three votes amid further accusations of improper
voter credentials. After 1761, however, tranquillity settled on the
recently divided county, and Henry Lee and two successive partners
became Prince William's permanent representatives until the Revolution.[22]

Tidewater counties of the Northern Neck were not the only communities to experience a general decline in competition; the Piedmont counties of Amelia and Prince Edward as well as the transappalachian county of Augusta did so. Local political squabbles in
Amelia swirled mainly around four families—the Jones, Bookers,
Tabbs, and Scotts—who battled each other for decades over the right
to represent the county in Williamsburg. A Scott edged out an incumbent Jones in 1741, and in 1748 another Jones lost when the
House reexamined voter qualifications. Formal polling remained
the norm through the 1761 election, when Thomas Tabb returned
to the hustings after a brief hiatus. Although the voters would be
asked again in 1768 to choose between four candidates, the elections
of 1765, 1769, 1771, and 1774 were noncompetitive.[23] Similar patterns of competition prevailed in Prince Edward from the county's
first election in 1754 through 1761; thereafter, signs of conflict disappeared.[24] West of the Blue Ridge, Augusta County witnessed challenges to voter qualifications in 1748 and such disorderly conduct
in 1755 that the sheriff stopped the polling and new elections had to
be held five months later. In 1758, newcomer Israel Christian took
advantage of incumbent Gabriel Jones' absence on election day and
defeated him. After 1758, long-serving burgess John Wilson and a
succession of partners represented this large frontier county, with
little or no opposition.[25]

In these Tidewater, Piedmont, and transappalachian constituencies, provincial and imperial developments reenforced an emerging

local consensus, producing a significant decline in local political tensions in the decades immediately preceding the American Revolution. Such was not the case in several Tidewater communities of the Northern Neck, where local controversies overshadowed outside events and electoral battles continued unabated until at least 1775.

Continuous Competition

On the surface, the political climate of Richmond County appears anything but competitive. John Woodbridge won nine consecutive elections and served continuously in the House of Burgesses from 1735 until his death in 1769. For nearly all of that period, he had just two fellow burgesses: William Fantleroy from 1735 to 1752 and Landon Carter from 1752 to 1768. Following Woodbridge's death, the voters of Richmond returned Robert W. Carter and Francis Lightfoot Lee, younger members of two of the Tidewater's most prominent families.

But despite the monopolization of burgess seats by a few individuals during this forty-year period, rival candidates continued to challenge, and sometimes defeat, incumbents. Incumbent Daniel Hornby lost to Woodbridge and Fantleroy in 1735, and Thomas Glascock upset incumbent Landon Carter in 1768 only to be turned out himself in 1769. After three consecutive terms, the voters rejected young Carter and Lee in the first election after independence. Following his loss in 1735, Daniel Hornby tried to regain his seat and lost by just three votes in 1741. It took Landon Carter seventeen years to achieve electoral success: he came in fourth in 1735, third in 1741 and 1748, and finally won in 1752. He failed by only seven votes in 1741. Finally, results of the 1771 election remained in doubt for months, as the House of Burgesses scrutinized and then reversed the original outcome. Competition among the local gentry dictated the level of electoral intensity in Richmond County throughout the eighteenth century, and only in the elections of 1765 and 1774 does it appear that imperial problems encouraged a laying aside of that rivalry.[26]

By 1741, if not before, the Essex County gentry had initiated a series of electoral battles that equaled or surpassed in intensity those of neighboring Richmond. No one served more than a few terms before either voluntarily giving up their seat or suffering defeat at the polls. William Dangerfield won in 1748, lost in 1752, and won again in 1754 and 1755; Francis Smith lost in 1748, won in 1752 and 1755, and lost again in 1758. James Garnett won in 1741, declined a poll in the next two elections, and tried again in 1755, only to come in third. Eight of the eleven men who represented Essex County from 1741 to 1775 saw defeat at some time during their political careers.

Even during the final decade of British control, when leaders and voters rallied around incumbents in most of Virginia's communities, the Essex gentry continued to fight over the county's two seats. Robert Beverly ran a respectable third in 1765, and Meriwether Smith challenged the leading candidates in 1768, 1769, 1770, and 1771 before finally achieving success in 1774. Few signs of a developing political consensus emerged within the county during the late colonial period, while no expression of patriotic solidarity against Britain surfaced except perhaps in 1774. The Essex political culture looked inward, not outward, rarely seeking outside help or encouraging interference in its brand of politics. Losing candidates never petitioned the burgesses to overturn polling results, accepting as a matter of custom and perhaps conviction the verdict of three hundred or so freeholders on election day.[27]

Cycles of Competition

While Richmond, Essex, and a few other counties sustained a highly contentious electoral system, other communities witnessed competitive and noncompetitive cycles that only occasionally coincided with provincial and imperial developments. In the tiny Tidewater county of Elizabeth City, for example, Merritt Sweney, John Tabb, and William Westwood easily monopolized burgess seats between 1735 and 1755. In the latter year, however, William Wager and George Wythe challenged Westwood and Tabb, and in the initial polling Wager received three more votes than incumbent Tabb. Tabb immediately challenged the results, claiming that Wager had both treated the voters illegally and received votes from questionable freeholders. While the House threw out the treating charge, investigators found seven illegal voters on Wager's poll list but also three on Tabb's. Tabb regained his long-held seat by a single vote and nullified Wager's election.

Wager continued to press, however, and topped the poll in 1758, unseating twenty-three-year veteran Westwood—but not Tabb. In 1761, George Wythe outpolled Wager, while a second challenger, James Wallace, received just two votes less. Wallace now disputed Wager's second-place finish, claiming illegal voters again. This time, the adding and subtracting and counting and recounting of voters produced a tie, but the House declared Wager the winner, apparently as a result of his incumbency! Wallace refused to give up and ran again in 1765 only to take a respectable third to Wythe and Wilson Cary.

The ten-year period of competitive elections ended as quickly as it began: Wallace and incumbent Cary easily won in 1768 and then had no opposition in 1769, receiving unanimous reelection. Henry King and Worlich Westwood took the 1771 and 1774 contests with little fanfare. The entry of Wager and Wythe into the electoral arena in the mid-1750s disrupted a long cycle of consensual politics and ushered in such highly competitive contests that the House of Burgesses had to resolve several. Wythe's departure from that same arena a decade later, after assuming duties as clerk of the House of Burgesses, combined with growing support for the stand against Britain to return Elizabeth City to the tranquillity of noncompetitive elections.[28]

Spotsylvania maintained a minimally competitive electoral environment until 1748, when Benjamin Grymes challenged incumbents William Waller and Rice Curtis. Although Grymes failed miserably in this and the 1752 elections, his activities apparently paved the way for others, culminating in a tight four-way contest in 1755. Three members of the Lewis family, William Johnson, and Grymes competed for seats until 1771, when George Stubblefield and Mann Page Jr. captured representation and held on to it throughout the final colonial and first state elections. Formal polling occurred at many of these late colonial contests, although only a token challenge surfaced during the Stamp Act crisis in 1765. Such was not the case in 1769: while most counties rallied around their representatives in the face of the governor's angry dissolution of the House, Spotsylvania voters tossed out incumbent Peter Marye. Grymes did win in 1761, 1765, 1768, and 1769, only to lose again in 1771.[29]

Norfolk County, on the other hand, experienced only one brief burst in electoral competitiveness—at precisely the time other communities were moving in the opposite direction. Until 1768, Norfolk's two seats had passed among a number of individuals with apparently limited competition. This group included George Veale, who won election in 1755 and 1758 but who resigned in 1759 to become county sheriff. In 1768, incumbent Robert Tucker Jr. decided not to stand a poll, and newly appointed county justices John Wilson and John Brickell as well as former burgess George Veale entered the contest against the other incumbent, Thomas Newton Jr. Wilson belonged to a prominent county family and easily topped the poll, with 330 votes, but the real contest occurred between Brickell, a lawyer from North Carolina, and Newton, who represented the long-established old guard. Newton captured the second seat with 303 votes in a closely fought race that attracted nearly 600 freeholders. Veale received 229 votes and accepted defeat gracefully, but Brickell, who lost by just 20 votes, did not and charged Newton with voter bribery and a variety of other offenses. Although the governor's angry dissolution of the House in May 1769 left Brickell's petition unresolved, it provided him another opportunity to challenge Newton. Again, the old guard prevailed, and Brickell polled a very respectable third to Wilson and Newton in the September 1769 general election. Thereafter, competition once more subsided, and Newton and new partner James Holt captured the final two elections of the colonial period.[30]

In nearby York and Warwick Counties, the only competitive elections of record occurred in 1735 amid the continuing controversy over the Tobacco Inspection Acts. Warwick's election resulted in defeat for incumbent William Harwood at the hands of challenger Thomas Haynes. Although Harwood asked the House to overturn the election, it declared Haynes duly elected. Haynes' political career ended as abruptly as it began, however, when Harwood regained his seat in 1741 and then kept it for the next thirty-five years.[31] In York, House Speaker John Randolph lost to Edward Digges and John Buckner and then complained that the county sheriff had attempted to increase the pool of eligible voters by executing nineteen life leases for tiny parcels just before the election. Although the election results stood, the House severely reprimanded the sheriff for "fraudulent Practice, contrary to Law, and tending to destroy the Rights of true Freeholders." Edward Digges continued to serve until 1752, when his relation Dudley Digges replaced him for the remainder of the colonial period.[32]

Not Competitive

As the following list shows, approximately two-thirds of Virginia's political communities held some competitive elections during the eighteenth century (date in parentheses is year the constituency was created):[33]

Competitive	*Minimally Competitive*	*Noncompetitive*
Accomack (1634)	Culpeper (1749)	Amherst (1761)
Halifax (1752)	Norfolk County (1634)	Williamsburg (1723)
Brunswick (1732)	Frederick (1743)	Botetourt (1770)
Amelia (1735)	Henrico (1634)	Buckingham (1761)
Westmoreland (1653)	Augusta (1745)	Charles City (1634)
Richmond (1692)	Loudoun (1757)	Charlotte (1765)
Prince William (1731)	Surry (1652)	Chesterfield (1749)
Essex (1692)	Gloucester (1651)	William and Mary (1718)
		Dinwiddie (1752)
King George (1721)	King William (1702)	Dunmore (1772)
Northumberland (1648)	Mecklenburg (1765)	Goochland (1728)
Elizabeth City (1634)	Jamestown (1684)	Hampshire (1754)
Lancaster (1651)	Prince George (1703)	Isle of Wight (1634)
Spotsylvania (1721)	Prince Edward (1754)	James City (1634)
Stafford (1664)	Caroline (1728)	Middlesex (1673)
Northampton (1643)	Warwick (1643)	Norfolk Borough (1738)
Fauquier (1759)	Bedford (1754)	Pittsylvania (1767)
		Southampton (1749)
Lunenburg (1746)	Cumberland (1749)	Sussex (1754)
Hanover (1721)	Louisa (1742)	Berkeley (1772)
Fairfax (1742)	Orange (1734)	Fincastle (1772)
Nansemond (1634)	Princess Anne (1691)	
Albemarle (1744)	New Kent (1654)	
	King and Queen (1691)	
	York (1643)	

The most competitive third sustained such activity over much of the period, while a second group experienced only intermittent competition. For another third, no competitive elections occurred. Silence in the historical record dictates this noncompetitive classification in most cases, but in several instances diaries, newspapers, and correspondence confirm the lack of electoral competition.[34] In Amherst County and the city of Williamsburg, for example, such evidence shows that candidates nearly always ran unopposed.

The noncompetitive political cultures of Amherst and nearby Buckingham County derive almost entirely from the overwhelming power and influence of the Cabell family. Dr. William Cabell (1699–1774), an English-born-and-educated surgeon, established the family power base in the 1740s in the then-large frontier county of Albemarle. As one of its founding fathers, Cabell not only served in local offices as justice of the peace, surveyor, and militia captain but also operated a medical practice and hospital, owned a tavern, store, and warehouse, ran a large plantation, and actively speculated in frontier land. By the early 1750s, he had accumulated more than twenty thousand acres in the county. In 1755, he won election to the House of Burgesses from Albemarle but in 1758 turned the seat over to his son, William Cabell Jr., a local vestryman and justice of the peace.[35]

When the colonial government divided Albemarle in 1761, creating Amherst and Buckingham, the Cabell family split its political and economic influence as well. William Cabell Jr. took Amherst County; his brothers, Joseph and John, took Buckingham. Joseph and John became vestrymen of Tillotson Parish, and both served on the Buckingham Commission of the Peace, although the prestigious quorum of eight justices initially included Joseph but not John. Joseph took one of Buckingham's first burgess seats in 1761 and represented the county for the following ten years. In 1771, he moved his political activities to Amherst County, leaving John to continue the family influence in Buckingham; by 1767, John had moved into the quorum of eight justices and in the 1770s took up duties in Tillotson Parish as churchwarden and collector. He represented the county in the fifth convention in 1776 and in several general assemblies following independence.[36]

The Cabells' domination of Amherst County became far more extensive and lasted far longer. Although Dr. William Cabell had been active throughout old Albemarle County, his power base remained strongest in the southwestern section, which became Amherst. Not only did he hold vast lands here but his son William Jr. eventually accumulated fifteen thousand acres in Amherst, as well. In fact, William Jr. and his offspring would monopolize legislative representation from the county for the next forty years. William Jr. had served as vestryman and justice of the peace in Albemarle and quickly assumed both of those roles in the new county of Amherst. He also became Amherst's first county surveyor and head of the militia as county lieutenant; all Commissions of the Peace of the period listed him first among the sixteen or so justices. After he had served one term in the House of Burgesses from Albemarle (1758–61), the voters of Amherst elected him to the six remaining sessions of the colonial House, to all five conventions (1774–76), and after the break with Britain, to four terms as representative to the state general assembly, and to several terms to the state Senate. He ended his career as a staunch antifederalist in the Virginia Ratification Convention of 1788.[37]

All six of Amherst's colonial elections appear to have been noncompetitive. William Jr. stood with fellow justice Cornelius Thomas in the first four elections; in 1769, we know for certain that they were "chosen by the View and Consent of the people without polling their being no Opposition." In 1771, brother Joseph dropped out of the race in Buckingham and replaced a possibly ailing Thomas on the Amherst ticket. In that year and again in 1774 the voters sent both Cabells to Williamsburg; the 1774 election was unanimous, and the 1771 one may have been so as well. Despite the noncompetitive nature of these elections, the Cabells and their political allies hardly took the results for granted. Treating the voters to large quantities of liquor demonstrated the gratitude and generosity of the Cabell family. In 1768, William Cabell "paid Mr. Joplin 31/6 for carrying my liquor to the Election." Two years later, he "sent up 120 gals. of Cyder and 110 Gallons of Bumbo to the Election in Wm. Joplin's wagon" and a week thence "paid Rich'd Alcock 20/. in full [for] expenses."[38]

While the Cabell family's control of Amherst may be without equal during this period, at least seven other non- or minimally competitive Southside and south-central counties came under the influence of powerful men or families. These men included Paul Carrington, who won all six of Charlotte County's general elections as well as two by-elections after he accepted the offices of deputy king's attorney in 1771 and county clerk of court in 1773. In a similar way, Richard Bland sat for Prince George County continuously from 1741 until his death in 1776, Archibald Cary entered and won eight of Chesterfield's nine general elections, Joseph and Edwin Gray represented Southampton in eight of ten assemblies, John Donelson served in three of four for Pittsylvania, and Robert Bolling journeyed to Williamsburg six of nine times for Dinwiddie County. Although Cumberland's first general election in 1752 saw three candidates battle for the two seats, thereafter the elections became noncompetitive, and George Carrington dominated representation until 1768.[39]

The family and personal career patterns of many of these men closely paralleled those of the Cabells: they or their families had already assumed positions of power and authority in the region when the creation of a new county provided alternative or perhaps more promising electoral opportunities. The creation of Cumberland County from Goochland in 1749 encouraged George Carrington to move his burgess service from the older county to the new one. At the same time, his fellow Goochland burgess, Archibald Cary, jumped to Chesterfield County, recently created out of nearby Henrico. Joseph Gray served Isle of Wight from 1735 to 1752, when the southern part of the county became the new county of Southampton, which he represented for nearly all of the following sixteen years. Moreover, the Bollings were well established in Prince George when Dinwiddie County split from it in 1752 and provided an opportunity for Robert Bolling to begin his legislative career in a new political community. Likewise, John Donelson already held considerable influence in western Halifax County as a vestryman, justice of the peace, and unsuccessful burgess candidate when the colonial government created Pittsylvania from Halifax in 1767.[40] The previously established local political power and the few, if any, qualified challengers in these sparsely settled areas produced noncompetitive local political cultures in which a handful of men stood for election year after year with little or no opposition.

In the long-settled Tidewater region, a more complex set of factors contributed to the development of noncompetitive political communities, but powerful individuals or families often formed part of the equation here as well. Middlesex County provides a case in point. In the first two decades of the century, Middlesex mirrored the highly contentious political environments of many Tidewater communities, where local issues and provincial politics mingled to ignite "the flame of burgessing." Intense rivalry among justices on the county court over the building of a new courthouse and the development of the town of Urbanna initiated the highly competitive climate and resulted in 1705 in the defeat of incumbents Gawin Corbin and William Churchill, who represented an older set of men who had run county affairs for years. Christopher Robinson and, later, his brother John led the younger, forward-looking, group and represented the county until 1715, when they suffered defeat after siding with the governor on a very unpopular Tobacco Inspection Act. By 1718, the old guard had recaptured power, and members of the Corbin, Grymes, and Berkeley families joined with the even more powerful Wormeleys to control representation for the remainder of the colonial period. After 1720, a noncompetitive electoral atmosphere prevailed in Middlesex County.[41] Similar patterns apparently held in Charles City, James City, and Isle of Wight, where hints of highly charged contests early in the century gave way to more tranquil elections, in which a few families dominated representation to the House of Burgesses.[42]

The three boroughs and the College of William and Mary provide a final set of constituencies that experienced little or no competition during the eighteenth century. The relatively small size of three of the four certainly hindered the development of opposing factions: the college electorate included only the president and the faculty, while Jamestown may have had no more than twenty or thirty electors and Williamsburg perhaps seventy-five to a hundred voters.[43] In addition, Williamsburg, the college, and to a lesser extent Jamestown came under the heavy influence of provincial affairs and provincial politicians. John Holloway, who served as speaker of the House from 1720 to 1734, alternated burgess service between Williamsburg and York County and won in both in 1728. His successor to the speaker's chair, Sir John Randolph, held the college's single seat from 1734 to 1737. As attorney general from 1755 to 1766 and then speaker of the House for the remainder of the colonial period, Peyton Randolph represented Williamsburg (1748–52), the college (1752–58), and Williamsburg again (1758–75). Philip Ludwell represented Jamestown from 1741 to 1751 before being elevated to the Council. John Page joined the Council in 1773 after two years as the college's representative. John Blair Jr. had served the previous term for the college before he became clerk of the Council in 1771. Finally, George Wythe, Williamsburg lawyer and later clerk of the House, held seats briefly in Williamsburg (1754–55) and the college (1758–61).[44]

These powerful and influential men apparently had little trouble securing—and keeping, if they wished—seats in one of these constituencies while concentrating most of their attention on the intricacies of provincial politics. According to available evidence, only in the Jamestown election of 1752 did competition occur, when

Lewis Burwell and Edward C. Travis battled for the seat being vacated by Philip Ludwell. Thereafter, the Travis and Ambler families amicably rotated service every two or three terms. In Williamsburg, unanimous elections became the norm by 1765 if not before; in August 1769, the *Virginia Gazette* assured local readers that Peyton Randolph would most certainly again be "the man of their choice."[45]

The borough of Norfolk remained noncompetitive as well but for somewhat different reasons. With a population surpassing several Tidewater and frontier counties, the borough electorate may have topped two hundred by the 1770s and could easily have become divided and contentious. Here, however, a long-established oligarchy continued to dominate local politics: the electorate placed its trust in the Hutchings mercantile family, which won ten of the twelve elections conducted after the borough received its charter in 1736. Most of these elections probably witnessed little or no opposition; in 1769, we know for certain that the citizens of Norfolk vowed to return Joseph Hutchings unanimously to a fourth term in the House.[46]

GEOGRAPHICAL PATTERNS

While the competitive level of elections fluctuated according to a curious blending of local conditions, broad institutional change, and provincial and imperial events, it is also abundantly clear that competitive, minimally competitive, and noncompetitive constituencies did not fall randomly across the Virginia countryside (see map 3.1). Among competitive counties, for example, three groupings are noteworthy: the four nearly adjoining and highly competitive counties in the southern part of the colony, the Eastern Shore counties of Accomack and Northampton, and the band of Tidewater and Piedmont counties stretching across northeastern Virginia. On the other hand, most of the Tidewater counties south of the Rappahannock River experienced either low or no competition, Elizabeth City and Nansemond excepted. Likewise, all counties on the western side of the Blue Ridge, as well as most of those immediately to the east, witnessed little or no competition.

A partial explanation for these patterns lies in the time of creation and the parentage of the constituencies. Newer regions, which were

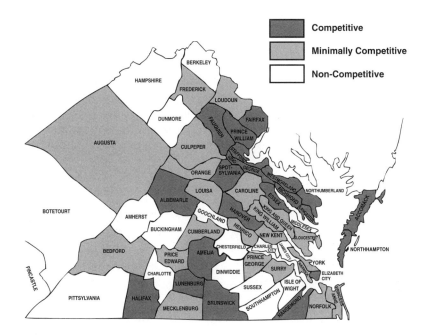

Map 3.1   Electoral Intensity of Virginia Constituencies, 1728–1774

settled in the second quarter of the eighteenth century and which acquired local government in the period after 1750, were increasingly less likely to give voters a choice at election time than some of the older sections. Created in an era of growing satisfaction with colonial elites and a developing dissatisfaction with imperial authorities, these counties initiated less-competitive electoral systems than those communities established a decade or two earlier.[47]

The stark contrast between the northern and southern Tidewater is more difficult to explain. One possibility is that the two sections exhibited major differences in leadership styles, which reflected, in part, local electoral environments. Northern Neck burgesses maintained a "maximum independence of the electorate" and acted as if they were responsible for the well-being of the entire colony, while those from the Williamsburg area exhibited a "representative" style of leadership, more closely attuned to the will of constituents.[48] What this may mean is that in the Northern Neck freeholders had their say at election time but rarely had direct influence on their legislators thereafter, while leaders in other parts of the Tidewater, usually elected with little or no opposition, were less concerned with the colony as a whole but were much more responsive to constituents.[49] In many southern Tidewater counties this explanation holds, but those men representing the college and the boroughs of Jamestown and Williamsburg hardly fit such a pattern.

A second explanation relates to landholding patterns: tenants in the Northern Neck represented a significantly higher percentage of the population than in the southern Tidewater and the Piedmont.[50] On the surface, high tenancy rates suggest a more docile electorate, but the opposite may have been true. Although long-term leases entitled many tenants to vote, the frequent transfer of such leases made for a continuous turnover in one segment of the voting population. When tenants became eligible to vote, however, they voted in appreciable numbers, making up a third to a half of the electors at some contests (see chap. 2). These leaseholders may have added an unpredictable and volatile factor, which was difficult for candidates to forecast or control.

Whatever explanations account for the differences in electoral competitiveness between the northern and southern sections of the Tidewater, settlers apparently carried these differences inland as new counties were established. The limited competitiveness of the Tidewater counties along the James River influenced the electoral culture of the newer counties formed upriver, while the highly competitive culture of the lower Northern Neck became part of the political heritage of Stafford, Prince William, Fairfax, and Fauquier Counties.[51]

The inherited political environments of Virginia's communities combined with a host of local issues and problems and specific provincial and imperial events to fan the flame of burgessing in some places and extinguish it in others. Where the flame burned bright for decades, we may observe in the sharpest detail the complex workings of local politics. In Accomack, Lancaster, Fairfax, and Halifax Counties, personal ambition, family rivalry, and a sense of duty among the gentry intersected at House of Burgesses elections with the equally strong desires of small freeholders for family well-being, responsibility in local leadership, and pride in neighborhood institutions and men.

Part II

Community Patterns

4

Accomack County

*Searching for Responsible Authority on the
Eastern Shore*

On April 11, 1771, the *Virginia Gazette* printed a lengthy letter reminding the citizens of Accomack County that the upcoming elections provided an "opportunity of exercising one of your most valuable Privileges . . . that of choosing your Representatives" to the House of Burgesses. Signing the letter "No Party Man," the writer recited the traditional eighteenth-century litany of qualities desirable in elected officials.

First and foremost, those selected must be persons of "Probity and Integrity [with] Fortitude . . . Strength [and] Independence of Mind" whose "Judgement . . . [could] penetrate through all the sinister Designs and secret Machinations of the Enemies of Freedom." Such attributes would lead legislators to do the right thing for their country—for Virginia—but a true representative also served the interests of his county and perhaps even his neighborhood. While it was critical that "Candidates are those of your old Acquaintance" and could represent "your true Interests," it was equally important that the responsible citizen not be swayed entirely by long-term friendship, kinship, or daily familiarity. "Say not he is my Neighbor . . . say not he is my friend," but rather choose those who know "that the publick virtue of each County consists of that of Individuals [and] the publick Virtue of the whole Province of that of each County."[1] The writer had hit upon the principal paradox of Virginia's local political culture: the often competing interests of neighborhood, county, and province. And he also knew from experience that working through that paradox had made Accomack County the most competitive electoral constituency in eighteenth-century Virginia.

Two broad themes dominated local political discourse during the final seventy-five years of the colonial period: who should hold positions of authority in the local community and how should those in power exercise the authority vested in them. The issue of longest duration involved the parish vestry and drew numerous candidates and hundreds of voters into the electoral arena, creating a divisive political climate, which often overshadowed the situation that brought it into being. While a brief hiatus in electoral intensity followed the resolution of the vestry controversy, a second, short-lived but lively, dilemma concerning the county court arose that both rejuvenated activities on the hustings and served to refocus political discussion to a higher, countywide, level.

VESTRY CONTROVERSY

By the early eighteenth century, the vestry of Accomack had excluded from membership several prominent gentry families and had alienated a significant segment of the county population with their inattentiveness to the location and repair of parish chapels. Beginning with an attempt to dissolve the vestry in 1710 and ending with the division of the parish in 1763, a continuing battle raged in Accomack between defenders and detractors of the vestry. The struggle took place at several levels, moving back and forth between the House of Burgesses and the Council in Williamsburg and the local political arena in Accomack. Although at one level this confrontation represented a struggle among the elite for prestige, authority, and power within the county community, the vestry's negligence in performing its duties and its utilization of House of Burgesses elections as a battleground brought the entire white adult male citizenry of Accomack into the fray. While the local controversy in Accomack remained a struggle over the membership and activities of the

Map 4.1 Accomack County, Eighteenth Century

Prepared from information contained in Ralph T. Whitelaw, *Virginia's Eastern Shore: A History of Northhampton and Accomack Counties* (Richmond: Virginia Historical Society, 1951; reprint, Gloucester, Mass.: Peter Smith, 1968); George C. Mason, "The Six Earliest Churches on the Eastern Shore of Virginia," *William and Mary Quarterly*, 2d ser. 21 (1941): 198; Charles Francis Cocke, *Parish Lines: Diocese of Southern Virginia* (Richmond: Virginia State Library, 1964), 273.

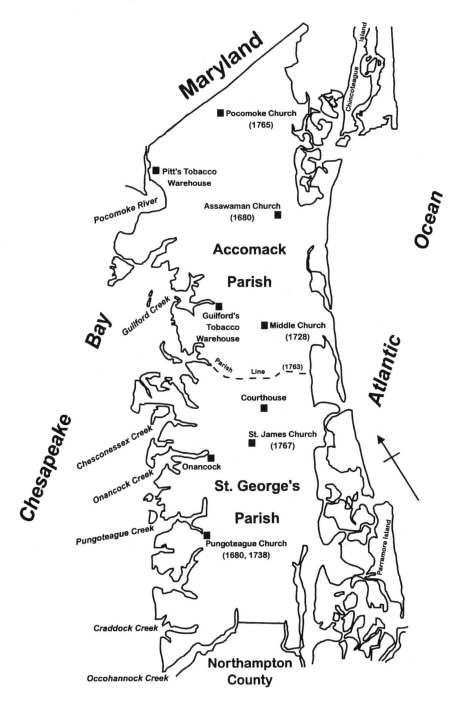

Maryland

Chincoteague Island

Pocomoke Church
(1765)

Pitt's Tobacco
Warehouse

Pocomoke River

Assawaman Church
(1680)

Accomack

Parish

Bay

Guilford Creek

Guilford's
Tobacco
Warehouse

Middle Church
(1728)

Ocean

Parish   Line   (1763)

Courthouse

Chesapeake

Chesconessex Creek

St. James Church
(1767)

Atlantic

Onancock Creek

Onancock

St. George's

Parish

Pungoteague Creek

Pungoteague Church
(1680, 1738)

Parramore Island

Craddock Creek

Northampton
County

Occohannock Creek

vestry, it also took on a significant geographical dimension as south-county leaders fought north-county elites and seaside gentry battled bayside patriarchs (see map 4.1). As voters became a permanent part of the fight, their natural loyalties to neighborhood leaders alternatively coincided and conflicted with an equally important desire for responsible authority in parish administration.

Parish vestries in Virginia wielded considerably more power than their counterparts in England, overseeing not only the relief of the poor but also hiring ministers, building and maintaining churches and glebes, and raising the necessary levies to pay for these activities. Such weighty responsibilities generally fell to twelve distinguished members of the county elite who had both the time and the wisdom to execute the charge placed upon them. For men interested in public office, the parish vestry along with the county court offered the best opportunities for local service as well as providing the best step toward eventual election to the House of Burgesses. In the early eighteenth century, Accomack County contained only one parish, also called Accomack, and thus just twelve vestrymen and another ten to twenty justices exercised such power across this forty-mile stretch of Virginia's Eastern Shore. As Accomack's adult white male population grew to approximately eight hundred by the 1720s, competition for these prestigious positions on court and vestry increased accordingly.[2]

Most men suited for service on the county court also saw themselves as viable candidates for the parish vestry, and vice versa, and in many counties membership in the two bodies overlapped considerably. Each group also controlled the selection of new members (de facto for the county court and de jure for the vestries).[3] The freeholders and householders of newly established parishes elected the initial vestry of twelve, but subsequently, the vestry selected and installed its own replacements. The House of Burgesses rarely tampered with this process.[4] As long as county inhabitants remained satisfied with those selected to fill vacancies and with the management of parish affairs, the vestry could operate peacefully for decades without interference from either local freeholders or authorities in the colonial capital. Dissatisfaction with the membership or proceedings of the parish vestry could bring bitter and prolonged conflict, as it did in Accomack for almost fifty years.

Initially elected in 1663, the Accomack Parish vestry spent the next century as a self-perpetuating body, hiring ministers, establishing tax rates, and managing church property as it saw fit.[5] Although the parish held no vestry elections for one hundred years, all was not well, and by the early eighteenth century discontent surfaced. Much of the controversy centered on the membership of the parish vestry and the apparent unwillingness of that body either to repair existing church buildings or to erect new ones in places convenient to the inhabitants. A formidable array of detractors emerged to challenge the vestry and its operations, but as the battle intensified the vestry put forward its own champion.

From the mid-1730s until his death in 1758, George Douglas vigorously defended the parish vestry against the challenges of several powerful nonvestrymen. Douglas had come to the Eastern Shore from England about 1715, combining the occupations of lawyer and planter. He first acquired land near Gargatha in the north-central part of the county but eventually established his permanent residence further north, just a few miles south of the Maryland border (see map 4.2). During his forty-year residency in the county, he bought and sold a half dozen tracts but probably never owned more than five hundred acres at a time. He held the office of colonel in the county militia, served as a vestryman and churchwarden by the mid-1730s if not before, and took a special interest in the affairs of the Assawaman Chapel (see map 4.1).[6]

Douglas's chief rivals during much of this period were several members of the Scarburgh family—initially, Edmund and Henry and, later, Henry's son, Henry. The Scarburghs (or Scarboroughs) had been among the original settlers on the Eastern Shore. Edmund I arrived in Virginia in 1621, moved to Accomack a few years later, and served as a burgess and county commissioner just before his death. His son, Edmund II, received legal training in England before his immigration, held the offices of county sheriff, burgess, speaker of the House, and surveyor general for the colony. He died with landholdings above thirty thousand acres. Substantial debts and a large number of heirs diminished this impressive estate, but a half century later his descendents could be counted among the largest landowners in the county: Henry I and his son Henry II held three thousand acres along the north shore of Pungoteague Creek, while Edmund owned more than fourteen hundred acres at the mouth of Occohannock Creek on the county's southern border (see map 4.1). Edmund joined the county court in 1711, held the office of sheriff in 1721, and entered the House of Burgesses for the first time in 1722. The elder

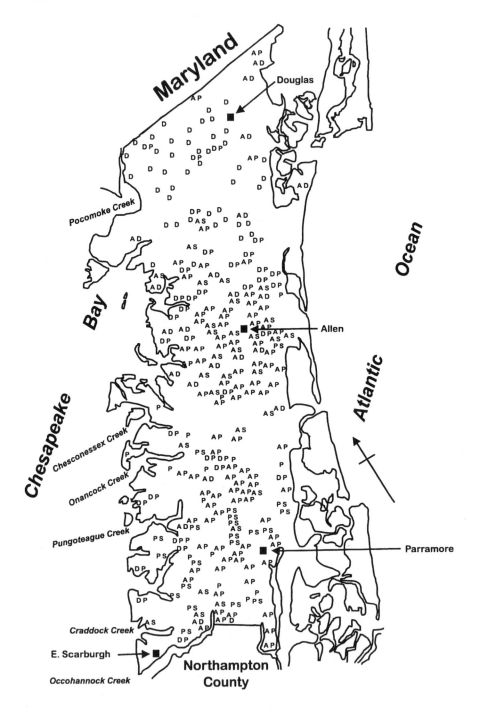

Henry also became a county justice in 1711; the younger Henry did so in 1732.[7]

Although the Scarburghs would spearhead the fight against the vestry during the second quarter of the century, fellow justice, non-vestryman, and burgess Richard Drummond fired the opening salvos a decade earlier.[8] During the 1710 session of the House, Drummond introduced a bill to dissolve the Accomack Parish vestry and hold new elections. The burgesses passed the bill, but the Council apparently rejected it. The next year, Drummond continued the fight with "A Bill to dissolve the *pretended* Vestry of the parish of Accomack," but it never came to a final vote. Undaunted, he tried again in 1715 with a "Proposition . . . for making a Law to Impower the freeholders of the Parish of Accomack to choose a Vestry for the said Parish and that they may have Liberty to Elect a new Vestry once in every Seven years." This attempt to pass a "vestry septennial act" failed to reach the floor as a formal bill.[9]

Drummond did not serve in the House for the next few years, but attempts to force the vestry into a specific course of action continued, nonetheless, with demands for a new church. Only two chapels served the county in the early eighteenth century: the so-called mother church at Pungoteague in the southern part of the county and Assawaman Chapel in the north (see map 4.1). Both were built about 1680 and were probably in poor repair.[10] To provide better service for the populous center of the county, Accomack burgesses John Teackle and Solomon Ewell introduced a bill in 1720 to erect a new church at "Long Love Branch" because the "upper inhabitants of Accomack County pray . . . that a Church may be built according to the Center of the Said County and not as directed by the Vestry and that the Minister may be obliged to preach at the Churches only and not at the Courthouse." The Council amended the bill, and it eventually cleared both chambers, receiving the governor's signature in 1722.[11]

Although the construction of a new church probably mollified some of the "upper inhabitants," direct attacks on the vestry did not

---

Map 4.2 Geographical Distribution of Votes for Major Candidates, Accomack County, 1748

Each freeholder could cast two votes; most did. Votes for seven minor candidates are not shown.

Key: P = Parramore; A = Allen; D = Douglas; S = Scarburgh

subside. The new round of skirmishes began even before completion of the new "middle church" in 1728 and again concerned both the membership of the vestry and their apparent lack of attention to the maintenance of church property. The renewed hostilities also coincided with the election of two members of the Scarburgh family to serve Accomack in the House of Burgesses. Accomack voters sent Edmund Scarburgh and Tully Robinson to the House in 1722, but Robinson died and Henry Scarburgh took his place in a by-election in early spring 1726.[12]

By the time Henry took his seat in late May 1726, several petitions complaining of the activities of the vestry had reached both the House and Council, but action on these grievances had been postponed until the next session.[13] On June 2, however, Henry and Edmund "in behalf of themselves and the Inhabitants of the Parish of Accomack" presented another petition "complaining of the unjust and Arbitrary Proceedings of the present Vestry of the said Parish" because "they refuse to repair the Mother Church with intent to induce A necessity of building a new Church." The only way to solve the problem, the petition continued, was to dissolve the present vestry. Why the vestry had neglected repairs is unclear; regular upkeep would have been costly, but presumably a new church would cost even more. It is certain, however, that this "mother church" served the Scarburgh families (Henry Scarburgh lived just two miles away and Edmund no more than seven), and they may have been especially affronted by the state of disrepair of "their" church. The House rejected the petition to dissolve the vestry but did resolve "that the Vestry of the said parish Ought to make all necessary repairs to the Mother Church."[14] One small battle of the conflict had been won, but as the Scarburghs, Drummonds, and others prepared for the next assault on the vestry, internal dissension among their group nearly ended this delicate coalition of non-vestrymen.

The principal squabble erupted during the 1728 general election (see table 4.1).[15] Edmund Scarburgh did not stand for reelection in the January 1728 contest, but his kinsman and fellow incumbent, Henry Scarburgh, did. Although Henry had won a by-election in 1726, he could not sustain a challenge from William Andrews, who had just become a justice, and Sacker Parker, who represented a family long active in county affairs.[16] Andrews resided in the north-central part of the county and undoubtedly drew strong support from his neighborhood, while Parker and Scarburgh lived twelve miles south, within a mile of each other, and probably split the votes of their neighbors.[17] Undeterred by his rebuke at the polls, Scarburgh petitioned the House of Burgesses, "complaining of an undue Election of Mr Andrews & Mr Parker." The basis for his complaint is unclear, but the House Committee of Privileges and Elections found Scarburgh's evidence lacking and affirmed the election of Parker and Andrews.[18]

Although the election dispute temporarily distracted the vestry's enemies, they nonetheless plunged ahead with their attack on the self-perpetuating body. On February 9, 1728, Accomack representatives presented a petition to allow the free election of a new vestryman upon the death of a vestry member; if the entire vestry could not be replaced in a single swoop, then perhaps the group could be infiltrated one position at a time. As before, the House rejected this attempt to circumvent the traditional method of selecting new vestrymen.[19] But once again, the Accomack burgesses fought back, bringing in a bill the next day to dissolve the entire vestry and hold new elections. Like its predecessors, the bill wound its way through the Committee of Propositions and Grievances, came back to the floor for several readings, and was eventually passed and sent to the Council for approval. The Council gave it a thorough hearing, which included testimony from Accomack burgesses Andrews and Parker, and ultimately sent it back to the House with amendments. The bill bounced back and forth between the chambers for several more weeks, but no agreement could be reached.[20] The vestry had survived again.

The vestry issue subsided for the next decade, as justices of the peace continued their intrabench squabbles and Accomack joined with other Tidewater counties in opposing the Tobacco Inspection Act of 1730. Both controversies swirled around William Andrews, who had defeated Henry Scarburgh in the 1728 election. In 1731, his fellow justices accused Andrews of "misdemeaning himself in his Office as a Justice of the Peace." The next year he resigned his seat in the House and became an inspector under the new tobacco law, only to be accused in 1734 of disregarding that law and accepting and reselling "a Considerable quantity of Trash Tobacco." Such abuses of the law as well as the all-too-subjective judgment of inspectors, who could reject one man's tobacco and accept another's, led Accomack to spearhead the unsuccessful fight to repeal the Tobacco In-

Table 4.1

Candidates and Election Results, Accomack County, 1728–1774

Candidate	1728	1732	1735	1738	1740	1741	1742	1744
William Andrews	W					L		
Sacker Parker	W		W					
Henry Scarburgh I	L							
Solomon Ewell		W						
Henry Scarburgh II			W		W	W		
Edmund Scarburgh				W				L
George Douglas				L	L	L	W	
John Snead				L				
Mitchell Scarburgh				L				
Thomas Parramore							L	W
Thomas Taylor								L
John Wallop								L
Edmund Allen								
John Wise Jr.								
Robert Pitt III								
Covington Corbin								
Ralph Justice								
Charles West								
James Rule								
Southy Simpson								
Henry Scarburgh III								
James Henry								
Isacc Smith								

Note: W = winner; L = loser.

spection Act. Although Andrews lost his job as inspector, he did not entirely disappear from county politics, as we shall see a bit later in the story.[21]

The general election of 1735 sent incumbent Sacker Parker back to Williamsburg, along with Henry Scarburgh's son, Henry Scarburgh II.[22] While Parker's position in the long-standing vestry controversy is unclear, we do know that the Scarburgh family deeply resented exclusion from parish governance. When Parker died in 1738, the fate of the vestry dropped into the hands of the county electorate. If an enemy of the current vestry joined Scarburgh in the House, the

1748	1752	1753	1755	1758	1761	1765	1768	1769	1771	1774
	L									
L										
L	W									
W				W	W	W	W	W	L	
W	W		W	W						
L	L			L						
L										
		L	L	L						
	L	W	W	L						
			L							
		L	L	L						
			L	L	W	W	W	W	W	W
				L						
							L		W	L
									L	W

chances of getting through a bill to dissolve that body increased substantially, while the election of a friend of the vestry could hinder if not prevent such legislation.

Parker had barely been laid to rest when longtime vestry nemesis and former burgess Edmund Scarburgh took up the contest for the vacant seat. Not waiting until late fall for the assembly to reconvene and a formal election writ to be issued, Edmund immediately began courting the county voters by providing liquor to any and all at a horse race and later at a muster of the county militia.[23] Lacking support from most of the county leaders, including his fellow justices,

Scarburgh relied instead on the backing of middling and small planters, who made up the bulk of the county's population.[24] Large public gatherings offered the perfect opportunity to cultivate such support.

The prospect of having two Scarburghs in the House of Burgesses did not sit well with the county leadership, especially those on the vestry, and several candidates soon came forward to challenge Edmund for the seat. Chief among them was Englishborn vestryman George Douglas, who lived in the extreme northern end of the county. Joining him in the contest were John Snead, an active member of the Pungoteague church and a resident of the west-central section of the county, and Mitchell Scarburgh, Edmund's cousin and neighbor on the county's southern border.[25] Not only would this contest pit vestry supporters against detractors, but the geographic dispersal of competitors would test the abilities of candidates to garner strong support from their own neighborhoods while at the same time appealing to a significant segment of county's entire population.

As the November 17 election approached, Edmund Scarburgh faced a seemingly insurmountable task: only 10 percent of the county leadership supported his candidacy, while George Douglas could count on the endorsement of a majority of the parish vestrymen and justices of the peace.[26] Edmund's only hope for success lay with a continued direct appeal to the average planter. Consequently, on the day of the election, he "cause[d] strong Liquor to be brought in a Cart, near the Court-house Door, where many People drank thereof, whilst the Polls of the Election were taking."[27] Edmund Scarburgh won the election, with 182 votes to Douglas's 173; Snead received 91 and cousin Mitchell Scarburgh only 11.[28] Douglas captured nearly every vote in the northern third of the county as well as a scattering of votes in other neighborhoods; but Scarburgh's appeal was more universal: he held a majority in the lower two-thirds of the county.[29]

Twelve days after his successful election, Edmund joined his kinsman Henry in Williamsburg and presented a petition from a group of county inhabitants requesting once again that the vestry be dissolved and that new elections be held. Again, a House committee seemed initially sympathetic, resolving "that unless the Vestrymen of the said Parish, shall then appear and justify their Proceedings, That the said Vestry be dissolved, and a new Vestry elected."[30]

The House instructed Edmund to prepare such a bill, which he presented on December 1. The burgesses eventually passed the bill on December 7 and sent it to the Council for concurrence.[31]

Even before the bill left the House, vestry supporters had begun to move against the proposal and its supporters. On December 4, defeated candidate George Douglas petitioned the House "complaining of an undue Election and Return of Mr Edmund Scarburgh." The Committee of Privileges and Elections examined the complaint, hearing testimony from Scarburgh, Douglas, and several other witnesses. They discovered "that the Liquors given . . . at the Race and Muster, and Liquor brought to the Election, and given whilst the Polls were taking, were given with Design to procure the sitting Member to be elected." Treating the voters to food and drink either before the election writ arrived in the county or immediately following the election fell within the letter of the law, but serving liquor during the election and for the express purpose of swaying individual voters violated not only the law but the committee's sense of propriety. Although the committee recommended the nullification of Scarburgh's election, the House did not concur and declared him "duly elected." A personal appeal by Scarburgh and a close examination of the 1705 law governing elections convinced the burgesses that no law had been broken.[32]

While Douglas and the vestry lost the battle in the House, the bill to dissolve the vestry still had to get through the Council. Scarburgh carried the bill to the councilors on December 7, where it received a first and second reading. On December 8, Henry and Edmund Scarburgh appeared before the Council to argue for the bill's passage, while George Douglas attended to represent the interests of the vestry. Three days later, the Council voted against a final reading of the bill. Despite Douglas's defeat in the election and the rejection of his petition against Scarburgh, he and the vestry had triumphed again; and once again the Scarburghs had lost.[33]

Yet the victory for Douglas and the vestry held no permanence; as long as the Scarburghs or their allies represented Accomack, a bill to dissolve the vestry could be brought in again and again and perhaps would eventually pass. George Douglas would have to obtain and hold a seat in the House of Burgesses.

His first opportunity came in 1740 when Henry Scarburgh accepted the office of tax collector. By law those holding an office of profit under the Crown could sit in the House, but only if their constituents formally approved the arrangement in an election.[34] The House requested an election writ on May 22, and on June 6 Sheriff Anderson Patterson conducted the polling. Scarburgh had a clear advantage: he had sat in the House for five years, and the voters were simply being asked whether he should be allowed to finish his current term. Douglas had to convince the voters otherwise. He did not. Henry Scarburgh easily won the election, with 259 votes to Douglas's 187.[35] As in the previous election, Douglas had strong support in his home territory, the northern third of the county, but limited backing elsewhere; Scarburgh drew voters from all sections.

Douglas's next opportunity for electoral battle came eighteen months later, when Governor William Gooch returned from a ten-month sojourn in the Caribbean (including the unsuccessful attack on Cartagena), dissolved the present general assembly, and called for new elections.[36] Henry Scarburgh again sought reelection and, based upon his strong showing in the 1740 by-election, would have an easy time retaining his seat. Edmund Scarburgh declined standing a poll, so the county's second burgess seat became the focal point of the November 1741 contest. George Douglas eagerly entered the race, but so did former burgess and controversial tobacco inspector William Andrews. Andrews was no ally of the Scarburghs, and though he now sat on the parish vestry, he and Douglas engaged in a spirited (though perhaps polite) contest for the vacant seat. As predicted, Henry Scarburgh easily topped the poll, but the voting between Andrews and Douglas was so close that it remained unclear for sometime who had won.[37]

County Sheriff Patterson returned the writ with the names Henry Scarburgh and George Douglas, and both took their seats in the House when it convened in May 1742. Andrews was certain, however, that he had won and on May 8 petitioned the burgesses to have Douglas's election set aside. An investigation by the Committee of Privileges and Elections quickly determined that the sheriff's count had been wrong. George Douglas then openly acknowledged before the House "that a greater Number of legal Freeholders voted at the Election for Mr Andrews, the Petitioner, than for him." The House amended the election writ, substituting Andrews' name for Douglas's.[38]

This third defeat at the polls provided only a temporary setback for George Douglas: only a few days later, someone reminded the House committee of Andrews' past indiscretions as a public official. An investigation revealed his "enormous Misdemeanours and male

Practices" as a tobacco inspector "in Breach of his Oath, and the Duty of his said Office." They discovered too that he had been "turned out of the said Office" in 1734 for these indiscretions and had been "left out of the Commission of Peace for Accomack County." The committee resolved and the House declared that William Andrews was "unworthy to sit as a Member of this House" and expelled him from the assembly. Douglas did not automatically get his seat back; the House decided to hold a new election. George Douglas would go before the voters of Accomack a fourth time.[39]

With William Andrews out of the way, Douglas's chances of success at the polls seemed excellent—that is, until Thomas Parramore entered the contest. Parramore had come of age in the 1730s, joined the county court in 1738, and acquired seventeen hundred acres along the Atlantic shore, including the large island that stills bears the family name.[40] As a dominant landowner in the southern half of the county and a nonvestryman, he represented a double threat to Douglas's electoral ambitions.

The election on June 2, 1742, attracted 485 voters, more than any other by-election of the period. Although the county elite supported Douglas's cause by a three-to-one margin, as they had in 1738, polling among the average freeholders was much closer. Ultimately, Douglas won, with 246 votes to Parramore's 235.[41] As in previous contests, Douglas did extremely well among his neighbors in the northern third of the county, but unlike other elections, this time he drew more evenly from the rest of the county. Conversely, Parramore received greater support in the south and a lighter but even distribution across the rest of the county. The electorate of Accomack County had finally sent a vigorous defender of the vestry to the House of Burgesses.

Thomas Parramore's impressive showing in his first electoral outing only whetted his appetite for further activity on the hustings. Parramore could certainly be counted upon to challenge Douglas in the next general election, perhaps five to seven years in the future, but an opportunity arose much earlier when Henry Scarburgh died in the fall of 1744. Scarburgh's death left the nonvestry interests and the southern half of the county unrepresented; the election called for November 13, 1744, would fill that gap.

The political leadership of the county strongly disagreed over the candidate of choice, but the wealthiest men in Accomack emphatically backed Parramore.[42] Although his election seemed secure, three other candidates decided to stand a poll, perhaps making the decision at the last minute. Chief among them was Colonel Edmund Scarburgh, who had served in the House between 1722 and 1726 and again from 1738 to 1741. As a longtime detractor of the vestry and prominent south-county resident, he may have felt some obligation to run for his dead kinsman's seat. Joining him in the contest were Thomas T. Taylor and John Wallop, both nonvestrymen and landowners in the extreme north of the county. Taylor and Wallop got 36 and 14 votes, respectively, from their immediate neighbors, while Edmund Scarburgh garnered 79 votes from supporters throughout the county. Parramore overwhelmed all comers, with 252 of the 395 votes cast.[43]

By the time this election occurred, the governor had already prorogued the assembly, and Parramore had to wait until February 1746 to assume his duties as burgess. Throughout the sessions of 1746 and 1747, Douglas and Parramore, as representatives of the vestry and nonvestry forces, seem to have maintained an implicit truce: no petitions reached the House, no controversial issues dealing with Accomack surfaced. The governor prorogued the assembly several more times in late 1747 and early 1748 and finally, on April 27, 1748, with the advice of the Council, formally dissolved it and called for new elections to be held before June 30.[44]

Incumbents Douglas and Parramore neatly balanced the county's geographical and political interests: one from the north, one from the south; one a vestryman, one not a vestryman; one an experienced leader, and one just beginning his political career. Such symmetry, however, made little difference to the gentry of Accomack. Beginning with the 1748 election and continuing through five elections over the next decade, the vestry controversy took a backseat to a series of intense electoral battles among eight or so of the county's prominent political leaders. A few men would win every race they entered, most would lose each time, and several would win a contest only to be turned out at the next election. The exact nature of this struggle is only dimly illuminated, but it is possible to see the vestry issue still lurking in the shadows and to find neighborhood loyalties and neighborhood rivalries moving in and out of focus.

Neighborhood rivalries had clearly existed previously: the 1738, 1740, 1742, and 1744 by-elections all exhibited localized voting patterns, and the 1741 general election may have. George Douglas had always been a sectional candidate of sorts, drawing heavily from his home territory in the northern third of the county. Likewise, in 1744, Thomas T. Taylor and John Wallop drew exclusively from their respective neighborhoods in the northern part of the county, while in 1738, Mitchell Scarburgh received votes only from his immediate neighbors in the southwest corner. These neighborhood conflicts sometimes obscured and occasionally intensified the continuing concern for vestry governance and for the location and maintenance of parish churches.

As the June 1748 election approached, all of these concerns surfaced, and a host of candidates stood ready to challenge both incumbents' right to represent the county. The most familiar face among the challengers was Colonel Edmund Scarburgh, who had run a distant second in the by-election four years earlier. Other contestants included Robert Pitt III, a thirty-four-year-old justice of the peace who owned 2,200 acres in the extreme northwest corner of the county, and John Wise Jr., another justice, with about 500 acres along Chesconessex Creek in the central bayside region. Finally, Edmund Allen entered the race. His domicile was a 275-acre farm on the central seaside, but he also owned 250 acres further north, on Chincoteague Island.[45] Residing near the geographical center of the county and holding the offices of justice and vestryman, Allen offered the voters an apparent neutral alternative in the ongoing battles between vestry and nonvestry, north and south.

Unlike most earlier electoral battles, in 1748 voters took an independent path, ignoring the preferences of the county elite. While county leaders favored Douglas nearly two to one over both Parramore and Allen, Douglas came in third, with 211 votes.[46] Incumbent Thomas Parramore topped the poll, with 304 votes, newcomer Edmund Allen received 262, Edmund Scarburgh was fourth with 114, Pitt had 99, and Wise got 66.[47] Geography, however, continued to play a major role in this contest as it had in previous ones (see map 4.2). Pitt and Wise were very much neighborhood candidates drawing the majority of their support from the northern one-quarter and southern one-third of the county, respectively. Although Douglas received nearly unanimous endorsement from his neighbors in the northern quarter as well and got considerable support from voters in the entire northern half, this could not offset Parramore's and Allen's strong showing in the more densely populated southern region. Six years earlier in 1742, George Douglas had demonstrated that he could just barely outpoll Parramore in a one-on-one contest

(248 to 235), but with old-timer Edmund Scarburgh back on the hustings and with newcomers Allen, Pitt, and Wise in the fray his countywide following dissipated.

Douglas's defeat and thus his absence from the House of Burgesses when it convened in late October 1748 provided another opportunity for a direct attack on the membership of the parish vestry. Allen's stance on the vestry issue remains obscure, although it seems likely that he was either neutral or considerably less adamant in his opposition to change than was his fellow vestryman George Douglas. Thomas Parramore, on the other hand, probably favored a more accessible membership system, which would benefit gentry families, like his own, that remained closed out of parish governance. Moreover, he probably held a genuine concern for the upkeep of convenient places of worship in the county, especially the Pungoteague church, a few miles from his home. Whatever the position of Accomack's two burgesses, someone from the county—possibly with the assistance of Parramore or Allen—presented a petition to the House seeking a specific law that would require vestry elections every three years. As with the proposal presented in 1715 asking for elections every seven years, the House rejected this petition—on December 15, before it became a formal bill.[48]

Although Virginia followed the provisions of the English Septennial Act requiring a general election at least once every seven years, the elite of Accomack had to wait only half that time before returning to the electoral arena. In May 1749, Governor William Gooch prorogued the short-lived assembly and left for England for health reasons. He never returned, and in July 1751, Robert Dinwiddie received appointment as the new governor. While Dinwiddie did not formally dissolve the assembly and call for new elections until December 12, 1751, his arrival in Virginia in November and his appointment five months earlier triggered preelection campaigning in a number of Virginia constituencies and may have done so in Accomack as well.

Such preelection activity in Accomack seems highly likely, as Thomas Parramore became county sheriff in June 1751, making him ineligible to sit in the House during his tenure in that office.[49] Although Edmund Allen would stand again for reelection, four candidates declared for the seat being vacated by Parramore. George Douglas would attempt to recover what he had lost in 1748, and again John Wise, who had come in fifth in the previous contest, would try his hand before the voters. Colonel Ralph Justice and William Andrews Jr. rounded out the roster of candidates. Justice had served on the county court since 1738 but had joined the vestry less than a year before this election; he also owned several parcels in the north-central part of the county, totaling about 825 acres.[50] The William Andrews in this election may have been either the controversial candidate and tobacco inspector who had won in 1728 and lost in 1741—or his son. The Andrews family owned about 800 acres as well and lived less than a mile from Justice.[51]

With strong support from the county's political and economic elite, incumbent Edmund Allen took first place in the January 23, 1752, election, with 298 votes. George Douglas, tallying 213, regained his lost seat. Newcomer Ralph Justice finished a very close third, with 201 votes. Wise improved his standing among the freeholders by moving from fifth to fourth place, with 122 votes. William Andrews garnered 118 votes.[52] Although Parramore's absence from the electoral arena certainly played some role in the successful return of George Douglas, Douglas also strengthened his own chances by appealing to a broader segment of the county population. Always popular among his neighbors in the northern third of the county, Douglas gradually widened that popularity with each election he entered. By 1752, his electoral center of gravity had moved far enough south that he appealed to north-county and south-county voters almost equally.

Following the election, Allen and Douglas headed for Williamsburg for the first session of the new assembly. They busied themselves first with a bill to regulate the use of liquor and other bribes during elections and then with gaining compensation for a number of planters who had lost tobacco at Guilford's warehouse during a recent wind and rain storm.[53] While these activities and burgess service in general proved rewarding, Edmund Allen readily put them aside when he received appointment as county sheriff the following year.[54]

Just as Thomas Parramore could not seek reelection when he became sheriff two years earlier, Allen now had to relinquish his seat in the House as well. When the second session of this assembly convened in November 1753, the burgesses requested and the governor issued a writ for a new election to be held later in the month.[55] Several Accomack politicians seemed likely candidates for the vacant seat. Thomas Parramore could certainly seek another term now that his duties as sheriff had ended. Losers from the previous election might also run; Ralph Justice had polled a close third in 1752, and John Wise and William Andrew had received respectable support. Of these four, only Ralph Justice sought the empty seat and might have achieved victory without a poll had not two newcomers decided to try their luck before the voters. One challenger, James Rule, owned a mercantile establishment in the bayside port town of Onancock and had served ten years as a justice of the peace. As a Presbyterian, he remained aloof from the parish controversy.[56] The other challenger, Covington Corbin, held no local offices at the time of the election but did own more than seven hundred acres scattered across the north end of the county. He lived about a mile from the Maryland border.[57]

The November 21 election attracted only mild interest from either the county gentry or the average freeholder. Only a few of the leading families even bothered to attend the election, and they favored Corbin by three-to-one over any of the other candidates. While voter turnout was the lowest of the period (see figure 2.6), the planters of Accomack overwhelmingly threw their support to Ralph Justice, not Corbin. Justice polled 231 votes to Corbin's 86 and Rule's 90.[58] Rule's support came primarily from his friends and neighbors in the southern end of the county, who were in all likelihood also regular customers of his mercantile business. Corbin appealed to a much broader constituency; he attracted support from voters in Rule's territory while capturing nearly every vote cast by his neighbors and acquaintances in the northern quarter of the county. Although Ralph Justice received few votes in Corbin's neighborhood, he overwhelmed all challengers in the populous central third of the county and made a respectable showing in the southern end as well. Two north-county vestrymen now represented Accomack in the House of Burgesses.

Douglas and Justice served together for a brief but intense two years, which included eight separate sessions of the House and a host of heated controversies between the burgesses, the governor, and imperial authorities in England. Squabbles started over the pistole fee Dinwiddie began collecting for placing his seal on each land patent issued by the secretary's office, then shifted to a debate over appointments to several important colonywide offices, and reached a boiling point when the burgesses continued to appropriate smaller sums than requested during the opening rounds of the war with the French and Indians. When, in December 1755, the burgesses passed a bill establishing a loan office to emit £200,000 in paper money—which the governor believed entirely outside their purview—Dinwiddie dissolved the assembly in the hope that new elections would bring in a more responsible and cooperative body.[59]

The colonywide elections held in mid-December proved disheartening to Dinwiddie but served to heighten the struggle among Accomack's elites for local prominence. Dinwiddie's unexpected dissolution of the assembly on November 8, 1755, gave potential candidates in Accomack just a month to declare and then prepare for an election, but the time was more than ample to bring forth a host of contenders.

In other parts of Virginia, incumbents often faced little or no opposition to a reelection bid, but neither Accomack's leading gentry nor the freeholders obeyed such rules of deference and courtesy. Instead, incumbents and new candidates expected closely fought contests in which the outcome often remained in doubt until long after the polling began. When George Douglas decided not to seek reelection, the contest became a wide open free-for-all.[60] Ralph Justice, who had finally secured a seat in 1753, would seek another term, but so would James Rule and Covington Corbin, who had both lost to Justice in the previous by-election. Moreover, Corbin's importance in the county community had increased recently, with his appointment to the Accomack court.[61] Joining these three were former burgess Edmund Allen, who had just completed his two-year term as county sheriff and was now again eligible to sit in the House. Yet even this formidable array of candidates did not discourage newcomers Southy Simpson and Charles West from also standing a poll. West owned several lots in Onancock, including one near Rule's as well as two hundred acres just outside of town; he had been on the county bench since 1744 and held a major's commission in the militia.[62] Simpson was probably the youngest of the candidates. He owned about four hundred acres, in the exact center of the county, but as yet had no local officeholding experience.[63]

The electors of Accomack received few clues from the county elite as to how they should vote; some of the leading gentry preferred candidates from their own neighborhoods, while others supported those who had the longest record of service as a justice of the peace. Allen, West, and Rule all had modest backing from segments of the gentry, although no county leader wanted Ralph Justice to succeed.

With six prominent candidates vying for the two seats, the election just nine days before Christmas produced relatively high voter turnout (see figure 2.6).

Allen easily regained his seat, with 257 votes; but despite the gentry's wishes, incumbent Ralph Justice took second, with 190 votes. Charles West lost by just 2 votes, polling 188; Simpson came in fourth, with 163, Corbin had 146, and Rule tallied 129.[64] Although there is just a hint of the vestry controversy in the election,[65] none of the six candidates appears to have run together in what might be called a slate, as freeholders mixed and matched their two votes in a seemingly endless array. Yet the political citizens of Accomack County applied their own brand of logic to their choices and did as they had in most past elections, selecting the candidates they knew most intimately. The freeholders along Onancock Creek, for example, overwhelmingly gave one of their votes to their neighbor Charles West, while they divided their second vote between another local resident, James Rule, and a more-distant contender, Edmund Allen. Covington Corbin, who lived more than twenty miles north, received just a single vote from the area. Similarly, Southy Simpson and Ralph Justice dominated votes from the north-central section of the county, where they both lived. Even Edmund Allen, who easily bested all comers and appealed to planters throughout the county, still drew the bulk of his support from those living less than eight miles from his home.

With only two votes separating second-place winner Ralph Justice from third-place loser Charles West, it is not surprising that West decided to follow a long-standing tradition among Accomack candidates and challenge the election results.[66] On March 30, 1756, just six days after the new assembly convened, West presented a petition to the House "complaining of an undue Election and Return of Mr Ralph Justice, to serve as a Burgess in this present General Assembly." West wanted the House to examine the landholding qualifications of some of the voters in the hope that a few disqualifications would give him a victory in the election. The House agreed to hear the petition and referred it to the Committee of Privileges and Elections for further study. On April 1, the committee recommended that an investigation proceed, but the House sent the petition back to the committee for additional review. A day later, the House agreed to the committee's recommendations but then referred it to the next session of the assembly. When the assembly met briefly the following September, the matter did not reach the floor. The House convened for a third session in April 1757 and resurrected West's petition but again postponed further consideration until the next session. West died at about this time, and therefore, on April 28, the House discharged the committee from any further action on the matter.[67] Two vestrymen continued to represent Accomack in Williamsburg.

With Charles West and his petition safely laid to rest, Accomack burgesses Allen and Justice again turned their attention to the local, provincial, and imperial problems of the day. Although the escalating conflict with the French and Indians on Virginia's western frontier occupied much of the burgesses' thoughts, local problems remained uppermost in the minds of the citizens of Accomack. Fire at two of the county's tobacco warehouses in 1755 and 1756 produced enough damage that planters sought provincial compensation through their representatives. Accomack's burgesses succeed in their efforts, and more than forty planters eventually received payment for their losses.[68] While some counties suffered Indian raids and remained jittery during the entire war, the conflict on the distant frontier just barely touched the lives of Virginia's Eastern Shore residents. A group of volunteers and another group of draftees left the county in 1756 and 1757 under the command of local militia officers, but these units may have totaled no more than a few dozen men.[69] Nor did the war dull the intensity of local political conflict; when a new governor arrived in early June 1758, the resulting general election produced a repeat of the highly contentious contest of 1755.

Although the newly arrived governor, Francis Fauquier, did not dissolve the old assembly and did not call for new elections until June 15, 1758, the departure of Governor Dinwiddie in early January may well have signaled the start of the electoral season in Accomack.[70] When the voters appeared at the courthouse in late June, they faced the largest slate of candidates ever placed before the Accomack electorate. In addition to incumbents Edmund Allen and Ralph Justice, 1755 losers Southy Simpson, Covington Corbin, and James Rule stood again for election. One newcomer with a familiar name also stepped forward: Henry Scarburgh III, who, like his father and grandfather before him, occupied the three-thousand-acre family seat on Pungoteague Creek in the southern end of the county. Joining these six was former burgess Thomas Parramore, who had

Table 4.2
Vote Totals, Accomack County,
by Candidate, 1755 and 1758

Candidate	1755	1758
Edmund Allen	257	250
Ralph Justice	190	183
Covington Corbin	146	143
Southy Simpson	163	39
James Rule	129	78
Charles West	188	
Henry Scarburgh		71
Thomas Parramore		272
No. of voters	555	562

occupied part of his seven-year hiatus from the House by serving as county sheriff.

Incumbents Allen and Justice and challenger Corbin replicated their 1755 effort with nearly identical polls (see table 4.2), but unfortunately for Justice 180 or 190 votes was no longer adequate to secure election. Parramore's 272 votes dramatically altered the final ranking and put Justice in third, not second, place. This resounding victory resulted in part from substantial support by the county elite, but it also had much to do with Charles West's death and a major erosion in support for Simpson and Rule.[71] Of the 125 West supporters who returned to vote in 1758, 107 gave one of their votes to Parramore; 20–30 percent of Simpson and Rule supporters also abandoned their candidate for Parramore. Ultimately, however, geography played a significant role in this election, as it had in many previous contests. Parramore's broad appeal across the entire southern half of the county gave him not only most of Charles West's support but also much of the local support that had belonged to fellow southsider James Rule. Moreover, Simpson's modest support in the south in 1755 had withered considerably by 1758, reducing him to nothing more than a favorite son of the north-central bayside. Parramore and Allen would again share the county's representation in Williamsburg as they had ten years earlier.

The next few years brought an end to the war with France but initiated the imperial crisis that would eventually abolish Virginia's colonial status. While local issues remained important to the citizens and burgesses of Accomack during the final decades of the colonial era, Eastern Shore planters also found themselves embroiled in a controversy that fused their continuing concern for responsible county governance with affairs in distant London.

Among the local problems addressed was the long-standing controversy over vestry membership and accountability. On March 26, 1761, the House of Burgesses once again received a petition to divide Accomack Parish.[72] However, protocol surrounding the death of one king and the accession of another brought the petition to nought. A change in monarch like a change in the colonial governor necessitated the dissolution of the provincial assembly. Elections for a new House of Burgesses took place in May.[73]

Little is known of the 1761 election in Accomack: Thomas Parramore and Southy Simpson were chosen to represent the county. Parramore's reelection needs little explanation, but Simpson's meteoric rise from his miserable showing just three years earlier remains a mystery. As far as we know, he was neither a justice of the peace nor a vestryman in 1761 and owned only an average-sized farm. Nor is it clear whether anyone opposed Parramore and Simpson. Edmund Allen did not die until 1768; he may have run in 1761 and been defeated, or he may have chosen not to run. Ralph Justice died in 1758, not long after his election defeat, but James Rule lived until 1763 and Covington Corbin until 1778. We do know that the squabbles among the elite, which began in the 1730s and resulted in five to seven candidates in every general election and often three in by-elections, came to an abrupt end in the 1760s. This lessening of tensions within the county coincides with a final resolution to the vestry controversy in 1762 and may, later in the decade, relate to the developing patriotic solidarity against Britain.

The vestry controversy that had plagued county politics for fifty years came to a head on November 5, 1762, when the House of Burgesses received a petition to divide Accomack Parish into southern and northern units. Despite a counterpetition presented the same day *not* to divide the parish, a committee report four days later supported the division and urged passage. The bill received a third reading on November 20, passed the House on the November 22, gained Council approval on the November 30, and obtained the governor's signature on December 23.[74] The northern half of the county continued as Accomack Parish, while the southern half became

St. George's Parish (see map 4.1). Vestry elections, held for the first
time in one hundred years, now gave each parish a separate governing body of twelve men. Among the prominent politicians gaining
a vestry seat for the first time were Southy Simpson and Covington
Corbin in northern Accomack Parish and Thomas Parramore, Henry Scarburgh III, James Henry, and Isaac Smith in the southern St.
George's Parish.[75] The issue of responsible parish governance had finally been laid to rest.

INTERLUDE

Although the burgesses and citizens of Accomack spent much time
in the 1760s petitioning and debating the location of ferry service to
and from the western shore and the removal and consolidation of tobacco warehouses, their remote location did not totally isolate them
from provincial and imperial problems.[76] In October 1766, "a number of principal inhabitants" addressed these concerns in the pages
of the *Virginia Gazette* in an open letter to their representatives,
Thomas Parramore and Southy Simpson. In what amounted to more
or less formal instructions to their burgesses, Accomack residents
described the ongoing Robinson affair and its aftershocks: a lack of
confidence in both the colony's monetary system and the current
and future management of the colonial treasury. By urging that the
House work to prevent a single person from holding both the offices
of speaker of the House and treasurer of the colony (as John Robinson had for more than twenty-five years), they hoped that Virginia
would be better governed and their own financial security stabilized.
But they also celebrated the "repeal of sundry late vexatious and op-
pressive laws" (principally the Stamp Act) and instructed their representatives to vote for "an elegant statue for our Most Gracious Sov-
ereign" and other appropriate memorials to "our kindest and best
friends in Great Britain" who had helped secure these repeals.[77]

The decade of the 1760s also witnessed three more general elections: 1765, 1768, and 1769. Two resulted from the governor's angry
dissolution of the assembly for passing the Stamp Act Resolves in
1765 and for opposing the Townshend Acts in 1769. The third occurred in 1768 following a change in the governorship. The first of
these elections took place in July 1765 and returned Thomas Parramore and Southy Simpson, with little or no opposition. The ex-

tremely short duration between the dissolution of the assembly and the general election gave potential challengers almost no time to mount a campaign and thus may account for the noncompetitive nature of the contest in Accomack. Yet Accomack was not alone in automatically returning its sitting burgesses; throughout the colony the general resolve to stand firm against the governor lowered the level of competition in many constituencies.[78]

The 1768 election was an entirely different matter, however. Governor Fauquier died on March 3, 1768, but the new governor, Baron de Botetourt, did not arrive until October 26 and waited until November 1 to call for new elections.[79] Accomack held its election on November 30, but clearly any potential challenger had had a full eight months to prepare for the contest. Only one did so: James Henry. Henry was born in Scotland, possibly in 1731, and first purchased land in the county in 1752. He surveyed and laid out the original plat for the town of Onancock in 1761, where he probably practiced law. He had accumulated more than 1,300 acres of land in the county by 1768. His home place, called Sea View, overlooked the Atlantic in the south-central part of the county. In 1763, he became a vestryman of the newly created St. George's Parish.[80]

Parramore and Simpson again ran for reelection and easily topped the poll, with 370 and 379 votes, respectively; challenger James Henry received an admirable 224.[81] Of the 533 citizens who journeyed to the courthouse of this late November day, 44 percent voted for the two winners (Simpson and Parramore), while 39 percent polled for Henry and one of the other gentlemen. The remaining 17 percent choose to plump for a single candidate: Simpson 47, Parramore 30, and Henry 16.[82] While geography played some role in this election, strong neighborhood allegiance to local candidates was less pronounced here than in many earlier contests. Whatever sectional animosities once existed in the past, they all but disappeared in this contest, as Simpson, Parramore, and Henry each drew significant support from every creek and inlet in the county.

The next general election occurred just nine months later, in September 1769, as a result of the governor's displeasure with House resolutions concerning the Townshend Acts passed the previous May. Following the example of many of Virginia's constituencies, Accomack returned the incumbent burgesses with little fanfare.[83] Parramore and Simpson would represent Accomack a fourth and final time.

A FINAL CONTROVERSY

Although no pollbooks or statistical data survive for the last two elections of the colonial era, 1771 and 1774, all evidence points to renewed contentiousness in the local political environment and intense competition in both contests. As in the earlier controversy over vestry membership and responsibilities, this late colonial matter also concerned the issue of local governance, but this time the dispute involved the composition and independent nature of the county court. Yet, unlike the earlier disagreement, this one reached far beyond the Eastern Shore of Virginia and became entwined in the escalating disagreements with imperial authorities.

The squabble began innocently enough. On October 15, 1770, Governor Botetourt died, and in January 1771, John, Earl of Dunmore, received His Majesty's Royal Commission as the new governor of Virginia. Dunmore did not reach Virginia for another nine months, leaving the Council in the hands of its president, William Nelson.[84] In the absence of a royal governor, the House of Burgesses and the Council continued to meet, to pass laws, to confirm appointments of officials, and to conduct all manner of routine business necessary to the orderly management of Britain's largest mainland colony. On February 1, 1771, one such routine matter came before the Council.

On this day, President Nelson reported to the Council that he had just received a complaint from officers of His Majesty's Revenues in the Port of Accomack that a good deal of illicit trade slipped in and out of the county in such a clever manner as to avoid detection, and he pleaded for assistance to stop this activity. Lack of adequate coastal patrols was part of the problem, but a general disrespect for revenue officers by local ship's masters added to the predicament. Flagrant avoidance of customs laws was a serious matter, and the Council immediately ordered His Majesty's schooner *Magdalen* to interdict such trade. But the Council went further, deciding "that it may be of Service to his Majesty's Revenues there by rendering the Officers more respected, if they were put into the Commission of the Peace issue for the County of Accomack"; therefore, collector Walter Hatton, customs comptroller Andrew Newton, and naval officer David Bowman were so added.[85]

It is hard to imagine that the Council had any inkling as to the firestorm these appointments would raise in Accomack. Rather than increase the respect held for revenue officials, the Council's action had exactly the opposite effect. When news of the appointments reached the county, the general population was much agitated, and the sitting justices of the peace refused to take the oath of office as required by law. Each side then communicated their concerns back to the Council—the revenue officials by letter, the justices through personal appeal. On April 7, 1771, Southy Simpson—as both county burgess and justice of peace—and two other county men appeared before the Council to explain their anxieties.

They objected to the revenue officials on numerous grounds. First, the officials resided in a part of the county that, according to Simpson, was already well represented on the county court. Second, "they were not men of Sufficient property" (Walter Hatton owned one lot in the town of Onancock, and there is no record of either Newton or Bowman owning any property in the county during this period).[86] Third, they would "hang together," meaning apparently that they would not act independently as justices but rather as a group. And fourth, and perhaps most important, these appointments had been made without the recommendation or consultation of the current justices of the peace. While Simpson admitted that by law the Council could appoint whomever they wished, he claimed that "a Recommendation had caused it to become a general practice." In other words, the Council had ignored a long-standing precedent operative throughout the colony.[87]

The Council decided, however, that most of these arguments were meaningless and that the real issue was that the new men were customs officials. Since the objections raised were superfluous and since four justices were no longer active due to age or infirmities, the Council simply reaffirmed their earlier position and sent a new Commission of the Peace back to the county, minus the names of the four nonfunctioning members.[88] Such firmness by the Council did nothing to deter the justices and residents of Accomack.

In early May, the Council received "Sundry papers" from Thomas Parramore and other justices of the county continuing their complaint against the appointment of the revenue officials. Not to be outdone, the customs officers filed a "cross complaint." To settle the matter, the Council ordered a formal hearing a month hence with both parties and subpoenaed witnesses present. The hearing, however, did nothing to change the Council's mind, and on June 13 it ordered another Commission of the Peace drawn up for the county, which continued to include the three customs officials.[89]

As the fight against the revenue officers continued before the
Council throughout the spring and summer of 1771, it also spilled
over into the local electoral arena. Governor Botetourt's death the
previous October and the delayed arrival of his replacement, the Earl
of Dunmore, provided Virginia—and Accomack, specifically—with
an extended campaign season. And the citizens of Accomack apparently used much of that season to stir up a hornet's nest of charges
and countercharges, almost all related to the affair of the revenue officials. Simpson and Parramore had taken a strong position against
the Council, and they would run again for election. James Henry,
who lost to the incumbents in 1768, would try again as well, but so
also would Isaac Smith. Smith had become a justice in 1762 and a
vestryman of the new St. George's Parish in 1763 and served as county sheriff from 1768 to 1770. He owned several lots in the town of
Onancock and a modest homestead of 160 acres nearby.[90]

The battle lines in this fierce campaign are not entirely clear, but
it does seem that the candidates' stand on the issue of revenue officials was of utmost importance. Everyone in the county, according
to one candidate, opposed the appointment of these men to the
court, and thus much political ground could be gained by accusing
an opponent either of sympathy for the Crown officials or of not
standing tough enough against them. Candidate James Henry was
the object of most of the accusations, with some cause, although
Isaac Smith was not entirely free of suspicion on the matter. To begin with, naval officer David Bowman had plumped for Henry in the
1768 election, and Henry and Bowman shared a pew in the parish
church. Furthermore, Smith was a neighbor of the three officials and
also shared a church pew with collector Walter Hatton. Henry's
stand was apparently the most suspect; to remove any hint of suspicion, he "produced a certificate of this having made an oath to his
innocence; and publicly promised that, in case he was elected a
Burgess, he would take every method in his power to have them left
out of the next commission."[91]

The campaign also turned on the issue of qualifications and on
how candidates should conduct themselves during the campaign.
There is some hint that Parramore stayed on the sidelines in the
campaign (possibly for health reasons) but that Simpson and his
friends plunged into the battle with great enthusiasm. Their first
ploy advanced the notion that the traditional virtues of wealth, in-

dependence of mind, and long-standing position in the community through service on court and vestry produced "Gentlemen, who are sensible and judicious, of incorruptible Integrity, firm and unshaken." The incumbents, so the argument went, possessed just such qualities and therefore could be given once again the public trust via the election process.[92] Second, they suggested that behind the "forced smiles [and] hearty shakes by the hand" of Smith and Henry lurked "self-interest and sordid avarice." Not to be outdone, the challengers, or those Simpson called the "little party," accused him of whipping the populace into an unjustified frenzy of fear about the revenue officials, which "prejudiced the people against them in order to carry [the] election."[93]

Neither side in this heated election campaign achieved complete success. The Earl of Dunmore finally arrived in Virginia in late September to assume his gubernatorial duties, dissolving the sitting assembly on October 12, and issuing writs for new elections on October 31. Accomack held its election in late November or early December. Simpson and Henry won; Parramore and Smith lost.[94]

Simpson's strong stance against the Council and his reelection remained bittersweet, at best; not only had he lost his long-time legislative partner, Thomas Parramore, and had to serve with a member of the "little party," but early in the following year he suffered the ultimate humiliation. On May 7, 1772, the Governor-in-Council ordered a new Commission of the Peace for Accomack County and specifically excluded Simpson. His sin, at least on the surface, had been to recommend his son-in-law for the position of tobacco inspector instead of a gentleman subsequently determined to be more qualified. Although Simpson fought back, petitioning the Council to regain his seat on the county bench, they would not budge, claiming "that he was a turbulent Man, & often Quarrelsome on the Bench, to the Hindrance of the Business of the Court." The three British customs officials, although extremely unpopular, would continue to serve on that bench, but one of the county's most popular burgesses would remain permanently excluded from the post.[95]

The final election of the colonial period showed no abatement of the squabbles that had dominated county politics and burgess elections for more than half a century. In the July 1774 contest, James Henry lost his seat to Isaac Smith in a very close race, but Simpson received some vindication for his earlier rebuke by the Council and easily bested all comers, to win a sixth term in the House of Burgesses.[96]

As the conflict with imperial authorities intensified that summer and over next few years, Simpson would again and again be called upon by his Accomack neighbors to represent their interests. He chaired the county Committee of Correspondence in 1774 and 1775, represented Accomack in all five revolutionary conventions (1774–76), served in the first state House of Delegates (1776), and ended his career as the state senator for both Eastern Shore counties (1777–78).[97] He may have been "a turbulent Man, & often Quarrelsome" and frequently absent from the legislative chambers to which he was elected, but that mattered little to the planters of Accomack County. He was their man, someone from the county, someone they knew, and someone who took care of their business and, perhaps most important, someone who stood tall against unwarranted outside interference.

The exercise of power in distant Williamsburg could dilute if not actually thwart local authority, as it did in the parish vestry controversy for the first half of the eighteenth century and in the debate over appointments to the county bench in the 1770s, but in one area of politics outside forces held neither legal authority nor actual power. As the writer of the 1771 letter in the *Virginia Gazette* told the citizenry of Accomack, the "Opportunity of . . . choosing your Representatives . . . is your greatest Glory, as well as your highest Privilege." "That you give Being to your Legislature, [and] from you they receive their political Existence . . . renders an American Planter superiour to the first Minister of an arbitrary Monarch." During the eighteenth century, the small landowners and tenant farmers of Accomack had greater opportunities than most Virginians to fulfill the writer's wish.

5

Lancaster County

Experiencing Parish Neighborhood
in the Traditional Tidewater

During the seventeenth century, two distinct rural neighborhoods formed in Lancaster County on the lower and upper sides of the Corotoman River (see map 5.1). Like a wedge driven into the heart of the county, the river provided a geographical barrier to daily interaction and fostered the development of separate economic, social, and religious communities. Separate tobacco warehouses catered to the planters of the respective neighborhoods, marriage arrangements occurred within each region, two well-established gentry families provided leadership for each area, and separate chapels served the spiritual needs of each community. The residents on both sides of the river thought and acted as if they belonged to two legally distinct communities.

Regular face-to-face interaction at religious services bound individuals to one of these two large neighborhoods. These Sunday gatherings witnessed a variety of social and economic activity, including the exchange of business documents, discussion of tobacco prices, arguments over the quality of horses, and the sharing of worldly news and local gossip.[1] Here also, small and middling farmers gained a certain familiarity with some of the large planters who served on the parish vestry and county court and who represented them in the House of Burgesses. When the governor called for colonywide general elections or a single by-election to replace a local burgess, these neighborhood gentlemen came first to the voter's mind. Although historians have demonstrated the social, economic, and religious cohesiveness of such rural Chesapeake communi-

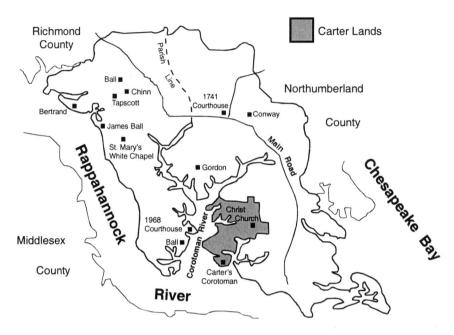

Map 5.1   Lancaster County, Eighteenth Century

Prepared from information contained in Catherine Hoover, comp., *Historic Sites of Lancaster Co, Virginia, and Vicinity,* rev. ed. (Lancaster, Va.: Mary Ball Memorial Museum and Library, 1972); *Lancaster County General Highway Map* (Richmond: Virginia Department of Transportation, 1987); Christ Church Vestry Book, 1739–86 (Richmond, Va.: Virginia State Library), 50; Herman Boyd, "Map of the State of Virginia . . . 1825 . . . corrected 1859" (Facsimile, Virginia State Library); "Carte de le Baie de Chesapeake . . . 1778" (Facsimile, Virginia State Library); Warren M. Billings, ed., *The Old Dominion in the Seventeenth Century: A Documentary History of Virginia, 1606–1689* (Chapel Hill: University of North Carolina Press, 1975), 72; *Atlas of Early American History: The Revolutionary Era, 1760–1790* (Princeton: Princeton University Press, 1976), 5.

ties, it is less clear how these neighborhoods shaped the political structure of Virginia counties.[2]

SEPARATION AND REUNION

For nearly ninety years the two neighborhoods also acted as distinct Anglican parishes. Some time after 1670, the names St. Mary's White Chapel and Christ Church came to refer to the upper and lower sides, respectively, of the Corotoman River. It seems certain that provincial law created the Christ Church Parish in 1666, encompassing the entire county, but how or when the upper parish, or St. Mary's, assumed separate status remains obscure.[3] Whatever the origins or their legal basis, by 1702, if not before, county and provincial records speak clearly of separate, fully functioning, parishes.[4] This separateness continued well into the eighteenth century.

About 1730, the vestry of Christ Church Parish began discussions on the construction of a new church. The expanding population of the parish had outgrown the old structure, built about 1670, and the parish desperately needed a new one. At the point in the discussion where the possibility of erecting the building at a new location came up, vestryman Robert Carter stepped forward and offered to finance the whole enterprise if the chapel remained in its present location. The vestry eagerly accepted Carter's proposal, and construction of a new church began immediately, reaching completion in late 1734, several years after its patron's death.[5]

A few years later, across the wide Corotoman River to the northwest, a similar scene took place. Here, the vestrymen of St. Mary's White Chapel made the decision to remodel their old church for probably many of the same reasons: the old building simply no longer served the needs of the local neighborhood. In this neighborhood, the name Ball replaced the name Carter. Members of this family had entered the county at about the time as the first Carter, establishing themselves on the north side of the Corotoman River. When the parish vestry decided to modify the church in the late 1730s, James Ball, Jesse Ball, Joseph Ball, William Ball Sr., and William Ball Jr. joined seven other vestrymen in approving the plan. The churchyard contained the graves of many members of the Ball family, and Joseph, Jesse, and William Ball had had private galleries constructed for their respective families.[6]

At about the same time that each of these religious communities and their respective leaders reaffirmed the importance of the local neighborhood by rebuilding their churches, other forces moved the two areas into closer cooperation. In 1738, the Virginia Council received "a Representation from the Inhabitants of Lancaster County Complaining of the Inconvenient Scituation of their Court house," and immediately thereafter the governor directed the justices of the county, "with all Convenient Speed," to erect a new building at the old militia muster field. The old courthouse was easily accessible only by water, which a number of freeholders (most probably those with inland farms rather than riverfront plantations) found intolerable. The new courthouse, completed in the early 1740s, sat on the main road through the county, giving easy access to persons from St. Mary's and Christ Church who resided away from the Rappahannock and Corotoman Rivers (see map 5.1).[7]

Shortly after completion of the new courthouse, the House initiated legislation to unite the two parishes. The burgesses rejected a bill to combine the parishes in 1744, but after another petition appeared in 1746, the legislators found the idea "reasonable." In 1752, the House received yet another petition from inhabitants of the county, but this time an investigation into old statutes revealed that, officially, St. Mary's White Chapel had never been a separate parish, and thus a formal merger of the two became unnecessary. Finally, in 1759 the inhabitants of Lancaster petitioned the House to have the vestry dissolved because it still contained twenty-four members, or twelve from each precinct. The dissolution occurred in March 1759, and thereafter voters elected six members each from the upper and lower precincts.[8]

This continued petitioning by "sundry Inhabitants of the upper and lower Precincts" suggests an unwillingness on the part of some of the freeholders to perpetuate a formal division in the county that had proved satisfactory to others for nearly ninety years. The identity of the petitioners remains unclear, but they probably represented inland families who had fewer ties to the older, separate, neighborhoods along the Rappahannock River. Weary of the "Disputes and Controversies" that had divided the county for years, these residents simply wanted the parish business handled smoothly and efficiently.[9] Yet despite the desire by some for greater harmony and unity, local politics in the prerevolutionary era reflected the attachment of most freeholders to the long-standing neighborhood communities.

GENTRY

If the term *gentry* has any meaning for the study of rural society in eighteenth-century Virginia, it certainly applies to the local elite of Lancaster County. Here, after all, resided Robert "King" Carter, perhaps the wealthiest and most influential planter of early-eighteenth-century Virginia. During his forty-year public career, he served as member and speaker of the House of Burgesses, member and president of the Council, treasurer of the colony, county lieutenant of Lancaster and Northumberland, rector of the College of William and Mary, and acting governor of Virginia. His sons and daughters married into the most prominent families of the colony, and as the principal agent for the Fairfax family, he managed the Northern Neck proprietorship and accumulated vast tracts for himself and his descendants. At his death he left an estate "above 300,000 acres of land, about 1,000 Negroes and £10,000."[10] His sons and grandsons continued to manage large plantations in Lancaster and served on the vestry and the county court well into the revolutionary period.

Here, surely, "county oligarchies" and "gentlemen of long-tailed families" dominated local activities, as Charles Sydnor describes in his classic study of eighteenth-century Virginia society.[11] Here, also, the same small handful of "slaveowning barons" sat on the county bench and the parish vestry, served as sheriff, and "took the lead in politics as they did in social affairs . . . and easily cowed all but the bravest freeholding farmers and named their own men for public office."[12] Evidence suggests that this classic model only partially fits the gentry of Lancaster County.

To begin with, the justices of Lancaster had always been recruited from the wealthier planters of the county. As early as the third quarter of the seventeenth century, justices owned twice as many acres of land and managed households with double the number of tithables of the average planter. Over the following forty years this ratio increased, and by the 1710s, justices headed households more than three times the size of the average planter.[13] This economic distance between officeholder and average planter continued for the remainder of the colonial period and may have increased in the last decades before the Revolution. Justices owned more than twice as much land as the average planter in the period 1735–55 and nearly four times as much in the years 1756–75 (table 5.1).[14]

Although little is known of the men who served on parish vestries in the seventeenth and early eighteenth centuries, by the 1730s and 1740s vestrymen exhibited substantial wealth. In the period 1735–55, their average landholdings exceeded those of their colleagues on the county bench, and by the 1760s and 1770s they held three times that of the average farmer. Similarly, those serving as county sheriff in the earlier period owned about 580 acres each, on average, a figure very close to that of justices and vestrymen. The

Table 5.1
Average Acreage Owned, by Officeholders,
Lancaster County, 1735–1775

Landowner	1735–1755		1756–1775	
	Acres	N	Acres	N
All landowners	241	223	251	253
Sheriffs	579	8	359	3
Justices	554	27	989	23
Vestrymen	588	18	726	14
Candidates	945	12	1,302	8
Winners	867	7	1,383	5

Sources: Lancaster County Rentals, 1748 and 1750, Brock Collection, Hunt-ingtton Library; Lancaster County Rental for 1773, Virginia Historical Soci-ety; "Public Officers in Virginia, 1702, 1714," Virginia Magazine of History and Biography 1 (1894): 368, 375; 2 (1894): 7–8; 8 (1901): 63; 10 (1903): 435–36; 21 (1913): 196; EJC, 4:129, 215, 233, 235, 238, 244, 286–87, 293, 320, 327, 336, 361, 368, 393, 397, 405, 421, 425, 429; EJC, 5:91, 93, 105, 108, 157, 259, 271, 303, 318, 329, 392, 422; EJC, 6:116, 405, 526, 559, 594; William Meade, Old Churches, Ministers, and Families of Virginia (Philadelphia, 1857), 2: 125; "Justices of the Peace of Colonial Virginia, 1757–1775," Bulletin of the Vir-ginia State Library 14 (1921), 56, 99–100, 107, 120–21, 126.

Note: Figures in this and subsequent tables do not include the main Carter plantation of approximately 8,000 acres, and therefore the averages are more representative than they would have been with such an extreme value.

limited information available on sheriffs at the end of the colonial period suggests a decline in average wealth.

The overlap between those serving on the judicial bench and on the vestry seems less than expected in this long-established Tide-water county. During the first half of the period, 83 percent of the vestrymen also served at some time as justices of the peace, al-though just 54 percent of the justices assumed vestry duties during their lives. Of the forty-one officeholders in this period, twenty served in both capacities at one time or another. In the last twenty years of the colonial period, however, the membership of the two bodies became even more distinct, with only 61 percent of the vestrymen also acting as justices and about a third of the justices re-ceiving election to the vestry. Fewer than 30 percent of the office-holders in this latter period had simultaneous membership in both local governmental bodies.

An actual reduction in the number of offices available accounts in part for this decline in multiple officeholding. The number of justices serving on the county bench at any one time varied somewhat but averaged about sixteen. However, the House of Burgesses cut in half the number of vestry positions available in the county when in the 1750s that body discovered that St. Mary's White Chapel was only a precinct of Christ Church Parish. For decades, each precinct had elected twelve vestrymen of its own, but after 1759 only six members came from each. In the 1760s and 1770s, the gentry had to share approximately twenty-eight positions rather than the forty or so available in previous decades, and this may have discouraged monopolization.[15]

Although by definition vestry service was divided evenly between the two precincts for the entire period (twelve each before 1759 and six each afterward), the county bench and sheriff's office might have been controlled by either side of the river. They were not. More justices resided on the upper, or St. Mary's, side of the Corotoman, particularly in the 1740s and 1750s and possibly earlier, but the imbalance is not so lopsided as to suggest domination (see table 5.2). Equally important, the prestigious quorum of eight or so justices who could conduct the court's business without all of the justices present remained nearly balanced between the two areas. Furthermore, of the sheriffs identified between 1730 and 1775, exactly half came from each precinct.

Whatever the size and geographic composition of the officeholding group, from within its ranks emerged the candidates for House of Burgesses elections. At least twenty-one individuals offered

Table 5.2
Officeholding and Precinct, Lancaster County (%)

Office and Year	Christ Church	St. Mary's
Justice		
1741	39	61
1752	44	56
1761	56	44
1774	47	53
Sheriff, 1730–75	50	50

Table 5.3
Candidates and Election Results, Lancaster County, 1728–1774

Candidate	1728	1734	1735	1741	1748	1752	1754
Charles Burgess	W						
Edwin Conway	W		W	W		W	
James Ball Sr.		W	W	L			
Robert Mitchell				W	L		
William Stepto				L	L		
Joseph Ball				L		L	
William Ball Sr.				L			
William Tayloe				L		L	
Joseph Chinn					W	W	
Peter Conway					W		
Thomas Pinckard					L		
James Ball Jr.							W
William Ball Jr.							L
George Heale							
Richard Selden							
Charles Carter							
Solomon Ewell							
Richard Mitchell							
Richard Ball							
James Selden							
Burgess Ball							

Note: W = winner; L = loser.

themselves to the voters of Lancaster County between the general elections of 1728 and 1774 (see table 5.3), and with perhaps only two exceptions these men had already distinguished themselves as either justices or vestrymen before seeking elective office.[16] Sixteen of the twenty-one had served as justices of the peace before seeking election, while nine accepted vestry duties. Only two served as county sheriff before running for office, while six assumed the duties of sheriff after their first attempt at the polls.

Although previous experience in major local offices became part of the career path for those wishing to try for a seat in the House of Burgesses, family connections and wealth also counted for much. Thirteen of the twenty-one candidates (62%) had fathers, grandfathers, or uncles who had represented the county in past assemblies,

1755	1755	1758	1758	1761	1765	1768	1769	1771	1774
		L							
						W			
W	W	W							
L	L		W	L					
L	W								
		W		W	W	W	W	W	W
			L						
				W	W		W	W	
					L	L	L	L	
									W
									L

with the Carter, Ball, and Conway families dominating in such matters. Further, candidates were, on average, substantially wealthier than those who attained only local office (see table 5.1). The twelve candidates who ran in the period 1735–55 and the eight candidates who ran in the following two decades owned 70 percent more land than other officeholders.[17]

When it came to actually winning an electoral contest, prior public service, particularly on the county bench, were clearly important attributes. Twelve of the thirteen winners had served on the county court before successfully contesting their first election to the House, six had had vestry experience, three had held both offices, and one had been a justice, a vestryman, and a sheriff.[18] Nine of the thirteen (69%) had ancestors who had also served in the House for the county, but unlike the group of candidates as a whole, differences in wealth did not separate winner from loser (see table 5.1).

Whether a man ran and whether he won may have had as much to do with where he lived as with the exact set of characteristics he brought to the electoral arena. Certainly, he had to be an officeholder, clearly he had to be a man of above average wealth, and probably the kinship group to which he belonged had much to do with his success at the polls, but his physical location within the county mattered also. The long-standing precinct-neighborhoods on either side of the Corotoman River formed not only social, economic, and religious neighborhoods but political entities as well. This de facto administrative separation (which lasted until 1759) and the psychological separation (which lasted much longer) also defined the way in which the county thought about its representation to the House of Burgesses.

With few exceptions, from the 1690s to the end of the colonial period (and at least partway into the revolutionary era), the gentry of Lancaster nominated and the freeholders elected one representative from each precinct. Only in the assemblies of 1700–1703, 1720–22, and 1755–58 did both burgesses reside on the same side of the Corotoman River. Of the twenty-six general elections held in the county from 1700 to 1774, twenty-three witnessed representation divided according to precinct. This split in representation could have resulted from a preelection agreement among county leaders (as occurred frequently in England during this period), but this seems unlikely here. The voting behavior of county leaders reveals that they only supported those candidates from their local area, and not until the forced merger of the precincts in 1759 did leaders begin to think in countywide terms. Thereafter, the representation remained divided, but the gentry tended to support a countywide slate that included a candidate from each side.[19] The voters, as described below, followed a similar pattern of behavior.

On the upper, or St. Mary's, side, the numerous descendants of the first Colonel William Ball (died 1669) dominated economic, vestry, and electoral activities. Four of the six largest landowners in the precinct in 1750 came from the Ball family, while five of the twelve vestrymen in the late 1730s shared that surname. A Ball represented the county from 1698 to 1728, and in most of the elections for the remainder of the colonial period at least one member of the family stood as a candidate (see table 5.3). When not running for election or serving in the House, members of the Heale, Mitchell, Chinn, or Selden families—related to the Balls by marriage—took their places.[20]

In Christ Church, or the lower precinct, the Carter and Conway families monopolized representation. Both families arrived with the earliest settlers in the area, and each initially took up land along the north bank of the Rappahannock, below the Corotoman River. The Conways had accumulated about two thousand acres by the middle of the eighteenth century and served as justices and vestrymen from the late seventeenth century until the Revolution. The Carters, principally in the person of Robert "King" Carter, built a colonywide dynasty from the first meager holdings in Lancaster County. By the time of "King" Carter's death in 1732, the family seat at Corotoman probably included nearly eight thousand acres and occupied much of the south-central section of the county (see map 5.1). Robert Carter represented the lower precinct and the county from 1691 to 1700, when the Crown elevated him to the Council. Edwin Conway assumed these duties in 1710 and served nearly continuously until 1755; Charles Carter (grandson of Robert) took over in 1758 and sat in the House for the remainder of the colonial period.[21]

Lancaster was clearly a county of "long-tailed families," and the Carter, Ball, and Conway clans had the longest tails. They had entered the county early, served as some of the first justices and vestrymen, and virtually controlled representation to the colonial assembly. While they certainly exercised countywide influence, their principal interests (to use the eighteenth-century term) operated at the precinct level. In these moderately large rural neighborhoods on either side of the Corotoman River, the respective families dominated economic, social, and religious activities to such an extent that a member of the kinship group nearly always became a legislative candidate and frequently won. Of course, members of other families served on the vestry and county court and ran for and won election to the House. They, like the Balls and Carters, were substantially wealthier than the average freeholder among whom they lived, and nearly all who sought election did so after some local public service. Although a fairly small percentage of the adult white male population shared county offices, Lancaster did not have nearly so tight an oligarchy as we are often led to believe.[22]

FREEHOLDERS

From the earliest stages of settlement, Lancaster County contained larger-than-average plantations and farms. Original settlers patented nearly a thousand acres each and managed farms with three laborers, on average, giving Lancaster the fewest one-man households of any Tidewater county. Although by the mid-eighteenth century the average size of farm had decreased dramatically (see table 5.4), average household size remained among the largest in the colony. Lancaster households averaged 4.3 tithables in 1745, 4.6 in 1750, and 5.7 in 1773. Much of this increase resulted from the steady growth in the number of black slaves in the county, which rose from about 1,600 in the late 1720s to more than 4,000 by 1774.[23] As contrasted with some Tidewater and Northern Neck counties, the owners of the land—not tenants—worked the majority of farms in Lancaster. At least 60 percent and possibly more of the householders owned the land they tilled, while life-lease and short-term tenants occupied something less than 40 percent of the farms.[24]

Although Lancaster had its paupers, transients, and short-term leaseholders who came and went from the county, the majority of householders (whether owners or tenants) operated modest-sized, highly productive farms. Furthermore, this group included the vast majority of adult white males in the county. The proportion who either owned or leased enough land to qualify as a freeholder fluctu-

Table 5.4
Landownership Patterns, Lancaster County, 1750 and 1773

Farm Size in Acres	1750[a]		1773[b]	
	%	N	%	N
Less than 100	22	48	29	72
100–150	29	65	25	62
151–250	25	55	25	63
More than 250	25	55	22	56

Sources: Lancaster County Rental 1750, Brock Collection, Huntington Library; Lancaster County Rental for 1773, Virginia Historical Society.

Note: Table excludes land in estates and land belonging to females and orphans.

[a]Range is 40 to 1,883 acres, with a mean on 241 and a median of 150.
[b]Range is 16 to 3,007 acres, with a mean of 251 and a median of 150.

Table 5.5

Electorate and Turnout, Lancaster County, 1741–1774

Election Year	Adult Males	Eligible Freeholders	Actual Voters	Turnout (%)	
				Adult Males	Eligible Freeholders
1741	412	313	203	49	65
1748	397	306	199	50	65
1752	381	293	185	49	63
1754 (by)	370	285	153	41	54
1755 (by)	365	281	114	31	41
1755	365	281	149	41	53
1758	373	291	217	58	75
1758 (by)	373	291	145	39	50
1761	381	297	203	53	68
1765	391	309	171	44	55
1768	399	319	188	47	59
1769	401	321	168	42	52
1771	405	328	165	41	50
1774	409	331	210	51	63

Sources: Lancaster County Deed Book 13, 249–50; Deed Book 14, 200–201; Deeds and Wills Book 15, 82–85, 167, 231, 232–33; Deed Book 16, 27–29, 49, 222–23; Deed Book 18, 42–43, 133–34, 154; Deed Book 19, 58a–59a, 112–13; Virginia State Library; Lancaster County Rentals, 1748, 1750, Brock Collection, Huntington Library; Lancaster County Rental for 1773, Virginia Historical Society.

Note: Number of adult males and eligible freeholders are estimates.

ated between 75 and 85 percent (see table 5.5). These freeholders also took an active part in the civic life of the community, and elections represented an important aspect of that political life. Turnout among eligible freeholders averaged 58 percent for all elections and 61 percent for general elections. Even participation among the larger adult white male population averaged just over 45 percent for the fourteen elections from 1741 through 1774, with the eleven general elections averaging 48 percent.[25]

Changes in turnout among eligible voters document the rise and fall of voter interest in the electoral process. Excluding by-elections, participation declined from the 1740s to a low point in a 1755 race that included only candidates from one of the county's two precincts (see table 5.5 and figure 2.2). With the entry of a candidate from the lower precinct (also a Carter) in 1758, interest in the electoral process jumped dramatically, remaining high through the next general election. Thereafter, a stable group of candidates and incumbents interested in continuing to seek office lessened the saliency of the contests, and a gradual decline in turnout occurred from 1765 to 1771. In 1774, however, voter interest again peaked as precinct rivalries surfaced once more in the final election of the colonial period.

THE POLITICS OF NEIGHBORHOOD

Lancaster's two distinct neighborhoods, or precincts, clearly defined the spheres of influence and areas of activity of local leaders. Countywide offices balanced neatly between the areas, and the choice of candidates for House of Burgesses elections somehow took precinct into consideration. Furthermore, the pair of winners in most electoral contests also included a person from each side of the river, but this process transcended elite control and depended upon the actions of two hundred or so freeholders at several dozen contests.

First, precinct loyalties remained the key element in determining voting behavior until the mid-1750s. Although lack of appropriate data obscures patterns in the 1730s, precinct loyalties operated in the elections of 1741, 1748, and 1752 and possibly earlier (see table 5.6). In these contests, members of both the elite and the electorate voted overwhelmingly for candidates from their own precinct: Christ Church freeholders averaged 72 percent, St. Mary's freeholders averaged 73 percent, and the leadership group (justices, vestrymen, sheriffs, and militia officers) averaged just slightly higher, at 74 percent. In 1741, for example, the seven candidates included three from Christ Church and four from St. Mary's. In Christ Church, freeholders gave 45 percent of their votes to the local pair, Edwin Conway and William Steptoe, 36 percent to Conway and William Tayloe, 2 percent to Steptoe and Tayloe, leaving just 17 percent for cross-precinct or countywide slates. Similarly in 1752, the St. Mary's freeholders gave 78 percent of their support to the local pair, Joseph Chinn and Joseph Ball, 19 percent to cross-precinct pairs, and only 3 percent to the pair from Christ Church.

Beginning with the 1758 election and extending through 1771, the level of support for precinct candidates dropped dramatically.

Table 5.6
Precinct Voting by Freeholders and Leaders,
Lancaster County, 1741–1774 (%)

Year	Christ Church	St. Mary's	Leaders
1741	83	74	75
1748	59	68	74
1752	75	78	74
1758	40		17
1761		42	15
1765		25	0
1768		37	18
1769		24	0
1771		30	7
1774		54	62

Support by county leaders for precinct-specific slates, which had averaged nearly 75 percent in earlier years, declined to an average of only 10 percent for these six elections. In 1765 and 1769, leaders voted only for countywide slates, casting no ballots for pairs of candidates from their local precincts. Similarly, support among the electorate for pairs of precinct candidates also dropped significantly, averaging only 33 percent between 1758 and 1771 (see table 5.6).

At least part of the explanation for this sudden change in voting behavior after 1752 derives from the absence of fully competing slates from each precinct. In 1741, three candidates stood from Christ Church and four from St. Mary's; in 1748, three from Christ Church and two from St. Mary's; and in 1752, a pair from each. Only St. Mary's candidates ran in the by-elections of 1754 and 1755 and in the general election of 1755, and thereafter each general election included only a single candidate from one of the precincts and two from the other: a single candidate from St. Mary's in 1758 and only one candidate from Christ Church from 1761 through 1774.

Yet, despite the reduction in the number of candidates, freeholders could have continued to vote predominantly for neighborhood men. A pair of candidates from Christ Church ran in 1758, and a pair ran from St. Mary's in the remaining elections. Furthermore, plumping occurred in other counties during these years, occasionally at a fairly high level, and therefore remained an option open to any freeholder who wished to limit his voting to precinct candidates only. Voters, however, chose neither of these options in very significant proportions: about one-third of the freeholders selected a precinct pair when available (see table 5.6), while plumping remained at the same low level before and after 1755.

The change in behavior occurred about 1755, probably the result of a combination of factors. The smaller number of candidates certainly had some impact; so did the entry into electoral politics in 1758 of Charles Carter, Christ Church vestryman, eventual justice, and heir apparent to his grandfather's social and economic position in the county. Further, the by-elections of 1754, 1755, and 1758, which concerned the replacement of a St. Mary's burgess, involved the entire county in selecting a successor and may have broadened voter interests into a countywide perspective. And finally, the law forced the two precincts, which had acted as separate parishes for sixty or more years, to form a single vestry, with six members from each area.[26]

The selection of countywide slates dominated electoral behavior among both leaders and freeholders for the six contests from 1758 through 1771. Charles Carter won all six races; Richard Mitchell won four. But when Mitchell decided not to run in 1774, a fifteen-year pattern of representation and voting behavior came to an abrupt end. Charles Carter continued as the Christ Church candidate, but two newcomers came forward in St. Mary's White Chapel. Both had just received appointments to the county court; one came from the Ball family and owned the third-largest estate in the county; the other represented the Selden clan, which had more modest landholdings. Burgess Ball's uncle and grandfather had served as the county's burgess in an earlier era; James Selden's father had won election to the House in the 1750s.

Three of the older and more distinguished members of the local gentry disliked both of the St. Mary's candidates and plumped for Charles Carter, three others thought Carter and Ball the best choice, while two selected Carter and Selden, and five favored the pair of newcomers. Nearly two-thirds of the elite selected only candidates from their own precinct. Such disagreement among local leaders had not occurred since the early 1750s.

The voters, for their part, responded to the election with an array of choices: Selden and Carter received 39 percent of the vote, Selden and Ball, 32 percent, and Carter and Ball, 20 percent. Another 9 percent voted for either Carter or Ball. Since 81 percent of the freeholders had selected Carter and Mitchell in the previous election, this represented a rather dramatic change in behavior. Moreover, while nearly unanimous support for the two winning candidates prevailed on each side of the river in the 1771, three years later voting broke along precincts lines. Fifty-four percent of the freeholders voted for precinct slates (see table 5.6), with Carter receiving 75 percent of his support from Christ Church and Ball getting 65 percent of his votes from St. Mary's. Selden, who ended up the top vote getter in the election, received 63 percent of his support from Christ Church and 37 percent from St. Mary's.[27] After lying dormant for nearly a generation, precinct loyalties clearly had surfaced again.

In short, a strong allegiance to candidates from the local neighborhood never completely died out between the mid-1750s and 1774. Approximately one-third of the freeholders in each of these elections had voted for a pair of candidates from their own precinct; more than half did so in 1774. Freeholders whose activities and interests probably did not spread much beyond their immediate neighborhoods on each side of the river accounted for such local favoritism. The most important elements in their lives lay nearby— church, tobacco warehouse, and wealthy neighbors who ran for election. Those freeholders who continued to prefer countywide slates operated within a wider economic and social circle.

If we use wealth as measured in size of landholdings to indicate roughly the breadth and level of economic and social activities, then socioeconomic status correlated with political perspective in eighteenth-century Lancaster County. In every election except one, those freeholders selecting the countywide slate owned substantially more land, on average, than their fellow voters who choose only precinct candidates (see table 5.7).[28] This held not only for the period after 1755 but in the earlier elections as well. In 1748, for example, countywide voters averaged 276 acres each, while those preferring candidates from the precincts averaged 179 acres and 186 acres, respectively. The gap widened after 1755, as the proportion of freeholders voting for precinct slates declined, culminating in 1771, when the very small minority selecting neighborhood slates averaged only 104 acres each, while countywide voters averaged 303. The world of the small farmer rarely extended beyond the local neighborhood, and his behavior in elections to the House of Burgesses reflected that perspective; the large planter, on the other hand, interacted with other large planters across the county,

Table 5.7
Average Acres Owned by Supporters
of Electoral Slates, Lancaster County,
1741–1774

		Slate	
Year	County	Christ Church	St. Mary's
1741	383	159	
1748	276	179	186
1752	203	191	236
1758	286	193	
1761	266		191
1765	291		150
1768	264		158
1769	296		114
1771	303		104
1774	257		164

and his electoral behavior mirrored his broader perspective.

The two large rural neighborhoods or precincts located on either side of the Corotoman River influenced the political structure of Lancaster County. The distinctiveness of the two neighborhoods defined the way in which large and small planters in each area thought about county politics: leaders supported candidates from their own precinct, and freeholders overwhelmingly voted for local men.[29] When in the mid-1750s the House of Burgesses forced the two areas to act in greater concert, the gentry and many of the freeholders from each section adopted a countywide political perspective, favoring a candidate from each precinct.

Although the period of county slates lasted more than fifteen years, the smaller farmers never abandoned precinct loyalties, while those of the middling planters were apparently only dormant. In 1774, while many counties responded to the governor's angry dissolution of the assembly by returning incumbents who faced little or no opposition, Lancaster residents rekindled old neighborhood rivalries by engaging in a closely fought contest between a veteran from Christ Church and two newcomers from St. Mary's. Even in the midst of deepening imperial crisis, many Lancaster County freeholders saw no farther than the boundaries of their familiar rural neighborhood.

6

Fairfax County

*Constructing Political Consensus
in the Northern Neck*

"I have not yet heard how you succeeded in electioneering," George Washington of Fairfax County wrote to his friend Burwell Bassett of New Kent, "I changed the scene from Frederick to this county and had an easy and creditable poll."[1] This election, held on July 16, 1765, marked an important point in the political career of the thirty-three-year-old planter: having aspired to the post for at least ten years, Washington finally became a burgess from his home county of Fairfax.

Washington's success was no mere quirk of fate, nor was it inevitable, but rather it was the logical extension of his economic, social, and political activities over the previous ten years. Washington had done all the right things to put himself in a position to run for office: he had become a major landowner in the county, had developed close social ties with the leading gentry, had achieved fame as a military leader, had assumed positions of leadership in the local community, had served in the House of Burgesses from another county, and had carefully studied the local electoral climate of Fairfax County.

The maturation of the young politician mirrored to a large extent the maturation of the county he now represented. Both came into being in 1732: Washington in Westmoreland County, and Truro Parish (the future Fairfax County) in Prince William County. By the mid-1760s, both reached a kind of maturity: Washington's activities over the past decade had prepared him to take on greater responsibilities in the regional and provincial community; and the Fairfax

County political system had reached a stage in which the local community began to understand that it wanted in its leaders precisely
what Washington possessed. It had taken more than two decades for
this consensus to develop. Both natural and political causes hindered its progress. Demographic phenomena in the form of a rapidly increasing population and geographic factors relating to a large
physical area with varying terrain did much to foster disunity
among the gentry and the population at large. Political conflict during this period centered on personalities, neighborhood loyalties, local administrative and economic problems, and imperial concerns,
and these issues set the agenda for political conflict within the county for a number of years. Following the division of the county in
1757, a smaller and more uniform geographic area provided the stage
for the achievement of political consensus.

Elections to the House of Burgesses provided the formal and
somewhat regularized mechanism for the resolution of some of
these local conflicts. These events also gave the county elite an opportunity to put forward their best members as candidates, with the
backers of various men feeling they had accomplished as much as
the winners themselves. The voters, for their part, judged the merits—usually personal rather than ideological—of the representatives of these competing factions. At each election over the thirty-
year period, the gentry and freeholders of Fairfax County came
together to develop and define one type of political community.

SETTING

Colonial Fairfax initially included all of the modern counties of Fairfax, Loudoun, and Arlington. Encompassing 950 square miles of
area, it stretched 50 miles from the flat Tidewater marshes below
Great Falls on the Potomac through rolling Piedmont hills to the
Blue Ridge in the west (see map 6.1). The county was part of the enormous Northern Neck Proprietary, which devolved to the Fairfax

---

Map 6.1   Fairfax County, Eighteenth Century

Based on information contained in Nan Netherton et al., *Fairfax County, Virginia: A
History* (Fairfax: Fairfax County Board of Supervisors, 1978), 10–41; Donald Jackson, ed.,
The Diaries of George Washington, vols. 1, 2 (Charlottesville: University Press of Virginia,
1976–78), esp. 1:8, 213, 220–21.

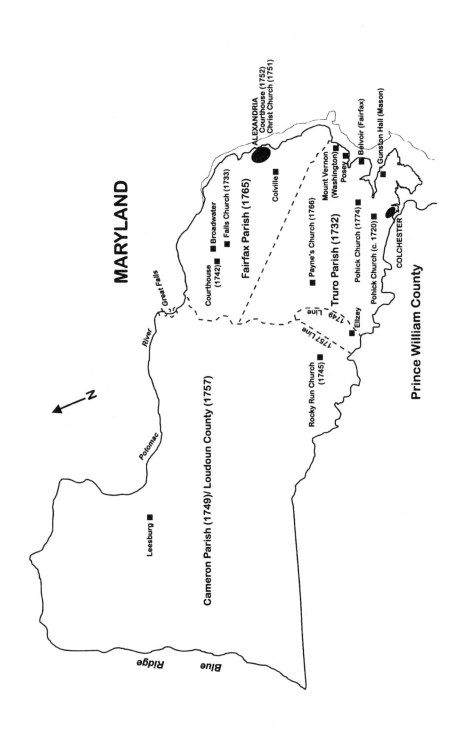

Table 6.1
White Male Population Structure, Fairfax County, 1744–1785

Year	White Tithes	Adult White Males	Eligible Free-holders	Male Land-owners	Male House-holders	Voters
1744	780	585	346			256
1748	917	688	465			318
1749	1,126	844	755		640	
1753	1,242	931	408			
1755	1,312	984	591			376
1757	1,345	1,009	550	326		
1761	925	694	341	162		281
1764	1,015	761	336	160		
1765	1,044	783	482		647	257
1768	1,130	847	403			211
1770	1,185	889	485	179		
1785	1,234	926		297	831	

Sources: Based upon a constituted adult white male population file of 2,084 individuals, compiled from Fairfax County Deed Book Liber A-1 (1742–46), Virginia State Library; George Washington Papers, Library of Congress; Prince William County Deed Book E, 524–524e, Virginia State Library; Julian P. Boyd, ed., *The Papers of Thomas Jefferson* (Chapel Hill: University of North Carolina Press, 1950), 1:43–48; Donald M. Sweig, "The Virginia Nonimportation Association of 1770 and Fairfax County: A Study in Local Participation," *Virginia Magazine of History and Biography* 87 (1979): 316–25; Fairfax County Lists of Tithables for 1749, Miscellaneous Manuscript Collection, Manuscript Division, Library of Congress; Fairfax Rentals for 1761, 1764, 1770, Loudoun Rentals for 1761, Brock Collection, Huntington Library; J. Estelle Stewart King, comp., *Abstract of Wills and Inventories, Fairfax County, Virginia, 1742–1801* (Baltimore: Genealogical Publishing, 1978); *Minutes of the Vestry, Truro Parish, Virginia, 1732–1785* (Lorton, Va.: Pohick Church, 1974); *Virginia Colonial Militia, 1651–1776* (Baltimore: Genealogical Publishing, 1965), 58–59, 72–73. Also Norma K. Risjord, *Chesapeake Politics, 1781–1800* (New York: Columbia University Press, 1978), 24–25.

Note: Number of adult white males is estimated. Eligible freeholders is number identified. County was divided in 1757.

family at the turn of the eighteenth century. The large land grants the Fairfaxes and their agents awarded to themselves and other prominent planters gave the Tidewater region of the county an aristocratic air, which survives today at Mount Vernon and Gunston Hall.[2] The presence of such large estates helps explain why landowners never constituted more than 25 percent of the adult white male population of Fairfax County even during the late colonial period. Furthermore, a remarkable stability in the size of the landholding class coupled with an increasing population meant that the proportion of owners probably declined in the 1770s. After the Revolution, however, the percentage of landowners again rose to about one-third and stayed at that level through the end of the century (see table 6.1).

Among the population that did not own land outright, more than half fell within some kind of tenancy arrangement. Those holding life leases were considered permanent rather than temporary residents and composed more than 40 percent of the adult white male population in the 1740s but perhaps no more than 15 percent in the 1770s.[3] The remaining third or so of the adult white male population of Fairfax fell into a group that probably occupied the lowest economic level in the county. This included various short-term tenancies on small parcels of land, laborers, servants, and outright paupers.

Like the 256 citizens who gathered in August of 1744 at the courthouse to elect the county's first set of representatives to the House of Burgesses, the electorate included both landowners and a considerable number of tenants. Some men were veterans of the electoral process, having voted previously in elections in other counties. Some were probably voting for the first time. Most resided in the new county, but a minority did not. This scene would occur eleven more times within the next thirty years; in some, many more voters would participate; in others, fewer electors would be present. On all but one of these occasions, the voters had to make an actual choice between competing members of the county gentry.

THE ELITE

Between this first election held in August 1744 and the last election of the colonial period in July 1774, at least sixteen men offered themselves to the voters of Fairfax County (see table 6.2).[4] Eleven of these candidates won at least once; five entered just a single election, lost, and never tried again. Only one person tried and failed more than once, although three men lost on their first attempt and won on their second. Only one incumbent suffered defeat during the colonial period.

Table 6.2
Candidates for House of Burgesses and Election Results,
Fairfax County, 1744–1774

Candidate	1741[a]	1744	1748	1752	1754
William Fairfax	248				
Thomas Harrison	234				
John Colville	175	148	108		
Valentine Peyton	141				
Richard Blackburn	29				
Lawrence Washington		139	193		
Lewis Ellzey		99			
John Sturman		59			
Bond Veal		20			
Richard Osborne			138		
George Mason			93		
Hugh West			46	W	
Gerrard Alexander				W	
John West Sr.					W
George William Fairfax					
William Ellzey					
George Johnston					
George Washington					
John Posey					
Charles Broadwater					

Note: W = winner; L = loser.

   [a]1741 data for Prince William County.

According to the most common interpretation of eighteenth-century elections, successful candidates—whether a George Washington, who would later achieve nationwide prominence, or a John
West, who never rose above the office of burgess—had to possess a
fairly specific set of attributes. Chief among them was membership
in the gentry, that real though somewhat fluid and not always definable body of men who had well-above-average wealth in land and
slaves, that set the social standards of the day with its dress and manners, and that exercised political power by its domination of local
judicial, military, and ecclesiastical commissions.[5] The gentry of
Fairfax County came fairly close to fitting this model. An analysis
of the 172 individuals who made up the Fairfax gentry during the pe-

1755	1758	1761	1765	1768	1769	1771	1774
251	W	W	148	142	W	W	
222							
224							
	W	W					
			201	185	W	W	W
			131	87			
	L						W

riod 1742–75 suggests a clear but not absolute correlation between officeholding and substantial wealth.[6]

On the other hand, the wealth of all officeholders far surpassed that of the average freeholder in the county. Fairfax County officeholders held six times as many slaves as the average householder in 1749 and owned two-to-three times more land than the average freeholder in 1757, 1761, 1764, and 1770. Although the wealthiest individuals in the county did not always monopolize local officeholding, some offices attracted persons with higher levels of wealth than others. More justices (57%) fell among the elite landowning class than vestrymen (47%). On the other hand, 49 percent of militia officers and 63 percent of sheriffs were among the elite landowners.

Despite these substantial differences between officeholders and the average planter, the gap between the two groups narrowed over time. County officials had six times as many slaves in 1749, three times as much land in 1757 and 1761, and just slightly over twice as much land in 1764 and 1770 (see table 6.3). The position of vestryman also fell relative to the average planter of the county, while justices declined for several periods, only to rise just before the Revolution.[7] Patterns for militia officers fluctuated widely after 1749, but even they had less wealth on average at the end of the period than at the beginning. Although the information on sheriffs is sketchy after 1752, there does appear to have been a significant decline in the wealth status of those holding this office as well.

Candidates for the House of Burgesses elections, on the other hand, represented for the most part an elite among the elite. In 1749, candidates owned an average of 14.7 slaves, more than ten times that of the average planter. Despite a slight decline in their relative economic position in Fairfax society, candidates for these elections held greater wealth throughout the period than any other group of local officeholders.[8] Candidates who won elections were even wealthier. Winners in the elections of 1744, 1748, and 1752 owned an average of 16.6 slaves—nearly twelve times that of the average household-

Table 6.3
Average Wealth of Elite Groups, Fairfax County, 1742–1775

Group	1742–1752		1753–1759	
	Slaves	N	Acres	N
Households	1.4	658	673	371
Sheriffs	7.8	5		
Vestrymen	8.1	23	2,421	14
Officeholders	9.0	38	2,256	39
All gentry	9.2	69	2,199	72
Justices	9.6	26	1,961	27
Militia officers	11.0	16	2,416	20
Candidates	14.7	7	3,682	4
Winners	16.6	5	4,352	3

Sources: See table 6.1.

Note: The time periods in the table are centered upon the five points in time at which householders, whether or not they owned the land they occupied; in 1757, 1761, 1764, and male population than householders.

er. This included the second- and third-largest slaveholders in Fairfax County: John Colville, who won in 1744, held 29 slaves; Lawrence Washington, who won in 1744 and 1748, had 27 slaves. Except for the election of 1761, where the two known candidates (and winners) only averaged three times the wealth of the average freeholder, winning candidates held approximately six times more land than those who voted for them during the last nine elections of the colonial period.

Yet despite a general decline in the relative wealth of most local officeholders, those who won election to the House of Burgesses maintained their lofty status right up to the Revolution. Winners after 1765 averaged nearly five thousand acres each, with their relative position actually on the rise in the last elections before the Revolution. Although the period witnessed an egalitarian trend among local officeholding in general, representatives to the colonial assembly always came from the wealthiest planters in Fairfax County.[9]

Service in a local office also was important for those seeking election to the House of Burgesses from Fairfax County. Only two of the sixteen candidates had no local officeholding experience when they sought election to the colonial assembly: Bond Veal, who ran in 1744, and William Ellzey, who ran in 1755. While 12 percent had

1760–1762		1763–1767		1768–1775	
Acres	(N)	Acres	(N)	Acres	(N)
809	197	905	181	788	204
		0	1	364	2
3,099	11	1,912	22	1,829	22
2,257	23	1,922	34	1,799	33
2,243	55	2,083	58	1,827	63
2,254	17	2,122	22	2,815	18
		4,294	6	509	3
2,389	2	3,562	3	3,673	4
2,389	2	5,141	2	4,762	3

wealth data are available: 1749, 1757, 1761, 1764, 1770. In 1749 *households* includes all
1770, *households* includes only landowners, a significantly smaller percentage of the adult

been sheriffs, service as either a justice of the county court, officer of the county militia, or vestryman of the local parish was crucial: 75 percent of the legislative candidates were justices, 69 percent were militia officers, and 68 percent had served on the parish vestry. Nearly 90 percent of the candidates had been either a justice or a vestryman, and 56 percent had served in both capacities.

Successful candidates had even more local officeholding experience. All eleven winners served as either a justice of the peace, militia officer, or vestryman before seeking elective office. Eight had been justices, seven vestrymen, and five militia officers. Losers, on the other hand, generally had less experience in local offices than the successful candidates. The two individuals who ran with no local officeholding experience lost, while half of those with just one office won, and 70 percent of those with two or more local offices succeeded at the polls. The more local offices held, the greater the likelihood of success (see table 6.4).

With perhaps one exception, every one of the sixteen individuals who sought election to the House of Burgesses from Fairfax County stands out from the freeholders and householders among whom they lived.[10] Their average wealth as measured in either slaves or land was two to five times greater than that of the ordinary planter. In those few cases in which personal wealth was not extraordinary, they (along with their wealthier colleagues) had made their mark on the local political scene with their service as vestryman, justice, militia officer, or sheriff.

In Fairfax County, degree of wealth correlated substantially with the level and responsibility of the office held. The economic status of militia officers and sheriffs fluctuated over time, with perhaps a significant drop in wealth in the immediate prerevolutionary era.

Table 6.4
Officeholding and House of
Burgesses Electoral Success

Offices	Winners	Losers
0	0	2
1	4	4
2–4	7	3

Note: More than sixteen cases are reported because several candidates both won and lost elections.

Next up the ladder came vestrymen and, just slightly above them, justices of the peace. Candidates for the House held even greater wealth, on average, and at the top were the winners of these legislative races. Wealth provided individuals with the opportunity to devote considerable time to local political offices, and the successful management of that wealth demonstrated to their peers as well as their economic inferiors that they could be entrusted with positions of responsibility. Wealth alone, however, could not buy a seat in the House of Burgesses, at least not from Fairfax County. Experience in one or more of the top local offices was necessary before an individual moved on to offer himself to the voters of the county. Whether this road to electoral success appeared obvious to the officeholder himself or to the average freeholder is unclear, but a fairly consistent pathway nonetheless existed.

The most common path for those who eventually won seats in the colonial assembly started with an appointment as vestryman. A few years later, a position on the county court followed. In a few more years, a successful election to the assembly occurred. Along the way, a few of these people also served as sheriff or militia officer, but such appointments did not prove critical. For those who obtained only one local office, that of justice ranked higher than vestryman.[11] But wealth and local political experience do not fully explain the success or failure of every candidate in each election. Events in Williamsburg or London dictated when elections occurred and thus offered a favorable moment in time to one man but denied it to another. Moreover, electoral success also depended upon hundreds of freeholders traveling dozens of miles over bad roads to cast their ballots.

ELECTORAL POLITICS

Fairfax County came into existence in 1742 and held its first election in 1744. That election took place within the context of the competitive heritage from its parent community, Prince William County. In the four Prince William elections between 1732 and 1741, three incumbents suffered defeat, two of the elections resulted in petitions before the House of Burgesses, coercion of voters through threats of physical violence reportedly occurred at one contest, and the House declared another election void because one candidate inappropriately used his office of tobacco inspector to influence the electors.[12] In the 1741 Prince William election, William Fairfax and Thomas Harrison won over incumbent Valentine Peyton and candidates John Colville and Richard Blackburn. These candidates and the competitive legacy from Prince William provided part of the setting for electoral developments in Fairfax.

The leadership structure just beginning to emerge in this part of the Northern Neck provided the rest of the setting. Through the creation of Truro Parish in 1732, that section of Prince William that became Fairfax County had already begun to develop a separate identity with separate leaders. Planters such as Richard Emms, Richard Osborne, John Sturman, and John Colville were early appointees to the vestry who sat ready to assume greater responsibilities with the formation of the new county.[13] Equally important in this formative period was the first set of justices of the peace appointed for Fairfax County. Those making up the prestigious quorum of eight of the new Commission of the Peace in 1742 (William Fairfax, John Colville, Richard Osborne, Jeremiah Bronaugh, Lewis Ellzey, William Payne, Thomas Pearson, and John Minor) included seven persons who had already served on the commission in Prince William. One year later, several additional appointments to the commission occurred, including that of Lawrence Washington.[14] These vestrymen and justices composed the group most likely to offer themselves as candidates for election to the House of Burgesses.

In late June or early July 1744, Governor William Gooch issued a writ directing the sheriff of Fairfax County to conduct an election to select two representatives to the House of Burgesses. Those elected from Prince William before the county division would continue to represent the older county until the next general election.[15] However, unsuccessful candidates from 1741 and those already assuming positions of local leadership in the new county provided the pool from which candidates for this election emerged. Defeated candidates Valentine Peyton and Richard Blackburn were very much a part of the leadership structure of the now smaller Prince William and had no equivalent position in the new county.[16] Only one of the unsuccessful candidates from 1741, John Colville, resided in the new county and had the necessary background as a vestryman of Truro, a justice of old Prince William, and a justice of newly created Fairfax.[17] He was the most likely candidate for the 1744 election and appears to have had unanimous support from the new county's elite.[18] And, in fact, he did run.

The other four candidates who ran in the 1744 election varied substantially in wealth, social position, and previous officeholding experience. Lawrence Washington had recently returned from service in the War of Jenkins' Ear, had married William Fairfax's daughter, and had begun rebuilding his father's old farmstead on the Potomac at a place he would soon name Mount Vernon. Six months before the election, he became a member of the county court. Lewis Ellzey, who lived fifteen miles inland on Pope's Head Creek, had been a member of the Prince William county court, had served as the first sheriff of the new county of Fairfax, and had served on the Fairfax Commission of the Peace. Before the election of 1744, John Sturman had held just one office, that of vestryman. Bond Veal was an average freeholder who held no local offices.[19] Previous experience as a legislative candidate, local officeholding, and connections to the right families in the county provided the key ingredients for election in 1744. Justice and vestryman John Colville topped the poll, with 148 votes; Lawrence Washington, with his new position on the county court and his marriage into the Fairfax family, came in a close second, with 139. Justice Lewis Ellzey was third, vestryman John Sturman, fourth, and common freeholder Bond Veal was last (see table 6.2).

At least two factors influenced the way voters polled in this election. First, the core of support for Fairfax and Colville in 1741 probably came from persons residing primarily in Truro Parish (the future Fairfax County), and thus a significant number of voters in the new county already favored at least one, if not two, of the candidates running in 1744. In the 1744 election, 37 percent of Colville's 1741 supporters, 33 percent of Fairfax's 1741 supporters, but only 12 percent of Harrison's 1741 supporters voted. Further, of the 106 who returned, 68 (64%) supported Colville, while 38 voted for other candidates. Similarly, Washington received 40 votes from those who had supported his father-in-law in 1741, although perhaps surprisingly Colville outpolled Washington among former Fairfax adherents.

Second, despite support from previous voters, the key to success in 1744 lay in attracting new voters who may have been eligible to vote in previous elections but had not voted because of the distance they had to travel to the courthouse.[20] One-hundred and fifty new voters participated in the 1744 election; the distribution of their votes reflects the complexity of voting behavior in this era. While Ellzey and Sturman received the same level of support from both old and new voters (Ellzey 39%, Sturman 23%), Colville and Washington obtained different levels of endorsement from the two groups: Colville got 64 percent of the old votes and 53 percent of the new votes, while Washington polled only 46 percent of the old votes and 60 percent of the new. Although Colville topped the poll in this election, Washington's support from newer votes would serve him well in the future.

These voters, old and new, made their selections based upon their personal associations with the various candidates and the opinions on these candidates held by other members of the county gentry. Freeholders may have attended the same chapel as, leased lands from, served on a jury that evaluated the conduct of, or sold tobacco to one of the candidates and, therefore, developed a view as to the worth of the man running for office. What these contacts told them about the five candidates who ran in 1744 comes to the surface by examining the actual votes cast. If, on the other hand, the gentry had expressed their opinions on the candidates and if the voters had listened, then the choice was absolutely clear: Colville and Washington. All thirteen of the local leaders who voted in 1744 gave one of their votes to Colville, while ten gave their second vote to Washington.[21] Ellzey received only two votes from these leaders. None of them voted for Veal. Although the elite gave overwhelming support to the winners, they did not speak with a united voice. All members of the county court, for example, voted for fellow justice Washington, while only four of six vestrymen did so. Furthermore, Sturman's two votes came from those serving on the vestry with him and not from those on the county bench. The tendency of previous voters to adhere to allegiances formed earlier and the cues taken from the local gentry ultimately determined the winners of the 1744 election. Such was not the case in the next election.

When the electors of Fairfax County assembled again in June 1748, the first votes came, as they had in 1744, from members of the Fairfax family. In 1744, William Fairfax voted for Washington and Colville, foreshadowing the near-unanimous vote of the local leaders and the strong support of the freeholders. In 1748 he selected Washington and Colville again. At this election, his cousin, English peer Thomas Lord Fairfax, joined him at the head of the poll; he also selected the incumbents. Three more local leaders voted for Washington and Colville, but the support ended there. Eight other leaders voted for a different combination of candidates—and so did the voters.

The final poll showed Washington leading the field, with 193 votes, but Colville came in third, with only 108. Richard Osborne took second, securing a seat with 138 votes, while George Mason ran a strong fourth, with 93, and Hugh West polled last, with 46 (see table 6.2). More voters selected the Washington-Colville combination than any other, but this was not enough, as it had been in 1744, to carry the election. In 1744, Washington and Colville received support from 94, or 37 percent, of the voters; in 1748, they received only 77 votes, or 24 percent of a much larger electorate. Other combinations attracted the voters' support in 1748, including Washington-Osborne (49 votes), Osborne-Mason (46 votes), Washington-Mason (31 votes), and five other pairs who received fewer than 20 votes each. These fragmented voting patterns reflect the entry into the electoral arena of three additional significant candidates and a lack of consensus among local leaders as to whom to support. Winner Richard Osborne was the most distinguished of the three newcomers. He had been a justice of the peace in Prince William County, a vestryman of Truro Parish since 1732, and a member of Fairfax County's first Commission of the Peace, and as the owner of five slaves, he qualified—just barely—for inclusion among the wealthiest 10 percent of the population. Hugh West had been a member of the vestry since 1744 and was a good deal wealthier, with ten slaves. The youngest of the three, twenty-three-year-old George Mason, owned eleven slaves and had become a justice the year before the election.[22]

The support given to these five candidates by the eleven local leaders who voted in 1748 suggests anything but the level of consensus observed for 1744. Only one leader voted for the winning pair. Three selected Washington-Colville, two Washington-West, two Osborne-West, one Osborne-Mason, one Osborne-Colville, and one West only. Six of the eleven leaders supported Washington, five Osborne and West, four Colville, and only one Mason. Most justices favored Washington, while the vestry split their allegiance between Osborne and West. Had the voters followed the examples set by the local elite, Washington would have been first, Osborne and West tied for second, Colville fourth, and Mason a very distant fifth. Although Washington and Osborne received the about same level of support from the electorate as they did from the elite, Mason had a much greater following among the voters and West much less.

The key to Washington's rise and Colville's decline in 1748, as observed in the earlier election, lay in the degree to which old voters maintained their allegiance and new voters flocked to the cause. Both Colville and Washington had 69 supporters from 1744 who returned to vote in 1748, but while 53 of Washington's remained loyal, only 30 of Colville's did. Similarly, 25 persons who had voted for other candidates in 1744 returned in 1748 to vote for Washington, while only 11 persons switched their votes to Colville. Among previous voters, Washington had a net gain of 9 and Colville a net loss of 28. Finally, those who had not voted in 1744 overwhelmingly threw their support to Washington; 115 (60%) of new voters, as opposed to the 67 (35%) who supported Colville.

Not only did Colville lose ground to his fellow incumbent, Washington, but his support fell so drastically that another candidate outpolled him. Old and new voters alike preferred new candidate Richard Osborne to incumbent and three-time candidate John Colville. Osborne received thirty more votes than Colville: eighteen more from previous voters and twelve more from new voters. Osborne's support from old voters came from nearly every quarter, but most important were the twenty-two persons who switched from Colville to Osborne and the high proportion of Ellzey's 1744 supporters who moved to the Osborne camp in 1748.

The final outcome of the 1748 election is less easy to explain than the previous one. The county elite, who had been solidly behind Colville in 1744 (100%), now supported him to a much lesser degree (36%). Voters, for their part, either knew of the gentry's decreasing interest in the man or had developed their own reasons for withdrawing support. Lawrence Washington, on the other hand, continued to be the favorite of local leaders (but only at the 55% level), and the voters reflected this by giving him a clear victory in the election. Osborne, who won with a second-place finish, also received modest support from the gentry (45%), but clearly he was no rising star in the local political scene. Ultimately, however, lack of consensus among the local elite coupled with a field of five very respectable candidates produced a multitude of voting patterns that may have unintentionally toppled an incumbent.

A 25 percent increase in the county's population since it's founding and the expansion of that population into land farther to the west
probably affected political consensus. The expansion also spurred
demands from these newly settled "upper inhabitants" for improved access to county and parish administration. The process began in the parish immediately following the 1748 election. On December 2, 1748, a proposition reached the House of Burgesses to
divide "the parish of Truro . . . by a Line to be run from the Mouth
of Difficult Run, near the great Fall of Patowmack River, to the
Mouth of little Rocky Run, on Bull Run." The bill reached committee a week later, but a mid-December adjournment postponed
legislative action until the following April, when the assembly reconvened. It then quickly passed the House and the Council, receiving the governor's signature on May 11, 1749. The new Cameron
Parish included the western two-thirds of the county and approximately one-third of the county's total population. The much-reduced Truro Parish comprised the long-settled, densely populated,
Tidewater section of the county (see map 6.1).[23]

The "upper inhabitants" now had their own twelve vestrymen,
who could more easily tend to their many problems and concerns,
but the county courthouse and all its important functions (including burgess elections) remained at Spring Field, in the Lower Parish.
Accessibility to those county services would decline even further in
the next few years.

In January 1752, the voters returned to the polls again. Incumbent
Lawrence Washington, in all probability, was not a candidate for reelection. His deteriorating health had forced him to leave the country for Barbados in September 1751, and he did not return to Virginia
until June 1752.[24] The fate of Richard Osborne is less certain; he
probably did not seek another term in the House, although it is possible he ran for reelection and lost. Limited information survives for
this election; we only know for certain that Hugh West and Gerrard
Alexander won. Because five candidates ran in the previous two
elections, it seems very likely that other candidates ran in 1752, but
their identity remains a mystery.

West and Alexander fit the traditional profile of Fairfax candidates. Hugh West had served on the Truro Parish vestry since 1744,
was one of the original trustees of the new town of Alexandria in
1748, and owned ten slaves and more than two thousand acres of
land. He was also one of the three unsuccessful candidates of the

1748 election. Gerrard Alexander had no previous experience as a legislative candidate but had served on the county court since 1742, was a trustee of Alexandria (named for his family), and held even greater wealth than his fellow candidate, West.[25]

With two residents and trustees of the town of Alexandria now serving Fairfax County in the House of Burgesses, inhabitants from that part of the county lost little time in petitioning for the removal of the courthouse to their booming port on the Potomac. The town had grown rapidly since its establishment three years earlier and could boast of eighty lots sold, a church built, and wharves and warehouses constructed. As early as 1750, town planners had reserved a lot for a future courthouse. Although some residents of the county (most probably those from Cameron Parish) strongly objected to abandonment of the old courthouse site, they had little political power in either the county or Williamsburg. The Council and the governor agreed to the move in late April 1752; the county court met in Alexandria for the first time a month later.[26]

Hugh West died during the spring or early summer of 1754, and on August 30, the House of Burgesses requested a writ to elect a replacement. The by-election occurred in the county some time in September, and Hugh's brother, John West (also of Alexandria), won the by-election.[27] Family connection made him a likely candidate and successor to his brother, but John West was very much a strong contender in his own right. Although less wealthy than his brother, John West had been a tobacco inspector, had served as a Truro Parish vestryman and county justice of the peace, and held the rank of captain in the county militia.[28] Whether West had any opposition in the contest is unclear, but it seems likely that at least one other candidate appeared before the voters.

John West had hardly begun his term when a petition arrived in the House to divide Fairfax County. Although the House delayed action on the petition until the next session of the assembly, a bill to that end began its way through the House of Burgesses in early May 1755. A new county would mean an adjustment in the local power structure: a new Commission of the Peace would be issued for both the new and old counties, a burgess election would be held in the new county, and eventually, when the governor called for new elections throughout the colony, the gentry and voters would redefine political relationships in the now smaller county of Fairfax. As the bill passed the House on May 26 and moved on to the Council for approval, talk of future elections was already stirring in Fairfax.[29]

Gerrard Alexander let it be known that he would not seek another term, while Col. George William Fairfax, nephew of Lord Fairfax and currently a burgess from Frederick County, announced his future interest in a seat from his home county, should one become available. At the same time—no doubt spurred on by the bill in the House and by Alexander's announcement—young George Washington wrote his brother on May 28 to ask what he knew of the open seat in Fairfax.[30] Could he discover "Colo. Fairfax's Intention's?" What would be the opinion of important members of the gentry like John Carlyle, John Dalton, William Ramsay, George Mason, the Reverend Green, Daniel McCarty, John West, and John West Jr.? Would they support him if he ran? Or would they likely favor someone else? The views of these leading gentlemen and his brother's advice on the matter remain a mystery, but it is likely they told him that it was not yet his time. Although he had recently assumed control of his late brother Lawrence's plantation at Mount Vernon and appeared to be the up-and-coming military commander in the colony, he had no experience in local affairs. He was neither a vestryman nor a justice, and he was just twenty-three years old.

The Council rejected the bill to divide the county, and talk of elections waned for the remainder of the summer and fall. However, on November 8, 1755, the governor showed his displeasure with a public credit act passed by the House, dissolved the assembly, and called for new elections in December.[31] John West, now serving out his brother's term, would stand a poll, but Gerrard Alexander declined, as he indicated he would earlier in the year. Potential candidates for the open seat abounded. George William Fairfax decided to run for the seat being vacated by Alexander, and this more than anything else probably discouraged Washington from pursuing his own candidacy. As a member of the Fairfax family, a local justice of the peace, and currently a burgess from nearby Frederick County, young Fairfax seemed a perfect running mate for incumbent John West. John Carlyle, Daniel McCarty, William Ramsay, the Reverend Green, John West Jr., and most of their fellow justices on the county court and fellow vestrymen of Truro Parish also thought the pair ideal.

Leaders in Cameron, or Upper, Parish had different ideas, however. The failed attempt to have Cameron Parish separated from Fairfax had been only a temporary setback for Cameron residents. To pursue the matter again in the new assembly, the Upper Parish needed its own spokesman. The man chosen for the task was a young attorney named William Ellzey, whose family owned substantial land on Pope's Head Creek, the dividing line between the parishes. His father, Lewis Ellzey, had run unsuccessfully in 1744 and was a vestryman, justice, militia officer, and former sheriff. Young William was one of the original trustees of the town of Colchester in 1753 and may have been a vestryman of Cameron Parish.[32] The vestrymen of Cameron Parish and the Fairfax County justices who resided there all strongly backed Ellzey, although they reached no consensus on whether West or Fairfax should be their second choice.[33]

The county sheriff conducted the general election for Fairfax on December 11; West received the largest number of votes, but the race between Fairfax and Ellzey was so close that documents differ as to which candidate actually received more votes.[34] Moreover, the closeness of the election apparently caused tempers to flare between supporters of the two candidates. George Washington, who cast only a single vote (for his good friend Fairfax), received an insult in such a manner (possibly by being knocked to the ground by an Ellzey supporter) that a week later his friends "were ready and violent to run and tear [his] Enemies to pieces."[35] Once the poll ended, however, Fairfax had clearly won, even if by the smallest margin; he showed up in the assembly as the representative from Fairfax County, and Ellzey did not protest the results.

As in several previous elections, the voters followed—although rather loosely—the voting preferences of their local leaders. While John West received almost exactly the same level of support from both leaders and freeholders (71% and 67%, respectively), the latter thought less of Fairfax than the former (59% and 75%, respectively) and a good deal more of Ellzey (59% and 38%). Despite the strong support for Ellzey among leaders in the Upper Parish and almost none for him among Lower Parish gentry, voters in the two sections remained less committed in their choice of candidates. Fairfax was the first choice of voters in the Upper Parish, while West was first among Lower Parish voters. Ellzey, however, did run considerably ahead of West in Cameron Parish, but he polled a distant third in Truro Parish.[36] Geography clearly dictated differences in the voting behavior of Fairfax County electors, but parish of residence played a smaller role with voters than it did with county leaders.

Furthermore, the heated rivalry between the backers of Ellzey and Fairfax disturbed the gentry more than it did the average voter. While the West-Fairfax combination received the highest number of votes (122) and the West-Ellzey pair the second highest (113), eighty-six voters (23%) remained oblivious to the rivalry and selected both Fairfax and Ellzey. Experienced voters followed most closely the dictates of the gentry, while newer voters and those more distant from the seats of power in the county tended to stray the farthest from the example set by their leaders.[37] From the gentry's perspective, a large, sprawling area with rapidly increasing population proved far more difficult to manage than a smaller stable unit.

The smaller unit soon became a reality. Despite Ellzey's loss, the inhabitants of the Upper Parish eventually accomplished their objective. A bill to divide the county at the current parish line surfaced again early in the new assembly, only to be deferred to the next session. A year later, on April 20, 1757, it appeared again, received temporary deferment, but then was resurrected and sent to committee. However, "sundry Back-Inhabitants" objected to the proposed dividing line and petitioned for an alternate plan that left a small parcel of Cameron Parish in the old county (see map 6.1). The House and Council accepted the revised dividing line, and the governor signed the bill on June 8, 1757. Although now much reduced in size and population, Fairfax County would face one more divisive issue before political tranquillity settled on the county in the final decade of the colonial era.[38]

Elections in the new county did not immediately occur, and when in January 1758 Governor Dinwiddie left for England, he still had not issued an election writ. The new governor, Francis Fauquier, arrived on June 5, and ten days later dissolved the old assembly and ordered writs for the election of a new assembly.[39] The writ reached the sheriff of Fairfax on or before July 1, and he set the date of the election for July 20. By July 6, everyone in the county knew the slate of candidates running in the election. For reasons that are not entirely clear, neither incumbent sought reelection. George William Fairfax's recent appointment as collector of customs for the port of South Potomac and his involvement in settling his father's substantial estate may have discouraged him from running again. John West simply chose not to run this time, although as we shall see he would represent Fairfax County for much of the remainder of the colonial period. In their place, George Mason, Charles Broadwater, and George Johnston offered themselves to the voters.[40]

When George Mason first, and unsuccessfully, sought election from Fairfax in 1748, he had only one year's experience as a justice of the peace and was just twenty-three years old. Now, ten years later, he owned more than eight thousand acres in the county and had served eleven years on the county bench and nine as a vestryman for Truro Parish. Charles Broadwater had a similar profile: he had sat on the vestry since 1744, had served as justice and as militia officer since 1749, had held the office of sheriff in 1751, and owned a large plantation of about seventeen hundred acres. The third candidate, George Johnston, could only point to militia service in the county, but he owned thirty-five hundred acres, was a trustee of the town of Alexandria, and had an extremely successful law practice in the county. Mason and Johnston won the election, although no information survives on the closeness of the contest.[41]

Two years later, King George II died, and when this news reached the colony in February 1761, the governor let the assembly finish the business at hand and—as was the custom at the death of a monarch—dissolved the assembly and called for new elections (to be held in late May). In Fairfax, George Johnston ran for another term, George Mason did not, and John West decided to return to the political scene again. Approximately 280 persons voted in the election, so opposition may have surfaced from at least one other candidate.[42]

The division of the county in 1757 had dramatically altered the leadership structure of Fairfax. A new Commission of the Peace, issued in May 1757, specified fourteen justices, who now all resided in an area one-third the size of the original county. Further, only Truro Parish (and a tiny piece of Cameron Parish) fell within the county, and thus just one set of twelve vestrymen attended to religious affairs. This smaller geographic unit with a smaller set of leaders provided the context for the elections of 1758 and 1761. The drop from five candidates in elections up to and including 1755 to just three candidates in 1758 may have been a partial reflection of this reduction in the leadership pool. Before the next election, however, a further reshuffling of the elite structure occurred.

This reshuffling resulted from dissatisfaction with the operation of the Truro vestry, additional adjustments to existing parish boundaries, and the establishment of yet another parish. These problems surfaced simultaneously in the early 1760s and related in part to continued expansion of the county's population, particularly in the area around Alexandria. First, a group of residents (perhaps from the Alexandria vicinity) asked the House to dissolve the Truro Parish vestry; the burgesses rejected the petition in early December 1762. Second, the small section of Cameron Parish left in Fairfax after the county division of 1757 proved troublesome to the affected citizens, and in November 1762 persons from both parishes petitioned the burgesses to add the parcel to Truro. A committee drafted an appropriate bill on November 30, 1762, and it passed the House and Council several weeks later, receiving the governor's signature just two days before Christmas.[43] Third and finally, the northern half of Fairfax County sought its own parish administration, but this task proved both protracted and contentious.

The process began in the fall of 1761 with a petition to divide Truro Parish, followed by a counterpetition opposing such a division. Postponed by the House for a year, the competing petitions arose again in November 1762, when the House voted against any division, accepting the counterproposal not to divide the parish. The proposal lay dormant for the next two sessions of the assembly but finally appeared on November 1, 1764. Strong opposition to a division had subsided, and now Fairfax burgesses John West and George Johnston prepared a formal bill. It passed the House and Council with no difficulties and received the governor's signature on December 5, 1764. A north-south division of the county took place on February 1, 1765, and elections of new vestrymen for both parishes occurred soon thereafter (see map 6.1). The sheriff conducted these elections on March 25 in Truro and on March 28 in the new parish, called Fairfax.[44] The results of these vestry elections provide a kind of popularity poll on nearly forty members of the gentry.

Both freeholders and householders participated in these elections, and thus the vestry electorate was perhaps twice the size of that for burgess elections. More than 400 persons cast ballots in the new northern parish of Fairfax, while fewer than 300 voted in the much-reduced southern Truro Parish. John West topped the poll in Fairfax Parish, with 340 votes, while his fellow burgess, George Johnston, came in seventh, with 254. Charles Broadwater, who ran unsuccessfully in 1758 and who would run again in 1774, took sixth. Future burgess candidates, George Washington and John Posey, polled fifth and eleventh, respectively. Although Henry Gunnell had served Truro since 1756, the voters in the new parish placed him a distant and unsuccessful twentieth. In all, at least twenty-three persons received votes in Fairfax Parish, with the top twelve becoming members of the new vestry.

The Truro elections also included several familiar names. George Mason, Fairfax burgess from 1758 to 1761, gained second place, with 210 votes, while another former burgess, George William Fairfax, took sixth place. Two members of the Ellzey family (although not the William who ran in 1755) came in eighth and ninth in the polling. Edward Payne was first, with 234 votes. Twenty-nine persons ran in this election, but again only the top twelve obtained seats on the vestry.

A month after these elections, the colonial assembly reconvened, and several local leaders headed for Williamsburg. Fairfax residents John West and George Johnston, who represented their home county, as well as George Washington, now serving for Frederick County, journeyed to the capital in early May. The burgesses finished their business by May 25, and a majority headed for home. George Washington and John West probably left the capital, but George Johnston stayed and on May 29 moved that the House go into a Committee of the Whole to consider the Stamp Act, which had recently been passed by the English Parliament. A series of resolutions passed the sparse assembly, whipped up "by a Mr. Henry a young Lawyer, who had not been a Month a Member of the House." On June 1, the governor had had enough of "this rash heat" and dissolved the assembly.[45]

Despite the wild ending to the assembly, the session had been an important one for the inhabitants of Fairfax County. The creation of the new parish in 1764 left the old parish of Truro at just one-third its original size and, more important, with only about a third of the tithables upon which parish revenues depended. Not wanting a greater tax burden than necessary, the residents of Truro petitioned the assembly on May 14 to adjust the boundaries, but in a counterpetition the inhabitants of Fairfax Parish asked for a somewhat different parish line.[46] Ultimately, they reached a compromise, perhaps worked out by Washington, whose lands fell in the disputed territory between the two parishes. The bill, which became law on June 1, provided for a nearly equal distribution of tithables and placed Washington back in Truro (see map 6.1).[47] Another consequence of the dispute, however, produced a substantial antagonism between the two parishes, which carried over into the next burgess election.

News of the governor's angry dissolution of the House probably reached Fairfax County within the first week of June, perhaps through George Johnston returning home. Some time in mid-June, the governor issued writs for July elections. At about the same time, Johnston announced he would not seek reelection, leaving John West as the only incumbent to run in the ensuing contest.[48] George Washington and John Posey let it be known that they would vie for Johnston's seat. Washington was thirty-three years old, a vestryman, a former military leader, a close friend of the Fairfax family, and a major landowner in the county. He had been a burgess from Frederick for seven years and now sought to represent his home county. John Posey had less-impressive credentials, but he owned 406 acres just south of Mount Vernon, where he ran an important ferry that crossed the Potomac to Maryland. He had been a business associate and hunting companion of Washington for at least five years. The only local office he held was the vestry position he had obtained three months earlier.[49]

The forthcoming election would not, however, be a contest between these two newcomers. Washington's previous activities, local contacts, family connections, and perhaps his recent work in the assembly to provide a satisfactory division between the parishes made him the nearly unanimous choice of the entire gentry of Fairfax County. Despite West's long tenure as justice, vestryman, and burgess and Posey's close association with Washington, both became parish candidates rather than countywide contenders. All of the vestrymen and justices who lived in the newly defined Truro Parish supported Posey, while West's followers came from Fairfax Parish. Posey was the candidate of the south half of the county, John West of the northern part.[50]

On July 16, the electors followed the general pattern set by the county leaders. Washington led the poll among Truro voters, followed by Posey, and then West as a very distant third. In the southern parish also, the Washington-Posey combination was the overwhelming choice of 76 percent of the freeholders. Only 14 percent of Truro electors gave their votes to the Washington-West slate. Less distinctive patterns occurred in Fairfax Parish. Washington's work in the assembly to produce a more equitable division of the county may not have found as much favor in the new northern parish. West topped the poll in Fairfax Parish, Washington gained second, and Posey came in third. Here, the Washington-West combination had

59 percent of the voters, while 12 percent voted for Washington and Posey.[51]

Within the entire county electorate, the Washington-Posey combination garnered the most support (40%), as it had among the elite. The number of those selecting Washington and West was only a few votes less (37%). The West-Posey combination, chosen by only one member of the gentry, did somewhat better among the average electors (11%). Washington clearly won, but plumpers, primarily from Fairfax Parish, turned the tide away from Posey to West: twenty-seven freeholders cast a single ballot for West, while only two did so for Posey. The final count stood Washington 201, West 148, and Posey 131.

Geography played a greater role in this election than it had in 1755. As in the earlier contest, neighborhood loyalties, countywide politics, the opinions of the local leaders, and the effect a division in county or parish would have on the taxes of the individual voter probably influenced the behavior of the freeholders at the election.[52] In 1765, however, both the leaders and the voters chose patterns of behavior that followed much more closely recently established parish lines. In little more than four years, however, animosities between sections of the county had disappeared so completely that both county leaders and voters agreed to reelect a set of incumbents without holding even a formal poll. Between the divisive 1765 election and this expression of countywide unanimity in 1769, an intervening contest demonstrates the transition from conflict to consensus. The 1768 election followed the arrival of a new governor, who dissolved the old assembly in October and called for early December elections.[53]

Although the burgesses had not been in session since the previous April, Fairfax incumbent George Washington was in Williamsburg to witness the governor's arrival and to hear firsthand of the new elections. Washington arrived back at Mount Vernon on November 9, probably about the same time that the official election writ reached the county. The sheriff set election day for December 1, and for the next three weeks incumbents Washington and West, along with other local leaders, met and discussed the forthcoming contest. Washington saw many of his neighbors at church on November 13 and 27 and no doubt talked of the election as he hunted fox with the Fairfaxes on seven different occasions. He asked for the continuing support of justices and vestrymen Edward Payne and

Daniel McCarty, whom he visited on November 17 and 18, and exchanged opinions with George Mason, who stopped by on November 30. He probably saw his fellow incumbent John West at court on November 21 and, at the vestry meeting on November 28, had an opportunity to discuss politics with a number of leaders, including John Posey.[54]

The local gentry remained united in their support of Washington, but West's backing now expanded beyond its 1765 base. In that year his support had been exclusively within Fairfax Parish; in 1768, most of the Truro gentry were behind him, as well. Influential leaders in Truro, including George Mason, Daniel McCarty, Edward Payne, Edward Washington, and George William Fairfax, switched their allegiance from Posey to West. Only one county leader moved from the West camp to the Posey camp. In all, twenty-four leaders supported Washington, twenty-two West, and only four Posey.

Despite the overwhelming support for Washington and West by the county gentry, Posey entered the race, hoping to fare better among the voters. He did, but not enough to win. Washington received 185 votes, West 142, and Posey 87. The anticipation of Washington's and West's victory helped produce the lower turnout at the election, but the freezing, snowy weather probably kept away many who had to travel substantial distances. This was particularly true of those in the southern parish of Truro, who lived farthest from the courthouse in Alexandria: 40 percent of the voters came from Truro, while 60 percent resided in Fairfax Parish.[55]

John West attained great advantage from the higher turnout in Fairfax Parish, where 80 percent of his supporters lived and where he had outpolled Washington in the previous election. Although in 1768 he and Washington ran dead even in West's home parish and he did somewhat better in Truro than previously, he still received 72 percent of his support from Fairfax Parish. John Posey actually picked up a few votes in the northern parish, but the low turnout in the south more than offset this slight gain. In 1765, 79 percent of the Posey voters resided in Truro, while in 1768 only 56 percent lived in the southern parish. Although Washington won the election handily, his reduced level of support resulted from low turnout in Truro as well.

Differences in turnout, however, explain only part of the declining support for John Posey among both the elite and the voters. While debt was a normal feature of planter life in the Chesapeake,

Posey had by 1768 taken his credit limit to extremes. George Washington held much of the obligation, including a £700 mortgage from Posey executed in 1763. By 1767, Posey had asked for another £500, and although Washington refused, he did pay the county taxes for Posey that fall and acted as security for a loan from George Mason. Despite his continued generosity, Washington expressed growing irritation with his neighbor's lack of financial responsibility, and many prominent men in the county probably shared his views by late 1768. The mismanagement of personal affairs also sent a negative message to voters, who had no desire to elect an incompetent, debt-ridden planter to represent them.[56] Posey's waning fortunes also meant that the Washington-West combination had greater appeal across the entire county than it previously had. Support in Truro Parish for the pair jumped from 14 percent in 1765 to 48 percent in 1768, while in Fairfax Parish it increased from 59 to 68 percent. The Washington-Posey slate dropped from 76 to 52 percent in Truro, while it remained nearly unchanged in Fairfax (about 12%).

Old and new voters alike followed these patterns, but it was primarily those who had voted in the previous election who affirmed overwhelmingly the choice of the county gentry: 60 percent of these returning voters selected Washington-West, while only 26 percent of them voted for Washington-Posey. New voters favored Washington-West, as well, but not by such a margin: 49 percent voted for Washington-West and 36 percent for Washington-Posey. Among old voters, 96 percent of Washington supporters and 91 percent of West supporters returned to vote the same way in 1768, but a third of Posey's old supporters switched their vote to another candidate. Among experienced, new, and switching voters, Washington polled first, West second, and Posey a distant third.

At the next contest, just nine months later, no one challenged incumbents Washington and West, who won the election without a poll. This contest, which occurred in Fairfax County on September 14, 1769, followed the dissolution of the assembly the previous May. Although the governor did not issue writs for new elections until mid-August, talk of an ensuing election must have occurred throughout the summer. Perhaps well before this, when Washington traveled about the county tending to social, vestry, and court duties in May and June, the gentry agreed to continue their support for him and Colonel West. Perhaps no one else's name came forward in discussions, or no one indicated an interest in running in the future election. Whatever the case, both leaders and freeholders seem to have been of a single mind by 1769 as to whom should represent the county, perhaps indefinitely.[57]

The next election occurred just over two years later, in December 1771, occasioned by the arrival of what would turn out to be the last colonial governor, John Murray, Lord Dunmore. Although Dunmore saw "no good reason" for the election because it was "productive of much riot and disorder . . . as in England," he reluctantly dissolved the old assembly on October 12 and called for early-December elections. Whether anyone opposed Washington and West at the election or whether the sheriff polled the voters is not known. Washington simply recorded in his diary almost matter-of-factly that he "went up to the Election & the Ball I had given at Alexa. Mr. Crawford & Jno. P. Custis with me. Stayd all Night." John West and George Washington would serve their fourth term together.[58]

The final general election of the colonial period occurred in July 1774, under rather strained circumstances. The House of Burgesses had voted in late May to declare a day of fasting and prayer in sympathy with the people of Boston, who had had their harbor closed by the Boston Port Act. When the governor read of the House resolutions in a broadside, he dissolved the assembly on May 26. Dunmore wanted to continue without a legislative body for a while, but the Council persuaded him to issue writs for new elections to dispel "the growing discontents of all orders of Men" and to thwart "the Increase of danger from a savage Enemy when the Country is in a defenceless State."[59] Fairfax representative George Washington, who was in Williamsburg on June 17 when the writs appeared, may have been very surprised by the turn of events, as he had not expected elections until Dunmore received instructions from the ministry in England. Washington left for home on June 20, arrived at Mount Vernon on June 22, and within a few days found himself immersed in electoral politics.[60]

Most Virginians believed, with Richard Henry Lee, that there would be few real electoral contests and that "it is pretty certain that almost every Man of the late assembly will be chosen again into the New one."[61] Washington and John West had served Fairfax County since 1765, and there was every reason to believe that this would continue. However, on June 26, after church service in Alexandria, West publicly announced he would not seek reelection. Talk in the churchyard immediately turned to who would run in his place:

some thought Bryan Fairfax should, while others believed he had no interest in doing so. Washington wanted to find a proper running mate, but one did not surface immediately. During the next week, however, Charles Broadwater, who had been a vestryman since 1744, a justice since 1749, and an unsuccessful candidate in 1758, declared he would take the seat left open by John West. Washington found Broadwater "a good man," who perhaps was better "in the discharge of his domestic concerns" than "in the capacity of a legislator," and therefore he still wished for a more suitable companion in the assembly.[62]

On July 3, Washington appeared at Pohick Church actively seeking another candidate for the election. He encouraged "several gentlemen . . . to press Colonel Mason to take a poll" and still hoped Bryan Fairfax would consider running. Fairfax, however, felt he must decline such offers both because of the expense involved and because he believed his conciliatory view in the present crisis with Britain was very much the minority view in the county. Neither Fairfax nor George Mason ran, although someone did run against Broadwater. The identity of this third candidate remains a mystery, although West's nephew John West Jr. seems likely.[63] Washington and Broadwater won in an election poll that took just two hours to conduct. The winners provided punch after the election. That night, Washington "gave a ball to the Freeholders and Gentlemen of the town."[64]

CONCLUSION

The electoral history of Fairfax County provides a window through which to view the development of a particular political community of colonial Virginia. On twelve separate occasions between 1744 and 1774 the voters came together to select a set of burgesses to represent them in the colonial assembly. The candidates who stood before them on election day, with perhaps one exception, were men easily distinguished from the average freeholder. They were gentlemen whose wealth in slaves or land was many times greater than the average freeholder who voted every few years on the courthouse green. This wealth gave members of the gentry the time and the inclination to assume positions of responsibility within the local community. Many served on the parish vestry and county court and as officers in the county militia. However, a single office combined with modest wealth rarely ensured success at the polls: the county leaders selected, and the freeholders usually elected, men actively involved in several spheres of local government. Wealth and multiple officeholding provided the keys to electoral success in Fairfax County.

Those hundreds of individuals who gathered at each election to pick their favorites from among the gentry were small planters. Although they had to be freeholders to vote, only a third of them based their freehold status upon land they actually owned. The remainder were tenants and exercised their right to vote through the long-term lease of their land. When it came time to ride off to any election, less than one-half and often closer to one-third of these freeholders bothered to make the trip. A small handful made the journey election after election, a slightly larger group appeared for perhaps half of them, and the vast majority voted only occasionally. The most frequent voters had the strongest attachment to the local community through their outright ownership of land and service in minor offices.

The electoral history of Fairfax County, however, is more than the demographic characteristics of gentry and yeomen interacting at twelve successive events over a thirty-year period. It is also much more than a series of social occasions in which "the rivalry between backers of different candidates was often of the sporting kind . . . excited but inconsequential."[65] The gentry and the freeholders of Fairfax thought these elections decided important things—and so should historians.

At one level, Fairfax County elections became the mechanisms through which the gentry attempted to settle their personal squabbles for ascendancy within the local community. At a number of elections during the period, personalities and loyalties to particular local leaders probably dictated the behavior of both elites and voters. On the other hand, real issues, including potential increases in parish taxes, played a key role in 1755 and 1765, and the controversy with Britain in 1769 and 1774 certainly influenced these later contests.

Throughout the thirty-year period, however, there are clear signs of both leaders and followers groping to define a community consensus in the matter of politics. After several periods of disagreement, the gentry finally presented a united front at the elections of

Table 6.5
Voting Behavior, Fairfax County, 1744–1774

Year and No. of Candidates	No. of Voters	Plumpers as % of Voters	Percentage Voting for			Gentry Unity (%)
			Lead Candidate	Lead Pair	Losers	
1741 (5)[a]	432	9	57	21	8	
1744 (5)	256	18	58	37	25	77
1748 (5)	318	18	61	24	11	27
1755 (3)	376	15	67	32	7	50
1758 (3)						
1761	281					
1765 (3)	257	13	79	40	1	50
1768 (3)	211	3	88	56	1	84
1769 (2)		0	100	100	0	
1774 (3)						

[a]1741 data are for Prince William County.

the late 1760s. Voters only partially followed the sometimes erratic patterns of their leaders and gradually developed their own notion of agreement (see table 6.5): support for the lead candidate and the lead pair increased steadily after the 1740s, and votes for single candidates decreased as the community came to understand what it wanted in its leaders. Stability within the leadership core of the gentry and the population at large, a physically restricted and knowable geographical area, and the deepening crisis with Britain combined to produce political consensus in Fairfax County as the colonial era came to a close.

7

Halifax County

Sustaining Contention on the
Southside Frontier

At worst, Nathaniel Terry of Halifax County was a horse thief, character assassin, common brawler, forger, and embezzler of public funds; at best, he was a rough-and-ready frontier soldier, land speculator, astute businessmen, and as a public administrator an "indifferent Accountant," whose financial "Transactions sometimes appear[ed] awkward and confused." His first cousin believed he was "as damned a Rogue as any in this Colony" but so shrewd "that it would take 100 honest Men to find him out." Some thought him unfit for service in the House of Burgesses, "where none but gentlemen of character ought to be admitted." He made enemies quickly and reveled in controversy most of his life.[1]

Nathaniel Terry was also the most successful electoral politician in Halifax County during the colonial and revolutionary eras. Over a twenty-year period, he represented the county on fourteen occasions: in the House of Burgesses in 1758, 1761, 1768, 1769, 1772, and 1774, in all five revolutionary conventions (1774–76), and in the first three meetings of the general assembly (1776–78). Illness, not politics, ended this long career; he died in 1780.[2]

That someone like Nathaniel Terry exemplifies the successful politician confounds our view of prerevolutionary politics and the role of elections in Virginia society. Eighteenth-century county politics, according to the most commonly held interpretation, remained the sole preserve of a very small group of wealthy, well-educated planters from respected families. Individuals from outside this closely knit oligarchy won elections on occasion, but such was clearly not the norm. Like Mr. Worthy in Robert Munford's 1770 play, *The Candidates,* the virtuous gentleman of impeccable reputation is what freeholders in the end wanted, and it is who they nearly always elected.[3]

Yet a deeper look into *The Candidates* and into its author, Southside politician Robert Munford, produces a different interpretation. Perhaps the play's other legislative candidates, Sir John Toddy, Mr. Strutabout, and Mr. Smallhopes, dominated electoral politics in southwest frontier counties like Lunenburg, Mecklenburg, and Halifax. These candidates drank too much, bullied each other, said anything to gain the support of a freeholder, and had none of the genteel characteristics that Munford found attractive in a Mr. Worthy.[4] Nathaniel Terry was clearly no Worthy, so perhaps he and his fellow Southside candidates were indeed the reality behind the Toddy, Strutabout, and Smallhopes of Robert Munford's play.

In a similar way, Munford's descriptions of voters in this section of the colony offers two different views of Southside freeholders. At the end of the play, the electors vote overwhelmingly for the respectable incumbents, Worthy and Wou'dbe, rejecting the challenge of the "scoundrels" Strutabout and Smallhope. Gentility triumphs over vulgarity; virtue smothers vice—the world is as it should be. Or is it? Such an ending to the play may represent "an unfulfilled expression of hope" on the part of the dramatist rather than a reflection of reality. Perhaps Munford lamented the fact that these frontier freeholders responded to wild campaign pledges and promises of liquor more often than to the candidate's background and abilities.[5] A cursory glance at testimony in the House of Burgesses journals suggests that Southside voters rarely mirrored the apparently stable and predictable behavior of their Tidewater cousins to the east, but it is not altogether clear that they exhibited patterns of participation and voting behavior as changeable and unstable as the rough-and-tumble region they inhabited.[6]

While many frontier counties achieved political stability and electoral tranquility early in their histories, Halifax remained wedded to a combative style of county politics for most of the colonial era. The personal behavior and ambitions of Nathaniel Terry and his detractors certainly did nothing to quiet the political waters, but a large, loosely defined, and often divided gentry thwarted harmony, as well. With diverse signals coming from above, county voters had little choice but to find their own way through the thicket of warring candidates, often choosing to stay at home rather than vote. Yet a core of freeholders in this sprawling Southside county saw through the heated rhetoric and found and consistently supported men they liked. Pollbooks surviving from the elections of 1764, 1765, 1768, and 1769 allow detailed analysis of this remote political world. Additional data on wealth from the 1750s and 1760s, coupled with lengthy and lively testimony before the House of Burgesses concerning two of these elections and several other local controversies, furnish ample evidence of the stuff of local politics.[7]

SETTING

In February 1752, the colonial government divided Lunenburg County, forming the new county of Halifax and the new parish of Antrim. The new entity included "all that part thereof laying on the south side of Blackwater creek, to the confluence of the said river with the river Dan, and from thence to Aarons Creek to the county line," or what today are the counties of Halifax, Pittsylvania, Franklin, Patrick, and Henry along the southern boundary with North Carolina. It was large for a Virginia county, encompassing an area approximately forty by one hundred miles. This was *the* southwestern frontier at midcentury, with few inhabitants in the western reaches of the new county and still fewer farther west over the Blue Ridge (see map 7.1).[8]

Those who settled the area before 1750 were primarily of English stock and were members of established families from Piedmont and Tidewater counties. About midcentury, however, a new stream of immigration began flowing from Pennsylvania down the Valley of Virginia and then east into the western sections of the county. These new settlers included a significant element of Scotch-Irish with Presbyterian and Baptists leanings, who when combined with traditional Anglican residents produced a "strikingly diverse mix . . . at least by Virginia standards." A large and continuous movement of people in and out of the area in those early years resulted in a population turnover of nearly one-fifth per year.[9]

Despite the large turnover, the county's adult white male population grew enormously from 1752 to 1767, when the western sections became Pittsylvania County (table 7.1). Although slavery was introduced into the area very early, during these first fifteen years it

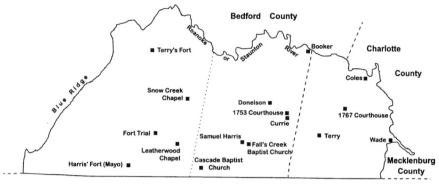

North   Carolina

Map 7.1   Halifax County, Eighteenth Century

The middle and western sections became Pittsylvania County in 1767. Based upon
information contained in Landon C. Bell, *Cumberland Parish: Lunenburg County,
Virginia, 1746–1816 and Vestry Book, 1746–1816* (Richmond: Byrd Press, 1930), following
22; W. W. Abbot, ed, *The Papers of George Washington, Colonial Series* (Charlottesville:
University of Virginia Press, 1984), 3:220–21; John Asplund, *The Universal Register of the
Baptist Denomination in North America for the Years 1790, 1791, 1792, 1793, and Part of
1794* (Boston, 1794), 24–31; Herman Boyd, "Map of the State of Virginia . . . 1825 . . .
corrected 1859" (Facsimile, Virginia State Library); *Atlas of Early American History: The
Revolutionary Era, 1760–1790* (Princeton: Princeton University Press, 1976), 5; John S.
Moore, "The Forgotten Story of Fall Creek Church," *Virginia Baptist Register* 10 (1971):
435–61; Halifax County Deed Books 2, 3, 4 (Richmond: Virginia State Library).

Table 7.1

Adult White Male Population Structure, Halifax County, 1750–1782

Year	Tithables	Estimated	Identified	Voters
1750	184	138	153	
1752	335	252		
1755	629	472	220	
1764	1,807	1,355	720	504
1765	1,918	1,438	1,067	837
1768	1,249	937	694	505
1769	1,252	939	510	338
1773	1,257	943	729	
1782	1,334	1,001		

Note: Tithables include all white males sixteen years of age and older and are based upon
baseline data for 1750, 1755, 1773, and 1782; *estimated* figure is 75 percent of tithables. The
1750 figure for *identified* is larger than that for *estimated* because 153 is the number of
heads of households identified while 138 is an estimate based upon the formula. The county was divided in 1767.

was much less of a factor in the county's demographic and economic structure than it would become later in the century. Blacks accounted for perhaps 13–16 percent of the population of the county up to the division in 1767; they had increased to 38 percent by 1790. In the more settled, eastern portions of the county, 25 percent of the households probably owned slaves in 1752, while few slaveholders lived in the more sparsely settled western regions.[10]

Little is known of Halifax voters during these early years. When the first election occurred in November 1753, more than three hundred white men qualified to vote; it is impossible to say whether anything close to that number actually appeared (table 7.1).[11] Like the population as a whole, the electorate grew considerably during the county's early history, reaching nearly sixteen hundred potential voters in the 1760s and representing one of the largest electorates in the colony. Following the division, the number of adult white males dropped to about nine hundred, still sizable by standards of the day. It was this massive electorate spread across a vast territory that Nathaniel Terry and his rivals had to "cajole, fawn, and wheedle, for a place that brings so little profit."[12]

LEADERS

Despite the aggressive, confrontational, and less-than-genteel nature of his personality, Nathaniel Terry possessed at least some of the characteristics found in local leaders in other parts of the colony. He was a member of both the county's first Commission of the Peace and the parish's first vestry and held both offices when he first ran for burgess election. Later, he was active in militia affairs and served for a time as county sheriff. Although the size of his early landholdings are uncertain, he did eventually accumulate more than seven thousand acres in the county.[13] At least sixteen additional men stood election to the House of Burgesses from Halifax County during the colonial period and, like Terry, became a part of the local community through their economic and political activities. Shortly after the formation of Halifax County, the governor appointed a county Commission of the Peace and the sheriff held elections to determine the vestrymen for the new parish of Antrim. A few additions to the county court occurred a year later, and both county bodies began meeting for the first time in 1753. With thirteen members common to the two groups, the leadership structure of the new county included approximately thirty individuals.[14]

As a group, these thirty men were reasonably undistinguished, although among them were a few very wealthy individuals and several with previous leadership experience. The most prominent member of the group was William Byrd III. He owned extensive tracts of land in the Southside, including forty thousand acres in Halifax. He was the largest slaveholder in the new county, had been elected burgess from Lunenburg in January 1752, and was now a member of the first Commission of the Peace for Halifax. Three men, Peter Fontaine Jr., Robert Jones, and William Wynne, had been justices of the peace in the parent county of Lunenburg, and Fontaine, along with Robert Wade Sr., had been a member of the Cumberland Parish vestry in that county as well. None of the remaining twenty-five individuals had any leadership experience.[15]

Many of the wealthiest men in the county were not among these initial leaders, including absentee landowners Richard Randolph, William Lightfoot, and Richard Bland and resident planters James Cooke, Luke Smith Sr., George Currie, and a Major Coles. Other than William Byrd, only vestryman Richard Echols (with 1,850 acres), justice Hugh Moore (with 1,588 acres), and justice and vestryman William Irby (with 600 acres and five tithable slaves) were men of modest wealth. Half of the remaining leaders held less than 500 acres and one or two slaves, while the rest do not appear as either landowners or slaveholders in the 1750 or 1755 tithables lists.[16]

With a lack of experience among the new leaders and with no clear-cut economic elite in place, it is not surprising that the earliest candidates for election to the House of Burgesses came from no single source within the community. Of the seven candidates who ran in the first six elections (1753–64), four were vestrymen or justices and two were militia officers. After 1764, every winner was a justice of the county court (table 7.2).[17] However, service in several local offices did not ensure electoral success, as in some other counties: some who won had served in only one local office, while several who lost had held two or three offices in the county.

Although some very wealthy members of eastern gentry families owned land in Halifax and might have chosen to become active in local politics, none did. William Byrd served as a burgess for nearby Lunenburg from 1752 to 1754 and was then elevated to the Council. Richard Randolph concentrated his political activity in Henrico

County, William Lightfoot in Charles City, and Richard Bland in Prince George. None of these gentlemen even voted in the Halifax elections of the 1760s, although their large holdings entitled them to do so. In some of Virginia's counties during this period, a specific pattern of local officeholding coupled with the accumulation of wealth became critical ingredients in the eventual election to the House. This was not the case in Halifax before 1764, and there are only the slightest hints that such patterns appeared thereafter.

ELECTORAL POLITICS

Halifax had been in existence for eighteen months before the governor issued a writ on November 1, 1753, to conduct the first House of Burgesses elections in the new county. Later in November the election took place at the newly constructed, but probably very rough, courthouse. Three candidates offered themselves in this first electoral gathering: George Currie, builder of the new courthouse, clerk of the court for the new county, vestryman, and one of only a handful of slaveholders in the area; John Bates, a small landowner, militia officer, and possibly a Quaker; and Samuel Harris, a former processioner and reader in Cumberland Parish in Lunenburg, modest land- and slaveholder, and recent appointee to the parish vestry and the Halifax County court.[18]

Samuel Harris and George Currie won the election, but on December 4, 1753, Bates petitioned the House of Burgesses to have the results overturned. Bates claimed, and the House agreed, that Currie did not meet the landholding requirements to serve in the assembly. Apparently the three-hundred-acre piece of land conveyed to him earlier in the year and upon which Currie based his right as a freeholder of Halifax County had not been owned by the man from whom he purchased it. Interestingly enough, in the late 1740s he took grants totaling more than seven thousand acres in Lunenburg and Albemarle Counties and had an overseer and five or six adult slaves in Lunenburg. George Currie was a wealthy man by the standards of the area, but the wealth was in the wrong county.[19]

The House resolved on December 7 that George Currie was "not duly qualified to serve as a Burgess in this present General Assembly for the County of Halifax" and issued a writ to elect a replacement. In a possible attempt to win back his seat, Currie petitioned

Table 7.2

Candidates and Election Results, Halifax County, 1753–1774

Candidate	1753	1753	1755	1758	1761
George Currie	W				
Samuel Harris	W		W		
John Bates	L	W	W		
Robert Wade Jr.				W	W
Nathaniel Terry				W	W
Edward Booker					
Hampton Wade					
Walter Coles					
John Donelson					
Thomas Tunstall					
George Watkins					
Thomas Green					
James Bates					
John Lewis					
Robert Wooding					
Isaac Coles					
Micajah Watkins					

Note: W = Winner; L = loser.

the Council on December 17 and received "all the Waste Lands between his own Lines and Sandy Creek, not exceeding Five Thousand Acres in Hallifax." Whether this grant qualified him to run again and whether or not he actually ran is not known. In late December 1753, Halifax voters elected John Bates to the fill the empty seat.[20] Samuel Harris and John Bates served out the remaining sessions of this assembly and ran and won in the general election held in December 1755. By the time of the next general election in the summer of 1758, one of the incumbents had substantially redirected his interests and activities, and other attractive candidates appeared on the scene.

Some time in 1757 or 1758, Samuel Harris began attending evangelical meetings, which occurred with increasing frequency in this part of the colony. At one such meeting he heard the preaching of the "Murphey boys," "saw the light," and became a Separate Baptist (a group more radical than many dissenters because they separated themselves completely from the Anglican establishment). Al-

1764	1765	1765	1768	1769	1772	1774
			W	W	W	W
W		W				
L		L				
	W	W	L	W		
		L				
		L				
		L				
		L				
		L				
			W	L		
			L			
				L	W	
						W

though Harris continued to improve the land he owned and to acquire additional properties in several counties, "upon being honored of God, he laid aside all worldly honors and became a laborer in the Lord's vineyard." He probably withdrew at this time from vestry, court, and burgess duties and devoted most of his time to preaching his new-found faith.[21]

A year or two earlier, Harris and several others in the county had begun to assume leadership roles in warding off Indian attacks along the frontier—activities that related to the North American phase of the Seven Years' War. In 1756, as part of a colonywide project to build a chain of eighty or so blockhouse forts along the frontier, Nathaniel Terry and his militia company constructed three in Halifax County. Samuel Harris, for a time at least, took responsibility for the defense of one called Fort Mayo (map 7.1). Terry had also captured and brought to justice "several Persons, who in the Disguise of Indians, had been robbing and plundering the Inhabitants in the Frontiers of this Colony."[22] By March 1758, however, matters had deteriorated, and a substantial panic had set in among the settlers along the frontier. In April, Indians killed or captured forty-seven people, and in May, Cherokee moving through the county stole horses from several settlers. Soon thereafter, the "Officers of Halifax" held a council of war and drew up a petition to the Council in Williamsburg "representing the distressed State of the County" and indicating "that the greater Part of the Inhabitants will quit their Plantations unless speedily and effectually defended." Consequently, young Robert Wade Jr. received orders to draft eighty men from Lunenburg and another company of eighty from Halifax.[23]

The activities of Nathaniel Terry and Robert Wade in the defense of the county during the early phase of the war probably put them in good stead with the freeholders of Halifax, and therefore it is not surprising that they ran in the general election held on July 12, 1758. Terry was also a justice of the peace and vestryman, and while Wade held no local offices other than militia captain, his father had been a vestryman in Lunenburg and his brother, Hampton, was a justice in Halifax. It seems unlikely that Samuel Harris sought reelection, but someone opposed Wade and Terry in the July contest, and it may have been the other incumbent, John Bates. Terry and Wade won the election "by a great majority."[24]

In 1761, the voters again elected Robert Wade and Nathaniel Terry, but nothing else is known of the election. Wade died in the early part of 1764, and when the House assembled on October 30, it issued a writ to elect a replacement. Two candidates offered themselves to the voters: Hampton Wade and Edward Booker. Hampton was the brother of the deceased burgess, lived on the Dan River in the east-central part of the county, and had been a justice of the peace since 1752. Booker resided near the northern boundary of the county, where his family operated a ferry over the Staunton River; he was a justice and vestryman, and his father and grandfather had been active politicians in nearby Amelia County.[25] A closely fought by-election occurred on November 28, 1764: Booker won 264 to 240. Overwhelming support from both the leaders and voters in the middle and western parts of the county assured Booker victory. Local leaders residing in these sections all backed Booker, while those living in the eastern part divided their votes evenly between the candidates.[26] Similarly, 70 percent of the western voters supported

Booker, while only 40 percent of those in the older, eastern section did so.[27]

The closeness of the contest encouraged Wade to petition the House to have the election results scrutinized. He believed that a number of unlawful voters polled for Edward Booker, and since only twenty-four votes separated the two, Wade could have become the winner if enough illegal votes could be found. Wade also claimed that one of the poll takers at the election, William Wright, accepted or refused voters in a manner that altered the outcome in Booker's favor. On December 12, 1764, the House agreed to look into the matter and to have Booker and Wade examine a number of the voters in the presence of three members of the Halifax county court. The House postponed action on the petition to the next session of the assembly, but when it reconvened in May 1765, Wade had not arranged for the examination of voters and witnesses and so the House declared Booker duly elected.[28]

Wade's failure to follow through on his petition may have been partially influenced by the appointment of Nathaniel Terry, the other Halifax burgess, to the office of county sheriff and therefore the certainty that another by-election would be scheduled soon to select Terry's replacement. The governor issued a writ on May 2, 1765, and late that month the by-election occurred. Whether Hampton Wade ran is not known, but Walter Coles became the county's new burgess. Coles was a twenty-six-year-old planter and recent appointee to the county judicial bench. He also served on the vestry during this period and held a modest estate of 1,530 acres in the eastern part of the county.[29] Coles' term of office was a short one, for on June 1, the governor dissolved the assembly because of the Stamp Act Resolves and issued writs for new elections in mid-June.[30] Since incumbents Edward Booker and Walter Coles had each served less than six months, they eagerly entered the contest. Other challengers, both old and new and with varying degrees of support from local leaders, also joined the race.

Incumbent Walter Coles was the first choice of the county elite. Thomas Tunstall, who owned just over four hundred acres and was Halifax deputy clerk of court and a vestryman, was the second choice of the county leadership. Their third favorite was recent loser Hampton Wade. Incumbent Edward Booker was fourth, and then John Donelson, a vestryman with a few hundred acres in the middle section of the county.[31] Although county leaders found something favorable in all five candidates, three more entered the race without apparent support from the vestry or the county court. Vestryman and justice George Watkins offered himself to the voters, as did Thomas Green and James Bates, who had recently joined the county court.[32] These eight candidates composed the election roster when the freeholders assembled on the hustings on July 17.

This election was unusual in several respects. First, more candidates ran than in any other Halifax election, and it was one of the largest recorded for any county during this period. Second, this election probably represented the largest physical gathering of voters in Halifax during the colonial era and one of the largest for the entire colony. Third, more than any other Halifax election of record, irregular and casual voters overwhelmingly dominated the contest. Fourth, factional allegiances played a smaller role in this election than in the other three for which information is available. And fifth, plumping was remarkably common. Of the 837 voters who participated, 609 (73%) had not voted in the by-election just seven months earlier. Furthermore, 485 of the 609 would not vote again in either the general elections of 1768 or 1769. Many of these freeholders, of course, lived in the middle and western sections, which after 1767 became Pittsylvania County, and therefore could not vote again in Halifax. Clearly, the large slate of candidates drew a significant number of persons into active participation who normally either lived too far away to vote on a regular basis or had little interest in politics much of the time.

These irregular voters brought into the electoral arena a mode of behavior less predictable and less orthodox than that of regular voters. Because Wade lost to Booker in the 1764 by-election and protested the results before the House, rival factions apparently developed around the two men. Geography further heightened the competition: Wade and his kin hailed from the long-settled eastern section, while the Booker family was centered along the Staunton River in the county's middle section. Donelson attached himself to incumbent and fellow westerner Booker; Wade allied himself with incumbent and fellow easterner Walter Coles. To the voters who voted in 1764, the discord between these candidates remained a political reality; 36 percent of them chose one of the two factions in the 1765 election. On the other hand, only 18 percent of those who had not voted in 1764 selected one of the two slates. Furthermore, returning voters remained reasonably loyal to their 1764 selection: 67 percent of the Booker voters and 62 percent of the Wade voters who showed up in 1765 held to their previous choice. Finally, the geographically based voting patterns of the 1764 election continued to be important: Booker received 56 percent and Donelson 77 percent of their support from the middle and western sections of the county; Wade and Coles each garnered more than 70 percent of their supporters from the eastern part. Most striking about this election—and about irregular voters—is the extent of plumping, which reached 41 percent. While only 24 percent of those who had voted in 1764 cast just a single ballot in 1765, 47 percent of the new or irregular voters did. Of the more than 300 voters who plumped in this race, 84 percent of them had never voted before.

Eight serious candidates, a relatively low degree of factional allegiance, and extremely high levels of plumping produced myriad voting patterns. The Coles-Wade and Booker-Donelson factions did receive the support of the highest number of voters, but these accounted for only 23 percent of the participants. Significant minorities of the electorate selected Coles-Tunstall, Coles-Booker, Wade-Watkins, and Coles-Donelson. In all, thirty-two different voting patterns occurred. The final results of the election, however, were a good deal less dramatic than the voting behavior that produced them. Incumbents Walter Coles and Edward Booker won the election, with 314 and 269 votes, respectively. John Donelson took third, with 236, Hampton Wade fourth, with 218, and Thomas Tunstall fifth, with 142, while George Watkins got 75, Thomas Green 58, and James Bates 22.[33]

The multiplicity of patterns as well as the results might suggest that electoral behavior was as random and unpredictable as frontier societies are often thought to be. Yet seen in another light, a very different image emerges. A leadership core spread over a large territory and with no consensus as to who should represent the county left to individual leaders in different sections the task of bringing forth suitable candidates for the election. Voters who participated regularly in this process knew of the continuing political conflicts within the county and followed fairly closely the voting patterns they had established in earlier contests. New voters or those who participated infrequently had less inclination to follow alliances from previous elections and were more likely to cross factional lines and to plump for neighborhood favorite sons.

The massive turnout for the 1765 election and the bewildering array of voting patterns (which often followed sectional and neighborhood lines) provided ample proof that a single parish vestry, one county court, and two burgesses could no longer serve the county's interests. Concern with the operation of the vestry had arisen a few years earlier, but when the new assembly met for the first time in the fall of 1766 Halifax residents pushed it with renewed vigor. Two petitions arrived in Williamsburg on November 22, one from a group of inhabitants asking for a division of the county and a second from the minister requesting a division in Antrim Parish. Both found favor with the burgesses, who combined them into a single bill— which passed the House on December 12. Walter Coles obtained the Council's consent, and the governor signed it a few days later.[34] The middle and western sections of the county became Pittsylvania County and Camden Parish, leaving Halifax with one-quarter of its original area. The reduced county lost half of its electorate as well and a portion of its leaders—changes that would substantially alter the electoral process for the remainder of the colonial period.

Within the group of eight candidates who ran in 1765, several were no longer active in the now smaller county of Halifax. Edward Booker died in late 1767 or early 1768, leaving Walter Coles as the only incumbent. John Donelson resided in the new county of Pittsylvania and would run in that county's general election of 1768. Hampton Wade probably died in 1766. The four minor candidates in 1765 remained residents of the county: Thomas Tunstall voted in 1768 and 1769; George Watkins and Thomas Green showed up in the 1773 fee book of the county clerk; and James Bates voted in 1768 and became sheriff in 1769. Joining these politicians from the old, larger, county were new leaders destined to play important roles in the reduced county. These included new members of the county court and new vestrymen appointed after the division. Among the new officeholders were John Lewis and Isaac Coles, a brother of burgess Walter Coles.[35]

As the 1768 general election approached, Walter Coles, the only incumbent, decided to run again; half of the county court backed his candidacy. Robert Wooding, who owned at least 2,500 acres in the county and had recently been named a justice of the peace, joined Coles as an apparent running mate. About a third of the justices favored this combination. Nathaniel Terry, former burgess and recent county sheriff, also entered the contest. The other half of the county court supported Terry and his apparent running mate, John Lewis. Lewis had served as a colonel in the militia, owned 1,880 acres in Halifax County and another 250 in Lunenburg County, and had joined the county court the previous year.[36]

A number of factors contributed to the formation of these two electoral factions, including a petition presented to the Council in June 1768 to have the courthouse moved, but most of the explanation falls squarely at the feet of Nathaniel Terry. Terry was a man of boundless energy, activity, and controversy. In the early 1750s, he sued burgess Samuel Harris over 2,680 acres of land; in 1756 he engaged a company of militia to help build several forts and probably pocketed the money provided for their pay; in 1758, when he first won election to the House, some in the county thought his personal attributes would disqualify him from service; and in 1762 he sued another landowner and was awarded 7,384 acres.[37] As county sheriff in 1764 and 1765, he got into further difficulties.

First, Nathaniel Terry altered the record books of his undersheriff and cousin, Champness Terry, to show a credit to the account of James Bates. While the adjustment probably corrected a previous error in the accounts, tampering with legal records under someone else's jurisdiction was highly irregular and stirred the ire of a number of prominent persons, including James Bates himself (a justice), Champness Terry (undersheriff), Benjamin Lankford (undersheriff and future Pittsylvania justice), and Thomas Yuille (justice). During this dispute, Moses Terry (undersheriff and vestryman) and Robert Wooding (justice) tried to help settle the issue and may have developed specific opinions about Nathaniel in the process. Second, attorney Paul Carrington (burgess from Charlotte County and future Halifax County clerk) asked Nathaniel Terry to turn over a sum of money Terry had received as sheriff that was part of a judgment concerning a runaway slave. Terry held on to the money for two years before finally turning it over, thus angering both Carrington and his clients. Finally, Terry threatened to sue burgess Walter Coles "to do Justice to his Character," because Coles said Terry's alteration of the account book issue was only "a little short of Forgery." This last dispute occurred in late 1768 and had much to do with the candidate lineup in the December 1768 election.[38]

The election occurred on December 2, 1768, under conditions of "confusion and inconvenience." Polling started at midday and "by the Throng of the Electors crowding in [to the courthouse], the Poll was several Times necessarily interrupted," and there was concern that it might not be completed before the day ended.[39] Eventually, everyone voted; the results clearly demonstrated the saliency of the two factions, not only from the perspective of the elite and the candidates but also in the minds of the voters. The Terry-Lewis faction received 178 votes; the Coles-Wooding faction received 149. Plumpers came in at about the same proportion, making the final results Nathaniel Terry 245, John Lewis 233, Walter Coles 209, and Robert Wooding 187. The Terry-Lewis faction had defeated incumbent Walter Coles (table 7.3).

Coles would have retained his seat in 1768 had he been able to rely exclusively on freeholders who had voted in the last election. Among the 203 who voted in 1765 and in 1768, Terry was first in the 1768 election (with 100), Coles second (with 98), Lewis third (with 96), and Wooding last (with 82). Yet given the substantial margin by which Coles had won in 1765, even a second-place finish among returning voters demonstrates an erosion of support. Although Coles had more returning voters than any other 1765 candidate (101), only 59 percent continued to vote for him in 1768. By contrast, 80 percent of returning Hampton Wade supporters became Terry adherents in 1768, and all but one of the 27 returning Watkins supporters

Table 7.3
Electoral Behavior, by Previous Electoral
Experience, Halifax County, 1768

Electoral Choice	Never Voted Before	Voted Once Before	Voted Twice Before	Total
Terry-Lewis	84	47	47	178
Coles-Wooding	75	44	30	149
Other pairings	13	18	11	42
Plumped	96	26	14	136
Total voters	268	135	102	505
Terry	122	68	55	245
Lewis	118	55	60	233
Coles	101	68	40	209
Wooding	99	53	35	187
Total votes	440	244	190	874

voted for Lewis in 1768. Returning backers of Edward Booker even gave Coles a larger proportion of their support (67%) than his own 1765 followers had.

Coles' real downfall came at the hands of other groups within the electorate. First, new voters (those who had not participated in either the 1764 or 1765 elections) gave Terry and Lewis a substantial edge over Coles and Wooding (Terry received 46% of this group, Lewis 44%, Coles 38%, and Wooding 37%). Second, those voters who had participated in both of the previous elections were also decidedly supporters of the eventual winners: John Lewis received 59 percent of this vote, Terry 54 percent, Coles 39 percent, and Wooding 34 percent.

At least one interpretation of this election suggests that Walter Coles was very much a flash-in-the-pan candidate. Having entered the House through a by-election in 1765 and then winning a factionless eight-candidate general election just a few months later, Coles was merely a leader of modest following who happened to be in the right place at the right time. When an experienced candidate like Nathaniel Terry returned to the electoral arena and a wealthy planter like John Lewis entered the race, Coles did not have a chance. New voters and those who participated regularly in the electoral process favored the old burgess, Terry, and his new running mate, Lewis. Coles' long-term supporters simply could not muster a large enough group to carry him through a serious challenge. Whatever his strengthens and weaknesses, his activities over the following year suggest a politician with a rather different view of himself.

Although Walter Coles could find nothing in the conduct of the 1768 election to enable him to challenge the outcome, this did not prevent him from doing everything in his power to unseat Terry. When the House assembled on May 8, 1769, Coles (now no longer a burgess) appeared in Williamsburg and spread stories about Terry's past behavior, particularly activities during his tenure as county sheriff in 1764 and 1765. By May 12, these stories had reached a number of burgesses, and the House assigned a committee to determine whether Coles was in "Breach of the privilege of this House" by telling such tales about a duly elected member. The investigation delighted Coles, who eagerly told the committee that these stories were not only true but that many more improprieties lurked in Terry's past. The committee now had to hold a full-scale investigation to determine the truth.[40]

No investigation occurred immediately, however, as the governor dissolved the assembly on May 17, sending the burgesses home to plan for yet another general election. Halifax sheriff William Hoskins received the governor's writ on August 18, decided to hold the election on September 15, and immediately sent a notice to be read at the several churches and chapels in the county. Incumbents Nathaniel Terry and John Lewis would stand for reelection. Walter Coles jumped at the change to get another shot at Terry and announced he would attempt to regain his seat. Robert Wooding, who came in last in 1768, would not run again, but Walter's twenty-two-year-old brother, Isaac Coles, took the remaining spot on the challenger slate.[41]

About September 1, Sheriff Hoskins informed Terry and the Coles brothers that he intended to open the poll at eight o'clock in the morning on election day rather than at the normal time of noon. The 1768 election had been such a wild affair and the voting so difficult that the sheriff wanted to start as early as possible. When election day came, however, the sheriff waited until about nine o'clock to begin. The Coles brothers urged the sheriff to start the election as soon as possible, for their "Friends live[d] nearer the Court-house than the Majority's of . . . Terry's" and presumably more were present at this early hour. Lewis and Terry both objected to this procedure, Lewis stating "that his Friends were at a great Distance, 20 and 30 miles, and could not possibly get there so soon." The sheriff wanted to start immediately but stated that he would keep the polls open until sunset to prevent "any Objections of Unfairness."[42]

Walter and Isaac Coles and John Lewis accepted the sheriff's plan, but Nathaniel Terry tried to stall the proceedings. He complained that the sheriff had not provided him with a clerk to take his poll (even though candidates usually arranged for their own clerks). When several freeholders declared that Terry's clerk "was at the Table in the Court-house, ruling the Columns in the Poll," the sheriff decided to start the election. Terry then stripped off his coat and waistcoat, unbuttoned his collar, declared "that he would be damned if he [the sheriff] should read the Writ yet" and that "he would be damned if he did not cane him," and he then attempted to hit the sheriff. Several freeholders deflected the blows, but the poll remained closed. Later, Terry wanted the sheriff to open the poll, but the Coles brothers urged him not to, and in the end the sheriff "declined proceeding further." The House of Burgesses investigated the matter when they met on November 8 and determined that "Nathaniel Terry, in obstructing Mr. Hoskins the Sheriff, in the Execution of his duty, is guilty of an Offense, and Breach of the Privileges of the People." Since no election occurred, the House requested a new election writ.[43]

The second attempt to hold an election in the fall of 1769 occurred on November 22, with apparently none of the controversy that surfaced in the earlier contest. Despite Terry's admonishment by the House, he remained a candidate for reelection along with fellow incumbent John Lewis and challengers Walter and Isaac Coles. Although clearly two opposing coalitions existed in the election, both the county elite and the voters demonstrated declining interest in the personal animosities between Coles and Terry and therefore became more willing to cross factional lines than they had been in 1768.

Among the twelve county leaders voting, eight supported Nathaniel Terry, six favored Walter Coles, five supported John Lewis, and just three supported Isaac Coles. Furthermore, the Terry–Walter Coles combination and the Terry-Lewis slate found the greatest adherence among the elite (four each), not the challenging pair from the Coles family. The county leadership had still not developed a consensus on the pair of representatives, but they were coming close to determining the individual candidates they thought best. The freeholders of Halifax County followed a nearly identical pattern.

Terry topped the poll, with 194 votes, followed closely by Walter Coles, with 189; Isaac Coles took third, with 134, and incumbent John Lewis was fourth, with 133 (table 7.4). Although two-thirds of the freeholders selected the two obvious slates as they had done in 1768, plumping had declined considerably, and other combinations of candidates received a significant share of the vote. The Terry-Lewis faction received the highest number of votes, with 112, while the Coles brothers followed close behind, with 110. Freeholders casting single ballots accounted for only 8 percent of the participants, as each of the four candidates received only four to six votes from plumpers. Of considerable importance were the 90 electors who ignored the two opposing factions and voted for either Terry and Walter Coles (60 votes) or selected one of the other three combinations (30 votes).

The overall results of the 1769 contest confirmed Walter Coles' staying power with the electorate, but his appeal, as before, remained strongest among the occasional voter. The Coles slate outpolled Terry and Lewis among those who had never voted before and among those who had only voted once in the previous three elections, while it lagged behind the incumbents among those who voted in two or three of the past elections (table 7.4). On an individual basis, Walter Coles also received more support from the irregular voters than did Nathaniel Terry: Walter Coles led among new voters and among those with only one previous electoral experience, tied with Terry among those voting twice before, and received considerably fewer votes from those participating in all four contests. Similar, but less clear-cut, patterns prevailed in the support given Isaac Coles and John Lewis.

The most significant factor in Walter Coles' successful reelection bid was his ability to get a substantial number of previously new and irregular voters who had supported him in 1768 to return and vote for him again in 1769. Although in 1768 Nathaniel Terry had outpolled him by thirty-six votes and John Lewis by twenty-four votes, Coles got considerably more voters to return in 1769 than either of the incumbents (table 7.5). Not only did Walter Coles have a far

Table 7.4
Electorial Behavior, by Previous Electoral
Experience, Halifax County, 1769

Choice	Never Voted Before	Voted Once Before	Voted Twice Before	Voted Three Times Before	Total
Terry-Lewis	27	33	28	24	112
Coles-Coles	29	37	25	19	110
Terry-W. Coles	14	19	18	9	60
Other pairings	7	8	7	8	30
Plumped	14	3	4	5	26
Total voters	91	100	82	65	338
Terry	48	56	49	41	194
W. Coles	49	60	49	31	189
I. Coles	34	44	30	26	134
Lewis	37	37	32	27	133
Total votes	168	197	160	125	650

Table 7.5
Voter Return Rates and Voting Consistency,
Halifax County, 1768–1769

1768 Candidates	1768 Votes	Voters Returning in 1769			
		%	N	% Voting Same	N
Walter Coles	209	52	109	91	99
Nathaniel Terry	245	35	86	92	79
John Lewis	233	34	80	76	61
Coles-Wooding	149	58	87		
Lewis-Terry	178	37	66	82	54
All candidates	505	39	199	90	179

greater return rate than either Terry or Lewis, but those who supported the Coles-Wooding faction in 1768 returned at a higher rate
than those voting for the Terry-Lewis slate. With freeholders from
the 1768 election accounting for 59 percent of the 1769 participants,
return voters played a much more critical role in this election than
they had in the previous three (table 7.4).

Getting voters from the previous election to return was only part
of the task in achieving victory; the returning freeholders also had
to remain loyal to individual candidates—and they did. More than
90 percent of the returning Terry and Coles adherents voted for their
1768 choice in 1769 (table 7.5). This represented a major change in
behavior from previous elections, in which Booker and Wade had,
respectively, only 67 percent and 62 percent consistency between
the 1764 and 1765 elections and Coles received only 59 percent support from his returnees in 1768. Even John Lewis's 34 percent return
rate and 76 percent consistency rate, which in the context of the
1769 election had much to do with his defeat, seem impressive when
compared to earlier races.

The 1769 election had the lowest level of voter turnout of any of
the three general elections of the period; at least four factors contributed to this. First, the 1768 general election had taken place just
twelve months earlier, and the short time span probably reduced
turnout. Second, both incumbents stood for reelection, a situation
that often encouraged freeholders to think there was very little to be
decided in a new election. Third, an attempt had already been made

to hold this election two months earlier, and some voters probably stayed away the second time fearing another inconclusive tumult. Fourth, the weather at this late November election could have discouraged some voters from attending, although the exact conditions on this particular day in Halifax County remain a mystery.[44]

All four of these factors probably influenced the general level of turnout among certain freeholders from certain sections of the county, and this in turn set the conditions for Walter Coles' return and John Lewis's defeat. These might have been particularly important if Lewis had done nothing in his brief legislative career to inspire the voter's continuing confidence. Further, because many Terry and Lewis supporters lived in the upper or western sections of the county, then either weather or general disinterest could have discouraged backers of the incumbents from attending. It also appears likely that Nathaniel Terry, as a longtime justice, vestryman, former sheriff, and burgess, had a greater countywide appeal than either Walter Coles or John Lewis and, therefore, remained insulated from geographical factors that influenced turnout. Lower turnout across the county in general coupled with higher levels of turnout among freeholders who lived close to the courthouse allowed Coles to attract more new voters to his cause, achieve a greater return rate from his old supporters, and keep a larger proportion of return voters solidly in his camp than incumbent John Lewis.

Although Walter Coles had won the late November election and now shared the county representation with Nathaniel Terry, this in no way lessened the antagonism between the two men. Less than three weeks after the election, Coles notified the House that he wanted to push on with the investigation of Terry's character initiated in the previous assembly. Consequently, the committee ordered that further testimony be taken in Mecklenburg County and that a report be prepared for the spring session. Of the eight original charges leveled against him, the committee found only one in which Terry "was guilty of a Breach of Duty in his Office of Sheriff" and that "there was nothing criminal or corrupt in his said Conduct." Although the burgesses censured him for only this one indiscretion, Terry had had enough and requested a leave of absence from the House for the remainder of the session.[45] Walter Coles had won more than the 1769 election.

The tumultuous elections of the 1760s gave way to relative tranquility for the final contests of the colonial period. Nathaniel Terry continued to represent the county until the late 1770s, but his fellow burgess changed in each of these last two elections. When the governor issued writs for new elections on October 31, 1771, Halifax County had no sheriff and, therefore, no election occurred. Once a sheriff had been appointed, the House ordered a second writ, and an election took place in early March 1772.[46] For some reason, Walter Coles declined another poll, and his brother, Isaac, stood in his place; Terry and Coles won.[47]

The results of the last colonial election provide a final testimony to the loosely defined nature of the Halifax elite. Terry stood again for election in the July 1774 contest and won, but Micajah Watkins captured Isaac Coles' seat. Whether Coles gave up the seat voluntarily is unclear, although he had just joined the county court and would remain an active vestryman until 1782. On the other hand, the Council dropped winner Watkins (who was probably related to unsuccessful 1765 candidate George Watkins) from the county court in 1773 because of inactivity![48]

CONCLUSION

The fact that local leaders still bitterly fought each other in 1770 and probably beyond suggests that a political consensus had not emerged in this Southside county on the eve of the American Revolution. In other places, local leaders sorted out their differences early in a county's history, but in Halifax this process lasted through the period of settlement and rapid growth and into the era of geographic and population stability. While weighty imperial or colonial matters and local issues like frontier defense, courthouse location, and the division of the county had some impact on these continuing disagreements, the personal behavior and ambitions of an ill-defined elite fueled much of the controversy. Elections to the House of Burgesses offered one battleground for these disputes, but when these contests failed to provide a clear-cut victor the feuds occasionally shifted to a higher arena through petitions to the House of Burgesses. In the 1760s, hotly contested elections between large numbers of candidates were the norm. Factions developed, disappeared, and reformed around specific contenders in a struggle for ascendancy in the local community. The county leadership sometimes lined up loosely behind specific factions, but a long-term commitment by the elite to a single pair of representatives never emerged before the Revolution.

This lack of agreement among the elite in the matter of political representation persisted because no single leadership core ever coalesced during the colonial period. Halifax never developed a definable gentry in the way counties like Accomack, Lancaster, and Fairfax did. County government in Halifax began with a hodgepodge of leaders, neither particularly wealthy nor especially experienced in local leadership, a situation that did not change dramatically over the next twenty years. Further, county courts, which figured prominently in most local governments in Virginia, did not play the same role in this Southside county. Instead, a rather remarkable turnover in the court's membership occurred, with at least eighty-seven men serving during the twenty-one-year period, 1752–73.[49] Rapid turnover in local officeholding provided little opportunity for the development of a clearly defined pathway to electoral success. Early in the county's history, some legislative candidates held the offices of justice and vestryman; others served only as militia officers. Although by the mid-1760s all candidates were either justices or vestrymen, membership in either court or vestry or both had little impact on success at the polls.

When it came to the selection of representatives to the House of Burgesses, instability and diversity at the top forced the freeholders of Halifax to ignore the opinions of those holding the highest local office, at least before the division in 1767. Although the elite and the voters agreed in general terms on the winner in the 1764 by-election, Booker garnered greater support from the elite than from the voters (table 7.6). With the exception of agreement on Walter Coles in 1765, voters and leaders had nearly opposite reactions to the rest of the candidates in that election. Following the division, however, preferences of the two groups began to move in the direction of congruence: in 1768 they agreed on the top and bottom of the poll, while in 1769 leaders and freeholders found nearly perfect agreement on the ranking of candidates.

Although these freeholders began to follow the lead of their betters only in the late 1760s, they were not as a group the whimsical, random, and haphazard voters that some believe inhabited the Southside. They participated in elections less often than freeholders in some other counties, and this fact has led to an interpretation of instability and randomness. Those who voted infrequently be-

Table 7.6
Elite Support and Voter Support, Halifax County, 1764–1769 (%)

Candidate	1764 Elite	1764 Voter	1765 Elite	1765 Voter	1768 Elite	1768 Voter	1769 Elite	1769 Voter
E. Booker	67	52	22	32				
H. Wade	33	48	33	26				
Tunstall			50	17				
W. Coles			55	38	50	41	50	56
Donelson			22	28				
Terry					50	49	67	57
Wooding					30	37		
Lewis					60	46	42	39
I. Coles							25	40

haved less predictably and in ways that seemed unlike their cousins in the eastern counties: they ignored long-standing political squabbles and crossed factional lines with their votes, or they wasted one of their two votes and plumped for single candidates. Regular voters, however, showed little of the capricious behavior that supposedly dominated these elections. Across any pair of contests, loyalty to particular candidates remained strong: 62 percent and 67 percent between 1764 and 1765, 59 percent between 1765 and 1768, and 76 percent, 91 percent, and 92 percent between 1768 and 1769.

The candidates who ran in Halifax County were clearly of a different breed from those who dominated elections in counties to the north and east. Few candidates with the gentility of Robert Munford's Mr. Worthy inhabited the humble plantations of the Southside, but neither did only simpletons and drunkards, like Strutabout, Smallhope, and Toddy, vie for office. Rather, the candidates in this Southside county had more in common with the character Wou'dbe. A bit below Worthy in status, he would "cajole, fawn, and wheedle, for a place that brings so little profit." He subjected himself "to the humours of a fickle crowd" to get elected, but he refused to make wild campaign promises or overindulge the drinking habits of some freeholders.[50] The two most active electoral politicians in Halifax County had much in common with Wou'dbe.

Nathaniel Terry and Walter Coles were hardly a George Washington or a Charles Carter, but they were the best their society had to offer. They rose to the top through modest economic successes, assumed positions of local leadership, which they sometimes executed imperfectly, and accepted the challenge of burgess election and office much as their legislative colleagues did elsewhere. Those freeholders who supported them in these electoral contests differed from freeholders in the east, but their participation and behavior was not nearly as erratic as sometimes imagined. Given the size of the county both before and after 1767, the degree of participation among all freeholders and the consistency of behavior among regular voters indicates a level of political interest and awareness often thought possible only in more settled regions of colonial America.

Conclusion

Elections and Political Community

Political community had meaning for all Virginians of the colonial era, although persons at each level of provincial society experienced it in distinct ways. Two nearly separate political worlds operated in the eighteenth century: one concentrated in Williamsburg and a second located in dozens of counties and parishes and hundreds of intimate neighborhoods of the Old Dominion. Governors and Council members occupied the first; justices, vestrymen, petit jurors, common freeholders, tenants, family members, servants, and slaves occupied the second. Members of the House of Burgesses held these two realms together, sharing constituent concerns with their fellow burgesses while bringing the political ideas and public culture of the provincial capital back to their friends and neighbors. The process of electing those representatives elicited responses unique in time and place but on occasion ignited a "flame of burgessing" that penetrated the most intimate neighborhoods and touched the lives of a significant number of Virginians.

For those at the pinnacle of this provincial world—the governor and his Council—political community operated among a handful of riverfront mansions along the James, York, Rappahannock, and Potomac Rivers and the Council chambers and governor's palace in Williamsburg. Within this circle, a well-established, nearly hereditary group executed their own high offices, sanctioned appointments of county justices and sheriffs, managed the distribution of western lands, and in general kept a careful watch over the activities of the popularly elected House of Burgesses. Weighty matters—what we easily recognize as real political issues—filled the lives of these men; political preferments and appointments, provincial revenues, military appropriations, major legal cases, as well as a broad sense of their place within the British Empire animated those at the top of Virginia's political system.

Those holding the office of burgess experienced two different forms of political community, one tied to the politics of the colonial capital and the other anchored in their home counties. For several months each year, these representatives adjudicated election disputes, weighed the merits of myriad local and private legislation, and debated and passed judgment upon measures affecting the entire colony. The leadership of the House shared much of the political world of the Council and governor as they drafted legislation, worked out compromises with the upper chamber, and in a few cases held provincial offices of their own. Some also had familial ties to the Council and to each other, adding further to a shared sense of community during their brief visits to Williamsburg.

Most burgesses, however, spent the bulk of their lives intimately entwined in the social, economic, and political fabric of their home counties. Here, they sat at the apex of a rural society containing anywhere from a few hundred to more than a thousand households. Wealth in land and slaves nearly always set them apart from their neighbors, but in Piedmont counties like Halifax such distinctions were less marked and sometimes blurred. The vast majority also held office as vestrymen of the local parish or justices of the county court, some were militia officers, and a few had taken a turn as county sheriff. In Lancaster and Fairfax all burgesses served in one or more of these local offices, although in Accomack a few had only limited experience in county government.

As the western reaches of established counties became separate entities during the eighteenth century, new political communities emerged and old ones were redefined. When Fairfax split from Prince William in 1742, it took with it a number of experienced leaders, who now blended the traditions of the older county with the realities of the newly developing area. In contrast, the creation of Halifax out of Lunenburg County in 1752 removed few leaders from the older county and forced the new unit to redefine its political community. While a fairly recognizable gentry of several dozen families emerged to lead most Tidewater counties by the early eighteenth century, turnover in local offices often remained high in newer areas, preventing the formation of a long-standing and stable leadership group.

The composition, stability, and public habits of the leadership core determined to a large extent how elites experienced political community in each locale. Where a finite and stable gentry—often closely linked by marriage—peacefully shared both major local offices and burgess service, the electoral arena remained tranquil, and few real contests occurred. Tidewater counties below the Rappahannock and especially along the James River typified such patterns, but a nearly equal number of Piedmont areas shared these traits. In these newer and still sparsely settled regions, one or two powerful families often captured county and parish leadership at an early stage and, with few rivals, held burgess service for decades. Campaigning rarely occurred, and only to demonstrate their munificence did candidates, like the Cabells of Amherst, treat the freeholders with food and drink. Political community here was primarily consensual and noncompetitive.[1]

The gentry in other locales witnessed a different form of political community. Geography frequently played a critical role. The Corotoman River divided Lancaster into two large, rural, and distinct neighborhoods, each revolving around a major family, a separate parish and church, and a separate tobacco warehouse. The vast expanse of Halifax until its division in 1767 fostered divisions between eastern and western elites, as did the agitation for greater access to parish and county services before Fairfax split in 1757. Similarly, the need for conveniently located and well-maintained places of worship helped divide the gentry of Accomack County for nearly half a century. The gentry here and elsewhere often viewed these geographically based, but local, problems from a selfish perspective, knowing that a new parish would create twelve new vestrymen and that a new county would create another county court and two more seats in the House of Burgesses.

While a few among Virginia's gentry complained about the burdens of public service, in most counties there was an ample supply of candidates for local and provincial office. Disagreements and rivalries between gentry families took many forms, including direct appeals to the governor and Council or petitions to the House of Burgesses in Williamsburg. Frequently, however, burgess elections provided a convenient local arena to settle disputes. Campaigning now became essential, and candidates sought every possible opportunity to ignite the flame of burgessing as they mingled with freeholders at militia musters, church services, court days, horse races, and other festive occasions. Although the Anglo-American code of civic virtue dictated that candidates stand on their character and not their position on issues, close contests often tempted men to make wild promises and to use food and drink to influence voting behavior. The gentry of these counties experienced political community as contentious, often bitter, heated, and highly competitive.

Rivalries among the leading families of the most highly competitive county communities encouraged the gentry to seek a consensual patriarchy within smaller, more manageable, arenas. In Fairfax and Halifax, for example, leaders in the westernmost parts of the original counties sought new administrative units—first parishes and then separate counties—where they no longer had to compete for power, prestige, and place with the established east-county families. Once formed into new counties, these smaller political communities often became a good deal more tranquil than the original and larger parent county. Loudoun was less competitive than older Fairfax, peaceful Pittsylvania contrasted sharply with contentious Halifax, while Amherst and Buckingham became essentially family preserves of the Cabells when each county split from moderately competitive Albemarle.

Nearly a century earlier, similar forces as well as geography had encouraged the development of separate communities within Lancaster County. Here, the personal ambitions of several powerful gentry families combined with a practical need for accessible places of worship and responsible local authority to create two Anglican parishes, which existed de facto if not de jure for three-quarters of a century. Similarly, the exclusivity and irresponsibility of the Accomack parish vestry shut out numerous gentry families from positions of power and authority and eventually led to the creation of a new parish within this Eastern Shore county.

While subcounty units such as parishes enhanced opportunities for the creation of consensual political communities, smaller units held even greater promise. Ensconced among several dozen families scattered along a Tidewater inlet or Piedmont creek, a man with moderate wealth and a local marital tie could emerge as the leader and spokesman for the smallest example of political community. As a member of the twelve-person parish vestry, he voted for repairs to the nearest church or lobbied for the erection of a new chapel close by. As a justice of the peace, he facilitated his neighbors' dealings with the court and showed compassion and understanding when they ran afoul of the law. In return, families in most Tidewater and some Piedmont neighborhoods showed him respect and deference but also looked to him to represent their interests to the larger world. The size, homogeneity, and stability of these rural neighborhoods as well as the existence of an easily identified gentry leader within them determined the level of political solidarity.

Most Virginians of the Tidewater and many from the Piedmont experienced community—social, economic, and political—within these intimate rural neighborhoods. Connected by kinship and economic ties, these families shared the perils of shifting tobacco prices, floods, droughts, crop blights, livestock diseases, and a host of other factors related to the annual agricultural cycle. The provincial and imperial world of Williamsburg and London rarely concerned or influenced them, but the activities of the parish vestry and the county court did. The construction or repair of churches, roads, and bridges affected their economic and religious well-being but also had an impact on the assessment of parish and county levies each year. The creation of a new parish or county might provide better access to local governmental services but was almost certain to raise taxes. As long as neighborhood families and the gentry who led them remained satisfied with the balance between services and taxes, then vestries and courts operated happily for decades. However, dissatisfaction with local government often spurred neighborhood gentry both to organize petitions addressed to the House or the Council in Williamsburg and to challenge those holding burgess seats.

A contested election for the House of Burgesses brought into being a political community that included rich and poor, free and slave, male and female. In addition to the candidates, the most important part of this political community was an enfranchised electorate composed of white adult male landowners and long-term tenants. On average, about half of the white adult males owned the one hundred acres of unimproved land or the twenty-five acres of improved land needed to vote, while another fifth held life leases to similar properties. Although only these subjects of the Crown voted, the rest of the community often became part of the election process. Disfranchised white adult males still received treats at militia musters, along with their enfranchised comrades, and many probably journeyed to the courthouse on election day to witness the polling. Some would eventually own or lease the requisite acres and one day join the electorate. Women served food and drink for their candidate husbands; voters' wives shared in the political discourse of the campaign; and through land they owned, women facilitated the enfranchisement of husbands under common-law coverture and of brothers and sons through outright deeds and gifts. Slaves and servants maintained the greatest distance from this political process, but they too helped serve treats and milled about on election day as their masters voted.[2]

A variety of factors conditioned the response of local families to countywide elections: distance to the courthouse, time of year, state of the roads, but also political calculations. If the neighborhood leader decided to stand for one of the county's two seats in the House of Burgesses, local freeholders streamed to the courthouse on election day to support him. Such loyalties grew out of more than deference; they combined an intimate knowledge of the man—his character, behavior, and reputation—with a sense of local pride. Their neighborhood voting bloc might be just enough to tip the countywide scales in the direction of their candidate, and thus someone they knew would be traveling periodically to interact with other burgesses in Williamsburg. A burgess who knew his neighborhood could also help solve local problems: he could facilitate the presentation of a petition to build a new tobacco warehouse, erect a new town, or split a parish or county. He could seek relief for local inhabitants from natural disasters, ask for new vestry elections, and help or hinder an applicant wanting to establish a new ferry service. An especially competitive election with local issues at stake or local men running sometimes encouraged more than 80 percent of the electorate to make the trip to the courthouse.

When local problems appeared minimal, when no familiar leader sought election, or when incumbents seemed likely to win, the number of persons venturing out of the neighborhood on election day decreased. In most locations, those staying home fell economically at the bottom of the electorate. Using credit obtained within the neighborhood and dependent upon their own labor on their hundred or so acres, these small planters maintained a narrow perspective on the world and reacted only to the most local of issues. Those making the journey to the courthouse for a minimally competitive election often owned well-above-average farms, had a few slaves or servants to help with the work, and in general interacted economically and socially with a broader segment of the county population. They also shared in the duties and responsibilities of the larger community, as they acted as processioners for the parish or jurors for the county court. Life-lease tenants, too, appeared at elections on occasion, sometimes voting less frequently than landowners but in some locales often exercising their tenuous franchise. While on average two-thirds of county electorates voted, elections with less at stake might muster as little as one-quarter of those eligible.

When freeholders gave their votes at the courthouse on election day, they did so in ways that mirrored their place in, and their perspectives on, their small corner of the world. Not surprisingly, and when given a choice, they tended to support candidates from their neighborhood rather than those who lived at the other end of the county. This was particularly true of the poorest freeholders, who adhered to neighborhood favorite sons in the face of what must have been overwhelming evidence that the local candidate had no chance of winning the countywide contest. To the contrary, larger planters with a broader circle of contacts were the first to abandon local candidates in favor of those who had shown success in the bigger arenas of county administration or in actual service in Williamsburg. Moreover, their regularized interaction with the county political community put them in the thick of intraelite squabbles and meant that, at election time, they were more likely than their poorer neighbors to follow the advice of county leaders and to understand and vote for factions or pairs of candidates running in concert. Ultimately, the remarkable consistency over time in voting behavior suggests that large and small freeholders alike took into account a variety of factors, including deference, respect, familiarity, pride, as well as their own social, economic, and political well-being.

Freeholders living along the inlets, creeks, and hillsides of colonial Virginia took only occasional notice of events in Williamsburg and rarely thought much about developments in the metropolitan center in London. Yet, despite their apparent isolation from both, provincial and imperial events had a considerable impact on the political lives of these men and the political communities they inhabited, especially in the final decades of the colonial era. In the 1730s, the controversy over the Tobacco Inspection Act brought provincial decision making into direct conflict with the economic well-being of small planters, initiating not only riots and protests in some counties but heated electoral contests that unseated numerous incumbents.

In a similar way, those frontier counties most worried about

provincial defense policies during the French and Indian War witnessed minor but measurable response in local electoral politics.
Following the war, however, imperial measures designed to increase
revenues and tighten the administration of the empire brought forth
determined resistance from the burgesses and then swift dissolutions of assemblies by angry governors. The accession of George III
in 1760 and the arrival of two new governors after 1765 further accelerated the frequency of general elections, producing myriad local
responses. The shorter intervals between contests and the emerging
patriotic solidarity against the mother country discouraged rising
local leaders from challenging sitting incumbents. In most counties,
fewer candidates ran, competition decreased, and only the most politically active of the freeholders bothered to vote. Yet, the competitive nature of elections in some locales as late as 1774 reminds us
that, even in the midst of a deepening imperial crisis, the small
planters of colonial Virginia often saw no farther than the boundaries of their familiar rural neighborhoods.

   Provincial politicians and long-established gentry families found
these final decades of the colonial period disturbing; their letters, diaries, and public utterances reveal a nervous uncertainty about the
future. Although the source of such anxieties was in part the developing imperial crisis, the increasing debt under the tobacco culture,
an expanding slave population, growing religious dissent, and perhaps a general weakening of patriarchal authority, these Virginians
also expressed concern that the civic-minded politics of their youth
were giving way to a less-virtuous and corrupting public culture.[3] In
the final decade before independence, they lamented unexpected defeat on the hustings, despaired over electioneering and treating, and
longed for "Gentlemen, who are sensible and judicious, of in-
coruptible Integrity, firm and unshaken."[4] Yet despite much grum-
bling, it is not entirely clearly that the provincial political culture
as a whole had turned sharply in some dark and ominous direction.
Landon Carter declared outrage at his own defeat in 1768 but had
spent the 1730s and 1740s trying to unseat established incumbents;
Theodorick Bland Sr. seemed shocked in 1765 that a friend had been
"swilling the planters with bumbo," but the practice had occurred
in his home county for at least a decade; and the writer who warned
in 1771 against candidates with "sinister Designs and secret Machinations" came from a county where long-established gentry families had engaged in less than virtuous activities for nearly a centu-

ry.[5] For most long-serving incumbents and even some newcomers, the 1760s and 1770s were more, not less, secure: competition subsided, contested elections decreased, and voter support solidified around experienced legislators. If some of the Virginia gentry seemed frustrated with the local political culture during these years, it was only because they had less opportunity than their fathers to stand and win a burgess poll.

The legacy of this colonial political culture continued to reverberate in Virginia and the nation for years to come. This localized and personal vision of politics apparently combined with patriotic solidarity (created before independence) and annual elections (mandated by the new state constitution in 1776) to keep electoral competition to a minimum during the war years.[6] While an occasional contest stirred the political waters in specific communities, competition remained low until the turn of the century, when developing national and state political party rhetoric began to penetrate the rural neighborhoods of the Old Dominion.[7] The lingering vision of those neighborhood, parish, and county political communities continued to hold for decades. Clearly, one side of the constitutional debate of the 1780s and the partisan bickering of the early republic centered on a vision of politics and representation firmly anchored in the intimate, personal, and familiar world of the colonial political community.

Notes

Introduction

1. J. Franklin Jameson, "Virginian Voting in the Colonial Period (1744–1774)," *Nation*, Apr. 27, 1893, 309–10.

2. Ibid.; Lyon Tyler, "Virginians Voting in the Colonial Period," *William and Mary Quarterly*, 1st ser., 6 (1898): 7–13.

3. Jack P. Greene, "Society, Ideology, and Politics: An Analysis of the Political Culture of Mid-Eighteenth-Century Virginia," in *Society, Freedom, and Conscience: The American Revolution in Virginia, Massachusetts, and New York*, ed. Richard M. Jellison (New York: W. W. Norton, 1976), 22–23.

4. For a long time, historians imagined communities existed only if they resembled, spatially and organizationally, the towns of New England. Even some recent work describes only a "dispersal of the bonds of society" and "intermittent . . . participation in community in Virginia." See Rhys Isaac, *The Transformation of Virginia, 1740–1790* (Chapel Hill: University of North Carolina Press, 1982), 116. The most detailed examination of the complexities of rural Chesapeake society are found in Darrett B. Rutman and Anita H. Rutman, *A Place in Time: Middlesex County, Virginia, 1650–1750* (New York: W. W. Norton, 1984), esp. chaps. 4, 5, 8; Allan Kulikoff, *Tobacco and Slaves: The Development of Southern Cultures in the Chesapeake, 1680–1800* (Chapel Hill: University of North Carolina Press, 1986), esp. chap. 6. The most important discussions of the concept of community and the implications for studies of regions outside New England include Darrett B. Rutman, "Community Study," *Historical Methods* 13 (1980): 29–41; Rutman and Rutman, *A Place in Time*, 12, 21–25; Richard R. Beeman, "The New Social History and the Search for 'Community' in Colonial America," *American Quarterly* 29 (1977): 422–43; Richard R. Beeman, *The Evolution of the Southern Backcountry: A Case Study of Lunenburg County, Virginia, 1746–1832* (Philadelphia: University of Pennsylvania Press, 1984), 8–9.

5. Alan Tully, *Forming American Politics: Ideals, Interests, and Institutions in Colonial New York and Pennsylvania* (Baltimore: Johns Hopkins University Press, 1994), 370–77, also notes the popularity of the client/patron and deference models in explaining the political culture of a number of British colonies.

6. Charles Beard and Mary Beard, *The Rise of American Civilization*, vol. 1, *The Agricultural Era* (New York: Macmillan, 1927), 109, 110, 127–28, 183.

7. Robert E. Brown and B. Katherine Brown, *Virginia, 1705–1782: Democracy or Aristocracy?* (East Lansing: Michigan State University Press, 1963), esp. 3–5, 308.

8. Isaac, *The Transformation of Virginia*, 56, 111–14.

9. J. R. Pole, *Political Representation in England and the Origins of American Democracy* (New York: Macmillan, 1966), 23, 136–37, 149–51, 155–56.

10. Edmund S. Morgan, *Inventing the People: The Rise of Popular Sovereignty in England and America* (New York: W. W. Norton, 1988), 174, 185, 197, 207.

11. Charles Sydnor, *Gentlemen Freeholders: Political Practices in Washington's Virginia* (Chapel Hill: University of North Carolina Press, 1952); reissued as *American Revolutionaries in the Making* (New York: W. W. Norton, 1965), 14, 20, 35, 62, 70, 73.

12. Those painting a static, although often differing, picture include Sydnor, *Gentlemen Freeholders;* Brown and Brown, *Virginia;* Richard L. Morton, *Colonial Virginia*, vol. 2, *Westward Expansion and Prelude to Revolution, 1710–1763* (Chapel Hill: University of North Carolina Press, 1960), 718–20; Edmund S. Morgan, *American Slavery, American Freedom: The Ordeal of Colonial Virginia* (New York: W. W. Norton, 1975), 364; Morgan, *Inventing the People*, 174–208.

13. Morton, *Colonial Virginia*, 2:490–513.

14. Jack P. Greene, "The Growth of Political Stability: An Interpretation of Political Developments in the Anglo-American Colonies, 1660–1760," in *The American Revolution: A Heritage of Change*, ed. John Parker and Carol Urness (Minneapolis: Associates of the James Ford Bell Library, 1975), 48–49; John C. Rainbolt, "The Alteration in the Relationship between Leadership and Constituents in Virginia, 1660 to 1720," *William and Mary Quarterly*, 3d ser., 17 (1970): 411–34. See also Jack P. Greene, "Reply," *American Historical Review* 75 (1969): 364–67; Jack P. Greene, "Changing Interpretations of Early American Politics," in *The Reinterpretation of Early American History: Essays in Honor of John Edwin Pomfret*, ed. Ray Allen Billington (San Marino, Calif.: Huntington Library, 1966).

15. Bernard Bailyn, *The Origins of American Politics* (New York: Random House, 1967), 87–90, 123.

16. Lucille Griffith believes that provincial and imperial affairs did influence local elections, but she does not make clear what the precise impact may have been. See Lucille Griffith, *The Virginia House of Burgesses, 1750–1774* (University: University of Alabama Press, 1970), 47–48. Robert Dinkin suggests that electoral battles declined during the confrontation with England. See Robert J. Dinkin, *Voting in Provincial America: A Study of Elections in the Thirteen Colonies, 1689–1776* (Westport, Conn.: Greenwood Press, 1977), 187.

17. See n. 12, above.

18. Griffith, *The Virginia House of Burgesses*, 66, 84; Richard R. Beeman, "Robert Munford and the Political Culture of Frontier Virginia," *Journal of American Studies* 12 (1978): 171.

19. Ibid., 176–79, 182; Beeman, *The Evolution of the Southern Backcountry*, 12, 21, 88–96.

20. Isaac, *The Transformation of Virginia*, 153, 163–64, 173, 259, 276; Isaac's argument is summarized in "Evangelical Revolt: The Nature of the Baptists' Challenge to the Traditional Order in Virginia, 1765 to 1775," *William and Mary Quarterly*, 3d ser., 31 (1974): 345–68. See also, Richard R. Beeman, "Social Change and Cultural Conflict in Virginia: Lunenburg County, 1746–1776," *William and Mary Quarterly*, 3d ser., 35 (1978): 455–76.

21. U.S. Bureau of the Census, *Historical Statistics of the United States, Colonial Times to 1957* (Washington, D.C.: Government Printing Office, 1960), 756.

Chapter 1: The Political Culture of Elections

1. The play, written by Robert Munford in 1770, first appeared in print in 1798, with a prologue by an unknown writer. See Jay B. Hubbell and Douglass Adair, "Robert Munford's *The Candidates*," *William and Mary Quarterly*, 3d ser., 5 (1948): 217–57.

2. Ibid., 257.

3. Varying interpretations of the play can be found in Sydnor, *Gentlemen Freeholders*, 44–47, 49–50, 133; Morton, *Colonial Virginia*, 2:720; Brown and Brown, *Virginia*, 169, 236–37; Griffith, *The Virginia House of Burgesses*, 61–63; Morgan, *American Slavery*, 363–64; Beeman, *The Evolution of the Southern Backcountry*, 88–93.

4. Hubbell and Adair, "Robert Munford's *The Candidates*," 222; Brown and Brown, *Virginia*, 237.

5. Morgan, *American Slavery*, 364.

6. Richard Beeman, "Robert Munford and the Political Culture of Frontier Virginia," *American Studies* 12 (1978): 169–83; Richard Beeman, "Deference, Republicanism, and the Emergence of Popular Politics in Eigh-

teenth-Century America," *William and Mary Quarterly*, 3d ser., 49 (1992), 407–8.

7. Beeman, "Robert Munford," 172–74.

8. William W. Hening, *The Statutes at Large; Being a Collection of All the Laws of Virginia, from the First Session of the Legislature, in the Year 1619* (Richmond, 1809–23), 1:412. Hereafter, Hening.

9. Hening, 3:244.

10. Theodorick Bland to John Randolph Sr., Sept. 20, 1771, Bryan Papers, University of Virginia Library. Hereafter, Bryan Papers.

11. H. R. McIlwaine and John Kennedy, eds., *Journals of the House of Burgesses of Virginia* (Richmond: Colonial Press, 1905–15), *1742–1749*, 266–67. Hereafter, *JHB*.

12. Halifax, 1753: *JHB, 1752–1758*, 153, 160.

13. Abraham Maury to Col. Theodorick Bland Sr., July 17, 1758, Charles Campbell, ed., *The Bland Papers* (Petersburg, Va., 1840), 1:12.

14. *JHB, 1766–1769*, 230–31.

15. Fincastle, 1773: *JHB, 1773–1776*, 86. Officeholders had to resign their legislative posts after such an appointment and had to stand a by-election to see if the voters wanted a representative not fully independent of governmental influence. Apparently, Doak sinned by running in a regular general election knowing that he would have to resign shortly.

16. *JHB, 1752–1758*, 436–37; *JHB, 1758–1761*, 5.

17. Jack P. Greene, *Quest for Power: The Lower Houses of Assembly in the Southern Royal Colonies, 1689–1776* (Chapel Hill: University of North Carolina Press, 1963), 187–88.

18. *JHB, 1727–1740*, 60, 62–63, 75; Hening, 4:292–93.

19. Morgan, *American Slavery*, 361.

20. *JHB, 1727–1740*, 80.

21. Ibid., 274–75, 258, 264–65.

22. Hening, 4:481–82.

23. *Executive Journals of the Council of Colonial Virginia* (Richmond: Virginia State Library, 1966), 4:618. Hereafter, *EJC*.

24. *JHB, 1766–1769*, 216–18.

25. *EJC*, 4:236.

26. See John Woodbridge, "To . . . the Freeholders of Richmond, July 5, 1765," Landon Carter Papers, University of Virginia Library. Hereafter, Landon Carter Papers.

27. *EJC*, 5:330–31.

28. Woodbridge was still alive in mid-May (*JHB, 1766–1769*, 199), but an estate sale occurred in late July. See Robert Wormeley Carter Diary, College of William and Mary Library. Hereafter, Robert Wormeley Carter Diary.

29. Robert A. Rutland, ed., *The Papers of George Mason, 1725–1792*

(Chapel Hill: University of North Carolina Press, 1970), 1:lxviii–lxix.

30. Jack P. Greene, ed., *The Diary of Landon Carter of Sabine Hall, 1752–1778* (Charlottesville: University Press of Virginia, 1965), 2:1008–9.

31. Landon Carter had also considered withdrawing from politics in 1765 and may have found the heated campaign polemics of 1768 not much to his liking. See Landon Carter Papers.

32. Robert Wormeley Carter Diary, July 14, 15, 30, Aug. 7, Sept. 22, 1769.

33. Richmond County Order Book 16, 491–97, Virginia State Library. Hereafter, VSL.

34. Rutland, *The Papers of George Mason*, 1:cvii.

35. Details of Washington's life follow the general outline presented in Douglas Southall Freeman, *George Washington: A Biography*, 7 vols. (New York: Scribner's, 1948–57).

36. Ibid., 3:222–25.

37. Donald Jackson, ed., *The Diaries of George Washington* (Charlottesville: University Press of Virginia, 1976), 2:153–54, 157–60.

38. Washington to Burwell Bassett, June 18, W. W. Abbot, ed., *The Papers of George Washington, Colonial Series*, 10 vols. (Charlottesville: University Press of Virginia, 1983–95), 8:217.

39. Jackson, *The Diaries of George Washington*, 2:165–68; George Washington to John Armstrong, Aug. 18, 1769, Abbot, *The Papers of George Washington, Colonial Series*, 8:240–41.

40. Jackson, *The Diaries of George Washington*, 2:173–77, 180–81.

41. *EJC*, 5:373.

42. Morton, *Colonial Virginia*, 2:596–98, 600.

43. Isaac, *The Transformation of Virginia*, 148–50.

44. *JHB, 1752–1758*, 61–62.

45. Ibid.

46. Ibid.; Hening, 3:243.

47. *JHB, 1761–1765*, 269–72.

48. Littlepage owned significant portions of land in several counties, including Hanover, Louisa, and Halifax, and first became a justice of the peace for Hanover in 1749; he may have still held that position in 1763. See *EJC*, 5:306, 317, 391, 455.

49. The Tobacco Inspection Act appears in Hening, 8:387–92.

50. *JHB, 1761–1765*, 269–72.

51. George Washington to John Augustine Washington, May 28, 1755, Abbot, *The Papers of George Washington, Colonial Series*, 1:290–91.

52. Dr. Theodorick Bland to John Randolph Sr., Sept. 20, 1771, Bryan Papers.

53. Edmund Pendleton to Joseph Chew, June 20, 1774, David J. Mayes, ed., *Letters and Papers of Edmund Pendleton, 1734–1803* (Charlottesville: University Press of Virginia, 1967), 1:94.

54. Mann Page Jr. to John Page, Feb. 2, 1771, Page-Walker Manuscripts, University of Virginia Library.

55. George Washington to Bryan Fairfax, July 4, 1774, Abbot, *The Papers of George Washington, Colonial Series*, 10:109–10; *The Journal of Nicholas Cresswell, 1774–1777* (New York: Dial Press, 1924), 27–28.

56. *Virginia Gazette*, June 1, 1769 (Rind).

57. *Virginia Gazette*, Sept. 14, 1769; *Virginia Gazette*, July 14, 1774. See also Isaac, *The Transformation of Virginia*, 253.

58. *JHB, 1727–1740*, 31–32.

59. Richard Adams to Dear Brother [Thomas], Oct. 19, 1771, Adams Family Papers, Virginia Historical Society. Hereafter, Adams Family Papers.

60. *JHB, 1770–1772*, 83–84.

61. *JHB, 1742–1749*, 34; *JHB, 1752–1758*, 457, 61–62.

62. *JHB, 1727–1740*, 251.

63. Two views of this practice prevail: one assumes that all candidates "with hardly an exception, relied on the persuasive powers of food and drink" during the election campaign. See Sydnor, *Gentlemen Freeholders*, 53–59; Griffith, *The Virginia House of Burgesses*, 64. A second view maintains that treating deviated from the norm and represented an unnecessary activity in the "ideal deferential social order" that characterized the political culture of the older sections of Virginia. See Beeman, *The Evolution of the Southern Backcountry*, 91.

64. Hening, 3:243.

65. Accomack, 1738: *JHB, 1727–1740*, 370.

66. Dinwiddie, 1765: Theodorick Bland Sr., July 27, 1765, Campbell, *The Bland Papers*, 1:27.

67. Mann Page Jr. to John Page Jr., Feb. 2, 1771, Page-Walker Manuscripts.

68. *JHB, 1758–1761*, 83.

69. Hanover, 1764: *JHB, 1761–1765*, 271.

70. John G. Kolp and Terri L. Snyder, "Gender, Property, and Voting Rights in Eighteenth-Century Virginia," paper presented at the conference The Many Legalities of Early America, Nov. 23, 1996, Williamsburg, Va.

71. King George, 1734, Prince William, 1735: *JHB, 1727–1740*, 209, 258; Prince George, 1752, Elizabeth City and Lunenburg, 1755: *JHB, 1752–1758*, 49–50, 360, 457.

72. Lunenburg, 1771: *JHB, 1770–1772*, 289.

73. Accomack, 1738: *JHB, 1727–1740*, 370.

74. Hanover, 1764: *JHB, 1761–1765*, 271.

75. *JHB, 1752–1758*, 50. Other examples of treats given during the actual election include Hanover, 1735, Gloucester, 1740: *JHB, 1727–1740*, 265, 426; Richmond and Orange, 1741: *JHB, 1742–1748*, 34, 50–51; Lunen-

burg, 1755 and 1758: *JHB, 1752–1758*, 456–57, *JHB, 1758–1761*, 83–84.

76. Account Books, 1767–70, Jefferson Papers, Library of Congress.

77. Ibid.; Thomas Jefferson Accounts, 1764–79, Huntington Library.

78. Diary of William Cabell Sr., Mar. 22, 1769, VSL; William Cabell Commonplace Book, 1771, Virginia Historical Society (hereafter, VHS).

79. *The Journal of Nicholas Cresswell*, 27–28.

80. Jackson, *The Diaries of George Washington*, 2:113; 3:74, 261.

81. *EJC*, 6:635, 432.

82. Hening, 3:236.

83. *JHB, 1770–1772*, 195.

84. Richard Adams to Brother [Thomas], Jan. 1 and Mar. 24, 1772, Adams Family Papers.

85. *JHB, 1770–1772*, 173, 195.

86. *Virginia Gazette*, Mar. 12, 1772; Richard Adams to Brother [Thomas], Mar. 24, 1772, Adams Family Papers.

87. *EJC*, 6:281; *JHB, 1770–1772*, 290–91.

88. *JHB, 1770–1772*, 291.

89. *JHB, 1727–1740*, 31–32.

90. Ibid.

Chapter 2: The Colonial Electorate

1. This election scenario was constructed from a number of sources, including Lancaster County Rentals, 1748 and 1750, Brock Collection, Huntington Library (hereafter, Brock Collection); Lancaster County Rental for 1773, VHS; Lancaster County Deed Books 13, 14, 15, 16, and 18, VSL; and Christ Church Vestry Book, 1739–86 (copy, Historic Christ Church).

2. Robert Stewart to George Washington, Feb. 15, 1761, in Abbot, *The Papers of George Washington, Colonial Series*, 7:12–13.

3. To use the term *citizen* in a colonial context is technically, of course, anachronistic, as all persons—male and female, white and black—were subjects of the British Crown. Americans did not become citizens until 1776. The pre-1776 Anglo-American world did make a clear distinction, however, between subjects and citizen subjects, the latter having political rights and responsibilities. The terms *citizen subject, political subject-hood*, and *citizen* are used hereafter to refer to those adult white males who held such rights and responsibilities. For a recent discussion of these concepts, see Richard D. Brown, *The Strength of the People: The Idea of an Informed Citizenry in America, 1650–1870* (Chapel Hill: University of North Carolina Press, 1996), esp. chaps. 1, 2. T. H. Breen also calls our attention to some of these distinctions in "Equality in the British Empire: James Otis's Radical Critique of John Locke," unpublished paper (1995).

4. The Reverend Andrew Burnaby, *Travels through the Middle Settle-*

ments in North America in the Years 1759–1760, with Observations upon the State of the Colonies (London, 1775), 46.

5. Sir Lewis Namier, *The Structure of Politics at the Accession of George III*, 2d ed. (London: Macmillan 1961), 62; Cynthia Miller Leonard, comp., *The General Assembly of Virginia, July 30, 1619–January 11, 1978: A Bicentennial Register of Members* (Richmond: Virginia State Library, 1978), 74–75. Hereafter, *GAV.*

6. Namier, *The Structure of Politics*, 62–63.

7. Ibid., 65, 76, 80–81.

8. Williamsburg had 722 white residents in the 1780s; Jamestown had only twenty to thirty houses in 1697. See Evarts B. Greene and Virginia D. Harrington, *American Population before the Federal Census of 1790* (New York: Columbia University Press, 1932), 153, 145.

9. William A. Speck, *Tory and Whig: The Struggle in the Constituencies, 1701–1715* (London: Macmillan, 1970), 11.

10. *GAV*, 36, 68, 74–75, 78–80, 86–87, 91–93, 105–7.

11. Namier, *The Structure of Politics*, 64.

12. Hening, 1:333–34.

13. Hening, 1:411–12.

14. Hening, 1:403. A 1658 law combined provisions of the 1655 and 1656 acts, including the affirmation that all freemen could vote. See Hening, 1:475.

15. Hening, 2:280.

16. Hening, 2:356, 380–81.

17. Hening, 3:26, 240.

18. *JHB, 1727–1740*, 251, 256, 282–83.

19. *JHB, 1727–1740*, 2.

20. Hening, 4:475–78.

21. Hening, 7:518–30; Hening, 8:305–17.

22. Hening, 3:172, 174, 243; Hening, 4:133–34; Hening, 3:172.

23. Namier, *The Structure of Politics*, 75; Speck, *Tory and Whig*, 9.

24. As the third borough constituency, Norfolk first elected a burgess in 1738.

25. Hening, 4:476.

26. *JHB, 1761–1765*, 126, 127, 129, 130.

27. *JHB, 1770–1772*, 158, 163, 251–52.

28. Population figures for 1725 and 1775 are extrapolated from data in U.S. Bureau of the Census, *Historical Statistics*, 756; Kulikoff, *Tobacco and Slaves*, 320, 322, 335, 340.

29. Life leaseholders received freehold status in 1684 and 1705. See Hening, 3:26, 240.

30. Not all of these men owned the land used as the basis for their enfranchisement; 5–7 percent employed property their wives had brought into

the marriage. Legally entitled to full utilization of these lands under common-law coverture, many of these men remained permanently dependent upon their wives for their economic and political standing. See Kolp and Snyder, "Gender, Property, and Voting Rights."

31. *JHB, 1761–1765,* 128.

32. *JHB, 1727–1740,* 251, 256, 282–83.

33. Research on tenancy is scattered in a number of works and is often in disagreement; a full-scale study of the subject is needed. An older, but useful starting point is Willard F. Bliss, "Rise of Tenancy in Virginia," *Virginia Magazine of History and Biography* 58 (1950): 427–41.

34. Kulikoff, *Tobacco and Slaves,* 131.

35. Brown and Brown, *Virginia,* 142. These authors used the extremely crude estimates of the number of freeholders who paid quitrents compiled by Council President John Blair in the early 1760s, which taken at face value do indeed suggest that the electorate comprised 80–90 percent of the adult white male population. See John Blair, "List of Virginia Counties and Estimated Number of Freeholders, 1763," British Library Add. Mss 38337, 321 (copy, Colonial Williamsburg).

36. Loudoun County was formed from the western two-thirds of Fairfax County in 1757 and probably exhibited similar tenancy patterns. One estimate suggests that in 1782 one-third of the adult white men in Loudoun were tenants. See Bliss, "Rise of Tenancy," 429. A detailed examination of county records after 1757 reveal more than two hundred life leases, of which 95 percent may have been eligible to vote. See Brown and Brown, *Virginia,* 144. Estimates of the size of the electorates in Fairfax in 1744–48 and 1765–68 and in Halifax in 1764–65 and 1768–69 are based on the number of persons actually voting in several elections in each of these periods.

37. A general discussion of the provincial and imperial factors influencing competition is found in chapter, 3, below and in John G. Kolp, "The Dynamics of Electoral Competition in Pre-Revolutionary Virginia," *William and Mary Quarterly,* 3d ser., 49 (Oct. 1992): 652–74.

38. Turnout rates can be calculated for one hundred elections held in twenty-two counties between 1735 and 1774; both total number of voters and the total adult white male population, or close estimations thereof, are available.

39. Kulikoff, *Tobacco and Slaves,* 110–13. The 1735 pollbook is found in the Brock Collection.

40. The 215 voters in this election represented 38 percent of adult white males and 53 percent of the electorate; Richmond County Order Book 13, 338–40, VSL.

41. Collation of the fourteen pollbooks from these elections as well as lists of landowners in 1748, 1750, and 1773 produced a list of 779 men who were eligible freeholders at some time during the period; 717 voted at least

once. See Lancaster County Deed Books 13, 14, 15, 16, 18, 19, VSL; Lancaster County Rentals, 1748 and 1750, Brock Collection; Lancaster County Rental for 1773, VHS.

42. Thirty-eight percent of voters in the eastern section of the county voted in both the 1764 and 1765 elections, as did 33 percent of those in the middle section, 25 percent of those in the western section, and 15 percent of those in the far western section. The eastern section is defined as that portion of the original county that would become the smaller Halifax County after the division of 1767; the middle section is present-day Pittsylvania County; the western section is Henry County; and the far western section is Patrick County. Residency is known for 434 (43%) of the pre-1767 voters. See also map 7.1, below.

43. Kulikoff, *Tobacco and Slaves*, 285. Kulikoff's analysis of published data on Lancaster County suggests that tenants voted less often than landowners (286). My analysis, however, makes a distinction between tenants who probably met the general freehold requirement (one hundred unimproved acres or twenty-five acres with a house), who could vote, and the majority of tenants, who probably did not meet this criteria.

Chapter 3: The Dynamics of Electoral Competition

1. Warren M. Billings, John E. Selby, and Thad W. Tate, *Colonial Virginia: A History* (White Plains, N.Y.: KTO Press, 1986), 234–36; *EJC*, 6: 151, 156.

2. Of the 882 elections examined here, 182 were by-elections.

3. Gilsdorf and Gilsdorf also emphasize the importance of choice as the determining factor in defining a competitive election. See Joy B. Gilsdorf and Robert R. Gilsdorf, "Elites and Electorates: Some Plain Truths for Historians of Colonial America," in *Saints and Revolutionaries: Essays on Early American History*, ed. David D. Hall, John M. Murrin, and Thad W. Tate (New York: W. W. Norton, 1984), 207–44.

4. In counting the number of candidates, a distinction is made between those who seriously offered themselves to the electors and those who received a handful of votes from close friends or respectful tenants but probably never announced a candidacy. It is, of course, impossible to know for certain whether all candidates actively sought election, but some criteria must be used to exclude unannounced candidates. Serious candidates are defined here as (1) any persons receiving at least 10 percent of the votes or a minimum of ten votes, or (2) any persons whose vote total is unknown but who are mentioned in documents from the period as contenders in an election.

5. Eleven percent represents 53 of the 468 contests for which information is available.

6. See, for example, the Prince William County election of 1761, *JHB, 1761–1765*, 126, 127, 129, 130; the Lunenburg election of 1771, *JHB,1770–1772*, 158, 163, 251–52.

7. See, for example, the Henrico election of 1771, *JHB,1770–1772*, 173, 195; the Westmoreland election of 1728, *JHB,1727–1740*, 31–32.

8. The presence or absence of competition can be determined for 491 of the 882 elections held during this period. Although the 35 percent figure may seem low, competition was probably lower in most colonies. Provinces with higher levels of competition usually experienced significant party or factional rivalry, a factor totally absent from the Virginia scene.

9. While the 1728 and 1735 figures are based upon data from only seven of thirty-one and twelve of thirty-eight elections, respectively, the remaining election tabulations include at least twenty elections; the 9 percent figure for 1774, for example, is based upon information from forty-seven of the sixty-five constituencies.

10. *JHB, 1727–1740*, 82; Billings, Selby, and Tate, *Colonial Virginia*, 237, 244; Kulikoff, *Tobacco and Slaves*, 110–13.

11. *JHB, 1727–1740*, 245–99 passim.

12. The British Septennial Act was passed in 1716; see J. H. Plumb, *The Growth of Political Stability in England, 1675–1725* (London: Macmillan, 1967), 174–75.

13. Billings, Selby, and Tate, *Colonial Virginia*, 245–47.

14. These two causes have also been noted by Griffith, *The Virginia House of Burgesses*, 47–48.

15. Francis Fauquier to the Board of Trade, May 12, 1761, George Reese, ed., *The Official Papers of Francis Fauquier, Lieutenant Governor of Virginia, 1758–1768*, 3 vols. (Charlottesville: University Press of Virginia, 1980–83), 2:524.

16. The southwestern frontier was especially nervous in the spring of 1758. See *EJC*, 6:91, 120, 124.

17. Morton, *Colonial Virginia*, 681–82.

18. For the most recent characterization of these elections as issueless and ritualistic, see Morgan, *Inventing the People*, 174, 185, 201.

19. *JHB, 1727–1740*, 18, 31–32, 189, 191, 210–11.

20. Westmoreland County Records and Inventories, 1723–46, 305–305a, VSL; Records and Inventories 2, 69a-71a, 184–186; Records and Inventories 3, 48a-49a, 70–72; Records 4, 25–28, 137–39.

21. *JHB, 1727–1740*, 258–65, 306, 334.

22. *JHB, 1752–1758*, 9, 57–58, 73, 81, 343, 348, 352; *JHB, 1758–1761*, 26, 29, 63, 98; *JHB, 1761–1765*, 17, 20, 23, 73–75, 80, 103–4, 122–23, 125–30; Prince William County Deed Book P, 68–73, VSL. In 1759, Prince William County was divided, the western two-thirds becoming Fauquier County.

23. *JHB, 1727–1740*, 245, 248, 252; *JHB, 1742–1749*, 8, 12, 36, 38, 51–52,

319, 321, 334–35; Amelia County Tithables, 1736–71, VSL; *Tyler's Quarterly Magazine of History and Biography* (1951) 33:54–59.

24. *Tyler's Quarterly Magazine of History and Biography* (1936) 17:244–47; Grigsby Papers, VHS; *JHB, 1761–1765,* 9, 15, 73–75, 83.

25. *JHB, 1742–1749,* 180, 197, 261, 264–65, 323; *JHB, 1752–1758,* 347–48, 381, 383, 422–23, 446–47. Gabriel Jones left Augusta County during the 1758 election to assist in the campaign, in nearby Frederick County, of his friend George Washington. Although Jones lost in Augusta, he had wisely put forward his name, and won, in Hampshire County. See George Washington to Gabriel Jones, July 29, 1758, Abbot, *The Papers of George Washington, Colonial Series,* 5:350.

26. *JHB, 1727–1740,* 189, 191; Brock Collection; Richmond County Account Book 1, 175–76; Order Book 12, 123–26, 353–55; Order Book 13, 338–40; Order Book 14, 264–68, 380–85; Order Book 16, 491–97; Order Book 17, 249–56, VSL; Robert Wormeley Carter Diary. See also John Woodbridge, "To . . . the Freeholders of Richmond, July 5, 1765," Landon Carter Papers.

27. Essex County Deed Book 22, 309–14; Deed Book 24, 275–80; Deed Book 25, 301–7; Deed Book 27, 248–52; Deed Book 28, 95–99; Deed Book 29, 1–7; Deed Book 30, 235–42, 243–48, 318–24, 385, 496–502, VSL.

28. *JHB, 1752–1758,* 339, 342, 344, 348–49, 358–61, 381; *JHB, 1761–1765,* 9, 15–16, 18, 37, 73, 75, 86–90, 94–96; Elizabeth County Deed Book E, 8–10; County Deeds and Wills, 1763–71, 77–77a, VSL; *Virginia Gazette,* Sept. 14, 1769.

29. Spotsylvania County Deed Book F; County Will Book B; County Will Book D, VSL.

30. Norfolk County Deed Book 24, VSL; Thomas M. Costa, "Economic Development and Political Authority: Norfolk, Virginia, Merchant-Magistrates, 1736–1800" (Ph.D. diss., College of William and Mary, 1991), 157–58.

31. *JHB, 1727–1740,* 248, 274.

32. *JHB, 1727–1740,* 276, 282–83. Randolph continued as speaker because he had been elected to represent the College of William and Mary.

33. See Kolp, "The Dynamics of Electoral Competition," 666–67.

34. For a discussion of the analytical ramifications of missing information and silence in the historical record, see ibid., 654, 663–64.

35. John Hammond Moore, *Albemarle: Jefferson's County, 1727–1976* (Charlottesville: University Press of Virginia for the Albemarle County Historical Society, 1976), 22, 25–30, 38–41; *GAV,* 86, 88; *EJC,* 6:51. Cabell family activities in the period 1747–51 are well documented in Robert Rose Diary, VSL.

36. "Justices of the Peace of Colonial Virginia, 1757–1775," *Bulletin of the Virginia State Library* 14 (1921): 64, 77, 113, 127; Tillotson Parish Records, VSL. The May 7, 1765, Commission of the Peace for Buckingham

listed a "Jacob" Cabell, which may have been another name for John.

37. Jackson Turner Main, "The One Hundred," *William and Mary Quarterly*, 3d ser., 11 (1954); William Cabell Jr. Papers, VSL; Amherst County Order Book, 1766–69, VSL; "Justices of the Peace of Colonial Virginia"; *GAV*, 88–174 passim; Norman K. Risjord, *Chesapeake Politics, 1781–1800* (New York: Columbia University Press, 1978), 300–301.

38. William Cabell Commonplace Book.

39. *GAV*, 74–124, passim; *Virginia Gazette*, July 14, 1774 (Rind); *JHB, 1752–1755*, 33.

40. *GAV*, 74–107, passim; further information on Donelson's activities are included in chapter 7.

41. Rutman and Rutman, *A Place in Time*, 223–24, 228, 247.

42. Controversies over representation occurred in Charles City in 1703 and 1710, but thereafter the Acrill, Kennon, and Harrison families dominated. See *GAV*, 62, 65. Three members of the Burwell family served James City after 1741. Two generations of Bridgers held seats in Isle of Wight County during the periods 1705–32 and 1755–74; two Bridgers were elected in 1758 and 1761. See *GAV*, 62–107, passim.

43. Greene and Harrington, *American Population before the Federal Census of 1790*, 145, 153; Thomas J. Wertenbaker, *Norfolk: Historic Southern Port*, 2d ed., ed. Marvin W. Schlegel (Durham, N.C.: Duke University Press, 1962), 6.

44. *GAV*, 62–107, passim.

45. *JHB, 1752–1758*, 41; Greene, *The Diary of Landon Carter of Sabine Hall*, 1:78–79; John Randolph Notebook, 1826, VHS; *Virginia Gazette*, Aug. 10, 1769, Nov. 21, 1771, July 7, 1774 (Rind).

46. Costa, "Economic Development and Political Authority," 86–87, 159; *Virginia Gazette*, June 1, 1769 (Rind); *GAV*, 77–106, passim.

47. Analysis shows that the electoral intensity of a particular era influenced the level of electoral intensity in newly created constituencies: 36 percent of the elections were competitive in counties created before 1728, 47 percent were competitive in counties created between 1730 and 1746, and only 19 percent were competitive in counties created after 1749. See John G. Kolp, "The Flame of Burgessing: Elections and Political Communities in Colonial Virginia" (Ph.D. diss., University of Iowa, 1988), 160–62.

48. These alternative styles of leadership were first articulated in Greene, "Society, Ideology, and Politics," 54–57, and are given a geographical dimension in Jack P. Greene, "'Virtus et Libertas': Political Culture, Social Change, and the Origins of the American Revolution in Virginia, 1763–1776," in *The Southern Experience in the American Revolution*, ed. Jeffrey J. Crow and Larry E. Tise (Chapel Hill: University of North Carolina Press, 1978), 62–63. See also Billings, Selby, and Tate, *Colonial Virginia*, 271.

49. The familiar interaction between burgesses and constituents in the southern Tidewater is best illustrated by the ways in which citizens greeted returning legislators from the borough of Norfolk, Elizabeth City, Williamsburg, and Prince George following the dissolution of the assemblies in 1769 and 1774.

50. On tenancy rates, see Bliss, "Rise of Tenancy"; Jackson Turner Main, "The Distribution of Property in Post-Revolution Virginia," *Mississippi Valley Historical Review* 41 (1954–55): 244–45, 248; Brown and Brown, *Virginia*, 13, 198–200; Kulikoff, *Tobacco and Slaves*, 135, 156.

51. On land acquisition and settlement patterns that followed these river basins westward, see "The One Hundred," 359.

Chapter 4: Accomack County

1. Letter, "My Dear Countrymen," signed "No Party Man," *Virginia Gazette*, Apr. 11, 1771 (Purdie and Dixon).

2. This estimate is from a report of total tithables in Accomack County Orders, 1724–31, VSL.

3. As vacancies on the county court occurred, the governor and Council appointed new members, although in practice the sitting justices usually recommended replacements. Periodically, a full "commission of the peace" was issued for individual counties, but again the sitting justices usually provided the list of nominees; see, for example, *EJC*, 5.

4. Beginning in 1740, the House attempted to address a growing problem of inoperative vestries by dissolving all of them throughout the colony and calling for new elections. The Council rejected this attempt and several others in the 1740s. See *JHB, 1727–1740*, 418, 420, 422, 423; *JHB, 1742–1749*, 334. The House and Council did agree to dissolve a few individual vestries—for example, those of Elizabeth City in 1728 and Prince William and Stafford Counties in 1757.

5. Charles Francis Cocke, *Parish Lines Diocese of Southern Virginia* (Richmond: Virginia State Library, 1964), 187–91; Ralph T. Whitelaw, *Virginia's Eastern Shore: A History of Northampton and Accomack Counties* (Richmond: Virginia State Library, 1951; reprint, Gloucester, Mass.: Peter Smith, 1968), 2:1396.

6. Whitelaw, *Virginia's Eastern Shore*, 2:1344; Accomack Vestry Order Book, VSL.

7. Susie M. Ames, ed., *County Court Records of Accomack-Northampton, Virginia, 1640–1645* (Charlottesville: University Press of Virginia, 1973), xv–xvi; Accomack County Orders, VSL; *EJC*, 4:12, 348, 361; Whitelaw, *Virginia's Eastern Shore*, 1:620–21; *GAV*, 72.

8. Richard Drummond owned six hundred acres along Guilford Creek

in the north-central part of the county. He represented Accomack in the House of Burgesses from 1703 to 1715, was a long-time member of the county court, served as sheriff in 1728, and died in 1731. See, "Virginia Quit Rent Rolls, 1704: Accomack Rent Roll," *Virginia Magazine of History and Biography* 34 (1926): 253; Accomack County Orders, VSL; Whitelaw, *Virginia's Eastern Shore*, 2:1111.

9. *JHB, 1702–1712*, 275, 278, 281, 322; *JHB, 1712–1726*, 138. Coincidentally, in 1716, the British Parliament passed the Septennial Act, which regulated elections to the House of Commons; the Virginia government adhered to this act for the remainder of the colonial period. See Plumb, *The Growth of Political Stability in England*, 173–74.

10. George C. Mason, "The Six Earliest Churches on the Eastern Shore of Virginia," *Willliam and Mary Quarterly*, 2d ser., 21 (1941): 198; Whitelaw, *Virginia's Eastern Shore*, 2:702–4.

11. *JHB, 1712–1726*, 279, 289, 291, 293, 304, 334, 336–37, 344, 353; Hening, 4:116.

12. *GAV*, 72.

13. *JHB, 1712–1726*, 406; H. R. McIlwaine, ed., *Legislative Journals of the Council of Colonial Virginia*, (Richmond: Colonial Press, 1918–19), 2:717. Hereafter, *LJC*.

14. *JHB, 1712–1726*, 418.

15. A puzzling dispute of unknown origin also splintered the justices of the county court in early 1728, when Henry Scarburgh and the rest of the bench brought suit against fellow vestry basher Richard Drummond. See entry for March 6, 1727–28, Accomack County Orders, 1724–31, VSL.

16. *JHB, 1727–1740*, 18; Accomack County Orders, 1724–31, VSL.

17. Andrews owned eight hundred acres. Although Sacker Parker had only two hundred acres, his brothers and cousins held dozens of tracts along the Pungoteague and Onancock Creeks in the southeast section of the county. See Whitelaw, *Virginia's Eastern Shore*, 2:1196–97, passim.

18. *JHB, 1727–1740*, 19.

19. *JHB, 1727–1740*, 14.

20. *JHB, 1727–1740*, 18, 20–22, 36, 47, 48; *LJC*, 2:730, 734, 736, 737, 748.

21. *EJC*, 4:243, 334; *JHB, 1727–1740*, 123, 253.

22. As sheriff of Accomack, Henry Scarburgh I supervised the election of his son in July 1735; he died a few months later.

23. *JHB, 1727–1740*, 370.

24. Elite support for Scarburgh was determined by examining the voting behavior of justices and vestrymen in this and subsequent elections; Scarburgh's supporters always held significantly fewer acres, on average, than his opponents.

25. Whitelaw, *Virginia's Eastern Shore*, 1:620–21; ibid., 2:1344.

26. Of the sixteen county leaders whose voting behavior can be traced, ten supported Douglas, two supported Snead, two supported Mitchell Scarburgh, and two supported Edmund Scarburgh.

27. *JHB, 1727–1740,* 370.

28. Accomack County Deeds, 1737–46, VSL.

29. Voter location is taken from the landholding records abstracted in Whitelaw, *Virginia's Eastern Shore.*

30. *JHB, 1727–1740,* 356.

31. *JHB, 1727–1740,* 357, 359, 362, 367.

32. *JHB, 1727–1740,* 364, 370. The 1705 election law is found in Hening, 3:240.

33. *LJC,* 2:872, 874.

34. Hening, 4:292–93.

35. Accomack County Deeds, 1737–46, VSL.

36. *EJC,* 5:71.

37. *JHB, 1742–1749,* 31.

38. *JHB, 1742–1749,* 8, 31.

39. *JHB, 1742–1749,* 33.

40. Whitelaw, *Virginia's Eastern Shore,* 1:766, 780; *EJC,* 4:417.

41. Accomack County Deeds, 1737–46, VSL.

42. A third of the justices and vestrymen supported Parramore, while the remainder divided their support among six others; ten of the thirteen wealthiest men in the county also backed Parramore.

43. Six other candidates received one or two votes each. See Accomack County Deeds, 1737–46, VSL.

44. *GAV,* 78; *EJC,* 5:249.

45. *EJC,* 4:266; *EJC,* 5:150; Accomack Vestry Orders, VSL; Whitelaw, *Virginia's Eastern Shore,* 2:854, 948–49, 1130, 1137, 1296–99.

46. Thirteen of the sixteen justices and vestrymen participating in the election gave a vote to Douglas, while seven supported Parramore, and only five, Allen; the wealthiest men in the county also supported Douglas and not Allen.

47. Five additional candidates received one to eight votes each. See Accomack County Deeds, 1746–57, pt. 1, 143–58, VSL.

48. *JHB, 1742–1749,* 325.

49. *EJC,* 5:348.

50. Whitelaw, *Virginia's Eastern Shore,* 2:1134, 1139, 1140; *EJC,* 4:417.

51. Whitelaw, *Virginia's Eastern Shore,* 2:1197–1200, 1220. There seems to have been both a William Andrews Jr. and a William Andrews Sr. during this period; the elder Andrews did not die until 1763.

52. Eight of twelve justices and vestrymen supported both Allen and Douglas, four voted for Wise ,and only one voted for Justice. Among the entire electorate, five additional candidates received one to seven votes each,

including Edmund Scarburgh. Accomack County Deeds, 1746–57, 367–70, VSL.

53. *JHB, 1752–1758*, 18, 51; Hening, 6:236–37, 241.

54. Allen probably became sheriff during the summer of 1753, although a record of the appointment has not been located.

55. *JHB, 1752–1758*, 107, 147.

56. Whitelaw, *Virginia's Eastern Shore*, 2:906, 917; *EJC*, 5:150.

57. Whitelaw, *Virginia's Eastern Shore*, 2:1356–66.

58. Accomack County Deeds, 1746–57, 473–76, VSL.

59. *JHB, 1752–1758*, xiii–xxiv.

60. Douglas's reasons for dropping out are unknown, although his health and age may have been factors. He was about sixty years of age and did die three years later, in 1758.

61. Accomack County Orders, 1753–63, VSL.

62. *EJC*, 5:150; Whitelaw, *Virginia's Eastern Shore*, 2:906, 910, 920–21.

63. Whitelaw, *Virginia's Eastern Shore*, 2:1082, 1083, 1085, 1088, 1093.

64. Accomack County Deeds, 1746–57, 623–29, VSL.

65. Allen and Justice were the only vestrymen; West, Corbin, and Rule served on the county bench; Allen served on both; and Ralph Justice seems to have been dropped from the court sometime between 1752 and 1755.

66. Candidates had challenged election results in 1728, 1738, and 1741.

67. *JHB, 1752–1758*, 349, 352–55, 421, 441.

68. *JHB, 1752–1758*, 323, 445, 472; Hening, 7:64–65, 127–31.

69. Majors Thomas Custis and John Wise and Sheriff James Rodgers received compensation from the provincial government for expenses incurred in housing and transporting draftees to Fredricksburg in 1756. See Hening, 7:200. The enlistment and size rolls in the Washington Papers for 1756–57 reveal only fifteen men listing Accomack as their place of enlistment. See George Washington Papers, Library of Congress.

70. *EJC*, 6:77–78, 103.

71. While approximatley half of the county's elite supported Parramore and Allen, there was almost no support for Justice among leaders voting in 1758. See Accomack County Deeds, 1757–70, 52–56, VSL.

72. *JHB, 1758–1761*, 231.

73. On February 11, 1761, Governor Fauquier passed along to the Council word of George II's death the previous October (*EJC*, 6:177–80), and on April 10 he dissolved the assembly and called for writs for a new election (*GAV*, 88).

74. *JHB, 1761–1765*, 72, 82, 99, 104, 107, 120, 165.

75. Accomack Parish Vestry Orders and St. George's Parish Vestry Book, 1763–86, VSL.

76. On ferry service, see *JHB, 1761–1765*, 237, 245; *JHB, 1766–1769*, 49, 60, 97, 103. The relocation of tobacco warehouses concerned Eastern Shore

residents well into the 1770s. See Hening, 8:77; *JHB, 1766–1769*, 332, 338, 346; *JHB, 1770–1772*, 20, 34; *JHB, 1773–1776*, 33, 82, 87, 185, 217.

77. *Virginia Gazette*, Oct. 17, 1766 (Purdie and Dixon); Billings, Selby, and Tate, *Colonial Virginia*, 309–14.

78. The governor dissolved the assembly on June 1 and issued new election writs shortly thereafter (*GAV*, 91, 94); elections took place in early July.

79. Reese, *The Official Papers of Francis Fauquier*, 1:xxxviii; *EJC*, 6:301, 304, 617.

80. Whitelaw, *Virginia's Eastern Shore*, vol. 2; St. George's Parish Vestry Book, 1763–86, VSL.

81. Accomack County Deeds, 1757–70, 593–98, VSL.

82. *Plumping* means casting only a single ballot for a single candidate.

83. The results of this election first appeared in *Virginia Gazette*, Sept. 28, 1769 (Purdie and Dixon).

84. *EJC*, 6:366–67, 430.

85. *EJC*, 6:388.

86. Whitelaw, *Virginia's Eastern Shore*, vol. 2.

87. *EJC*, 6:401–2.

88. Ibid.

89. *EJC*, 6:410, 426.

90. Smith's candidacy is confirmed in only one source, *The Defence of Injur'd Merit Unmasked; or, the Scurrilous Piece of Philander Dissected and Exposed to Public View. By a Friend of Merit, wherever found* (n.p., 1771), as quoted in Sydnor, *Gentlemen Freeholders*, 49. Sydnor refers to a copy of this pamphlet he located in the Yale University Library, but in response to my inquiry, the Yale library staff could not locate such a copy. For Smith's background, see "Justices of the Peace of Colonial Virginia," 61; St. George's Parish Vestry Book, 1763–86, VSL; *EJC*, 6:307.

91. Southey Simpson, letter, *Virginia Gazette*, Mar. 12, 1772 (Rind). The vestry reassigned church pews on March 16, 1767; see St. George's Parish Vestry Book, 1763–86, VSL.

92. Letter, "My Dear Countrymen," signed "No Party Man."

93. *The Defence of Injur'd Merit Unmasked*, as quoted in Sydnor, *Gentlemen Freeholders*, 49; *Virginia Gazette*, Mar. 12, 1772 (Rind).

94. *EJC*, 6:430, 432, 635. The Accomack election results were first publicized in the *Virginia Gazette*, Dec. 12, 1771 (Purdie and Dixon).

95. *EJC*, 6:461, 511–12.

96. *JHB, 1773–1776*, 201, 227; *Virginia Gazette*, July 28, 1774 (Purdie and Dixon).

97. Peter Force, *American archives: consisting of a collection of authentick records, state papers, debates, and letters and other notices of publick affairs, the whole forming a documentary history of the origin and progress of the North American colonies; of the causes and accomplish-*

ment of the American revolution; and of the Constitution of government for the United States, to the final ratification thereof, ser. 4, 1 (Washington, D.C., 1837), 1059; 2 (1839), 1111; 3 (1840), 935; also, *GAV,* 109, 112, 114, 117, 119, 122, 128, 132.

Chapter 5: Lancaster County

1. Activity before, during, and after Sunday services in nearby Westmoreland County is described in Hunter Dickinson Farish, ed., *Journal and Letters of Philip Vickers Fithian: A Plantation Tutor of the Old Dominion* (Charlottesville: University Press of Virginia, 1957), 167.

2. Rutman and Rutman stress the existence of such rural Tidewater neighborhoods as well as their economic, social, and religious importance in *A Place in Time,* esp. 53, 120–27. See also Isaac, *The Transformation of Virginia,* 60–61; Lorena S. Walsh, "Community Networks in the Early Chesapeake," in *Colonial Chesapeake Society,* ed. Lois Green Carr, Philip D. Morgan, and Jean B. Russo (Chapel Hill: University of North Carolina Press, 1988), 200–41.

3. Charles Francis Cocke, *Parish Lines Diocese of Virginia* (Richmond: Virginia State Library, 1967), 142–43, 152–54; *JHB, 1659/60–1693,* 35; Hening, 2:252.

4. References to two separate parishes appear in public documents between 1702 and 1750. See "Public Officers in Virginia, 1702, 1714," *Virginia Magazine of History and Biography* 1 (1894): 368, 375; 2 (1894): 7–8; "Tithables in Lancaster Co., 1716," *William and Mary Quarterly,* 1st ser., 21 (1912): 106–12; Lancaster County Rentals, 1748 and 1750, Brock Collection.

5. Robert Carter died in 1732. The completion date of the church is mentioned in John Carter to Micajah Perry, Aug. 8, 1734, Landon Carter Papers (this reference was brought to my attention by Ann Dorsey). Carter may have wanted the church to remain at its present site for several reasons. First, his father, John Carter, constructed the original building and lay buried, along with Robert's mother, in the churchyard. Brothers and sisters who had died young also rested in graves east of the church, and Robert Carter wanted to be buried with them. Second, a direct road lined with tall cedar trees connected the old church to Carter's home plantation of Corotoman, just three miles away. With the parish church so close, his large family, tenants, servants, and perhaps even slaves could easily attend services. See William Meade, *Old Churches, Ministers, and Families of Virginia* (Philadelphia, 1857), 2:117–18; "Christ Church, Lancaster County," *Virginia Magazine of History and Biography* 10 (1903): 208–10; Louis B. Wright, ed., *Letters of Robert Carter, 1720–1727: The Commercial Interests of a Virginia Gentleman* (San Marino, Calif.: Huntington Library,

1940), v–xiv; Louis Morton, *Robert Carter of Nomini Hall: A Virginia To-bacco Planter of the Eighteenth Century* (Williamsburg: Colonial Williamsburg Foundation, 1941), 3–30.

6. Christ Church Vestry Book, 1739–86, 5, 15; Meade, *Old Churches*, 2:125–27; *St. Mary's White Chapel* (Lancaster County, Va.: St. Mary's White Chapel Protestant Episcopalian Church, 1969).

7. *EJC*, 4:433; *EJC*, 5:9.

8. *JHB, 1742–1749*, 126, 127, 160, 181; *JHB, 1752–1758*, 39, 47, 49, 59, 63, 68, 77–78; *JHB, 1758–1761*, 104, 106, 109; Hening, 7:301–2. A general vestry, held for the entire county on November 17, 1752, formally adopted the terms *lower precinct* and *upper precinct*, not *parish*. Concern for equal representation from each precinct continued to be an issue for the remainder of the colonial period (Christ Church Vestry Book, 1739–1786, 50, 73). The term *precinct* also appears in the Lancaster County Rentals for 1773 (VHS).

9. *JHB, 1758–1761*, 104.

10. Morton, *Colonial Virginia*, 497–99.

11. Sydnor, *Gentlemen Freeholders*, 60–85.

12. Beard and Beard, *The Rise of American Civilization*, 1:127.

13. Robert Wheeler, "The County Court in Colonial Virginia," in *Town and County: Essays on the Structure of Local Government in the American Colonies*, ed. Bruce C. Daniels (Middletown, Conn.: Wesleyan University Press, 1978), 114; "Tithables in Lancaster Co., 1716"; "Public Officers in Virginia, 1702, 1714."

14. In nearby Middlesex County for the period 1650–1750, the median number of acres owned by officeholders at this level was 829. See Rutman and Rutman, *A Place in Time*, 145–47.

15. Ten of the sixteen appointments to the county bench after 1759 went to persons who had no connection to the vestry, while of the fourteen men already serving as justices in 1759, twelve were vestrymen. Alan Williams addresses this issue in regard to minor county offices in "The Small Farmer in Eighteenth-Century Virginia Politics," *Agricultural History* 43 (1969): 91–101.

16. Pollbooks survive for all fourteen elections in the period 1741–74, so there are only three elections in which the full slate of candidates is unknown. Probably one additional candidate stood in the 1728 general election, the 1734 by-election, and the 1735 general election whose identity remains obscure. Likely losers in the 1728 election include Major William Ball Sr., an incumbent burgess for the county who lost in 1741, and James Ball Sr., who served from 1715 through 1722 and won the 1734 by-election. William Ball may also have tried for election in 1734 and 1735.

17. The averages presented in table 5.1 partially mask the substantial diversity in wealth among candidates and winners. During the early peri-

od, candidates' landholdings ranged from 400 to 1,883 acres and winners' landholdings from 400 to 1,516 acres; in the latter period, landholdings of both candidates and winners ranged from 130 to 3,007 acres.

18. Richard Mitchell, who won in 1761, may have been the only winner who did not hold office before his election. His service as a justice probably did not begin until 1762, although it may have started a year or two earlier.

19. The extent to which local leaders supported precinct candidates, as opposed to countywide candidates, can be determined by looking at the voting behavior of these leaders in the fourteen elections for which poll books survive. If the leader voted for two candidates from his own precinct, his selection is considered a *precinct vote*; if he split his votes between candidates from both precincts, his selection is considered a *countywide vote*. In the elections of 1741, 1748, and 1752, 75 percent of the elite cast precinct ballots; in the six elections between 1758 and 1771, the precinct vote was 15 percent or less; and in the final election in 1774, it was 62 percent.

20. Meade, *Old Churches*, 2:125–29; Lancaster County Rentals for 1750, Brock Collection; "Marriage Bonds in Lancaster County," *William and Mary Quarterly*, 1st ser., 12 (1903–4): 96–103, 175–81.

21. Lancaster County Rentals for 1750, Brock Collection; Rutman and Rutman, *A Place in Time*, 49–50; Morton, *Robert Carter of Nomini Hall*, 3–30.

22. Sydnor, *Gentlemen Freeholders*, esp. chap. 6.

23. Wheeler, "County Court," 114; Morgan, *American Slavery*, 227–28, 342, 418–19. Household size for 1750 and 1773 were derived by dividing the number of known tithables in each of these years by an estimated number of households. The number of adult black slaves is estimated by taking a percentage (known for 1750, 1755, and 1790, and extrapolated for other years) of the total tithables for the years in question.

24. In 1720, tenants occupied 41 percent of the households in Christ Church precinct, although this is the area where Robert Carter owned eight thousand acres, much of which may have been tenant-occupied. See Morgan, *American Slavery*, 222.

25. For comparison, the average adult male turnout in Fairfax County during this period was 41 percent; in Halifax County it was 44 percent.

26. If vestry meetings acted as slate-making occasions, which they might have, then this formal opportunity would have been removed after the 1759 consolidation.

27. The actual totals in the election were Selden 151, Carter 138, and Ball 115.

28. Average acres are calculated from the rental lists (see above): the 1748 rental list, which includes Christ Church only, was used with the 1741 election, and thus average acres for the St. Mary's voters cannot be determined; the 1750 rental list was used for the elections of 1748–61; and the

1773 rental list was used for the elections of 1765–74. Only one candidate from Christ Church stood in the elections of 1761–74, and thus there was no Christ Church slate during these years.

29. Such countywide issues as the location of the new courthouse in 1740 and the drive to unify the parishes in the 1740s and 1750s must have had some influence on the behavior of county voters, but neighborhood loyalties appear to be the most dominant factor in electoral politics. Several other well-known controversies occurred within (not between) the respective parishes and, therefore, may have had minimum impact on voting. The riots against the Tobacco Inspection Act of 1730 and the burning of the Deep Creek tobacco warehouse in March 1732 involved primarily persons from St. Mary's White Chapel (*EJC*, 4:259–60; *JHB, 1727–1740*, 122), while additional protests against tobacco inspectors late in 1732 remained within Christ Church (*EJC*, 4:287–88, 293). Moreover, the long and heated controversy between young Thomas Pinkard and old Edwin Conway in the 1740s may have been a youthful challenge to established authority within Christ Church, although this spilled over into the election of 1748, when Conway's son and Pinkard both ran (*JHB, 1742–1749*, 261, 266–68; Robert A. Wheeler, "Lancaster County, Virginia, 1650–1750: The Evolution of a Southern Tidewater Community," Ph.D. diss., Brown University, 1972, 138–41).

Chapter 6: Fairfax County

1. George Washington to Burwell Bassett, Aug. 2, 1765, Abbot, *The Papers of George Washington, Colonial Series*, 3:386.

2. Thomas, sixth Lord Fairfax, set aside 12,588 acres for himself near Great Falls in 1737, while his agent, Robert Carter, had granted himself 30,000 acres in the previous decade, and Thomas's brother, William Fairfax, secretly obtained 5,000 acres in the 1740s. Although several additional grants to absentee landlords occurred in the 1720s and 1730s, numerous grants of less than 500 acres came to planters who planned to live on and work the land. See Nan Netherton et al., *Fairfax County, Virginia: A History* (Fairfax, Va.: Fairfax Board of Supervisors, 1978), 5–6, 11–19.

3. Bliss believes that the 33 perceent tenancy rate he found for Loudoun County in 1782 was unusually high. See his "Rise of Tenancy in Virginia," 429. However, Kulikoff notes that tenancy rates may have been as high as 55 percent in nearby Prince George's County, Maryland. See Kulikoff, *Tobacco and Slaves*, tables 5, 20, 22. Kulikoff's figures include both long-term leaseholders and short-term tenants-at-will.

4. All candidates can be identified for the elections of 1744, 1748, 1755, 1758, 1765, 1768, and 1769. It is likely, however, that there were at least five more candidates besides the winners running in the other elections of

the period, but it is uncertain as to whether they were some of the same six-teen already identified or five entirely different individuals. There was probably a single losing candidate in the elections of 1752, 1754, 1761, and 1771, whom we have not been able to identify; a third candidate ran in 1774, but his identity remains a mystery.

5. Most scholars see two distinct and easily definable groups in county society—the gentry and everyone else. See Sydnor, *Gentlemen Free-holders*, 83–85, 100–101; Isaac, *The Transformation of Virginia*, 65, 133, 143; Greene, *Quest for Power*, 24–26. More recently, "a complex layering of society" has been proposed. See Rutman and Rutman, *A Place in Time*, 143–47, 161–63.

6. The Fairfax gentry is defined by (1) wealth, and includes the top 10 percent of slaveowners or landowners at particular points in time, and (2) those holding the local offices of justice of the peace, vestryman, sheriff, and militia officer. Among the ninety-three officeholders who served before 1757, only forty-two (45%) were among the wealthiest 10 percent in 1749, and twenty (22%) were among the top 10 percent of landowners in 1757. Moreover, fewer than a fifth of the officeholders who served after 1757 were among the most wealthy individuals in the county.

7. Justices in the earliest period (1742–52) owned on average 9.6 slaves, while vestrymen held on average 8.1 slaves. This made them six to seven times wealthier than the average householder in 1749. This changed dramatically as the period progressed. Vestrymen declined from being 3.6 times as wealthy than the average landowner in 1757 to 2.4 times as wealthy in 1770. Justices dropped from being 2.9 times as wealthy in 1757 to 2.3 times as wealthy in 1764 but then jumped to 3.6 times as wealthy in 1770.

8. Candidates were 5.5 times as wealthy as the average landowner in 1757, 3.9 times in 1764, and 4.7 times in 1770. Furthermore, seven of the nine candidates who ran in the period 1744–52 fell among the top 10 percent of slaveholders, four of eight did so in the period 1753–62, but only three of the seven did so after 1763.

9. Winners were 3 times as wealthy as the average freeholder in 1761, 5.7 times in 1764, and 6 times in 1770. However, the high figures after 1765 are due in part to a single, very wealthy individual who successfully contested each of the last five elections of the period. This candidate—George Washington—owned 9,381 acres when he first ran for Fairfax in 1765 and had increased his holdings to over 12,000 acres by the 1774 election. The other two winners during these years were John West and Charles Broadwater, who each owned fewer than 2,000 acres. In the period before 1765, there appears to have been a group of winners who averaged just as much wealth but among whom there was less disparity (statistically speaking, there was a smaller standard deviation in the earlier period than in the lat-

ter). Furthermore, all five winning candidates in the period 1744–52 were among the top 10 percent of slaveowners, a level that was not achieved by any later group of winners.

10. Nothing is known of Bond Veal, who came in a rather distant fifth in the election of 1744. He does not seem to have served as a local office-holder in either Prince William or Fairfax Counties and was not among the householders in the tithables lists of 1749. He did, however, vote in the Prince William election of 1741 and the Fairfax election of 1748.

11. Sydnor believes that becoming a justice of the peace was the first step toward higher appointive or elective office. See Sydnor, *Gentlemen Freeholders*, 100–101. Rutman and Rutman found that in Middlesex County vestrymen, justices, sheriffs, and burgesses had similar degrees of wealth and were positioned as a third level in a four-level econopolitical hierarchy. Below them were jurors and appraisers, clerks, constables, and levy collectors. Above them were extremely wealthy individuals who were appointed to colonywide offices. See Rutman and Rutman, *A Place in Time*, 145–47.

12. *JHB, 1727–1740*, 258–65, 306, 334.

13. *Minutes of the Vestry: Truro Parish, Virginia, 1732–1785* (Lorton, Va.: Pohick Church, 1974); Philip Slaughter, *The History of Truro Parish in Virginia* (Philadelphia: Jacobs, 1908), 4, 7.

14. *EJC*, 4:339; *EJC*, 5:103, 122, 132.

15. Neither the date of the original election writ nor the exact date of the election are known. The county clerk copied the election pollbook into the county records immediately following a meeting of the county court on August 16, 1744. William Fairfax did not in fact finish the term to which he was elected in 1741; he was appointed to the Council during the summer of 1744, and a by-election was held to replace him early in the fall. Although several standard reference works on the House of Burgesses indicate that John Colville succeeded him, this seems not be have been the case.

16. Both were members of the new Commission of the Peace for Prince William County formed in November 1742, after Fairfax was formed. See *EJC*, 5:103.

17. Slaughter, *The History of Truro Parish*, 7; *EJC*, 4:299; *EJC*, 5:103.

18. Support before the election is reflected in the actual voting behavior of the county elite during the election; Colville, who received votes from all thirteen justices and vestrymen who voted, was clearly the choice of the gentry.

19. Abbot, *The Papers of George Washington, Colonial Series*, 1:7; *EJC*, 4:339; *EJC*, 5:103, 122, 132; Slaughter, *The History of Truro Parish*, 7.

20. This would have been particularly true of those residing on the upper sections of the Potomac or northwestward toward the Blue Ridge. Trav-

el time to the Prince William courthouse from these areas would have been a day or more. The new Fairfax County courthouse was located at Spring Fields (EJC, 5:93); see map 6.1.

21. Local leaders are defined as those serving as justices of the county court or vestrymen of the parish. Twenty-seven justices and vestrymen served during this period. Thirteen voted in the election, another four were candidates, and ten took no part in the election.

22. Fairfax Harrison, Landmarks of Old Prince William (Berryville, Va.: Chesapeake Book Company, 1964; reissue of private edition, 1924), 407, 663; EJC, 4:339; EJC, 5:103, 122, 231; Minutes of the Vestry; Fairfax County Lists of Tithables for 1749, Miscellaneous Manuscript Collection, Manuscript Division, Library of Congress.

23. JHB, 1742–1749, 298, 318, 320, 356, 358, 373–74, 405; see discussion of county population above and Netherton et al., Fairfax County, Virginia, 28–29.

24. Abbot, The Papers of George Washington, Colonial Series, 1:53; Jackson, The Diaries of George Washington, 1:24–37. Washington died within a few weeks of his return to Mount Vernon.

25. Minutes of the Vestry; Harrison, Landmarks, 139, 407; EJC, 5:103; Lists of Tithables for 1749; Fairfax Rentals for 1761, Brock Collection. Alexander owned twelve slaves in 1749; in 1761, the year of his death, he owned more than six thousand acres.

26. JHB, 1752–1758, 27; EJC, 5:379, 387; John W. Reps, Tidewater Towns: City Planning in Colonial Virginia and Maryland (Williamsburg: Colonial Williamsburg Foundation, 1972), 202–9; Netherton et al., Fairfax County, Virginia, 37.

27. Fairfax County Will Book B (1752–67), VSL; GAV, 83.

28. EJC, 5:25, 179; Minutes of the Vestry; Edith Moore Sprouse, ed., A Surname and Subject Index of the Minute and Order Books of the County Court, Fairfax County, Virginia, 1749–1802 (Fairfax, Va.: Fairfax County Historical Commission, 1976); Lists of Tithables for 1749; Fairfax Rentals for 1761, Brock Collection.

29. JHB, 1752–1758, 212, 243, 264, 265, 269, 272.

30. George Washington to John Augustine Washington, May 28, 1755, Abbot, The Papers of George Washington, Colonial Series, 1:289–93.

31. JHB, 1752–1758, xiii–xxiv.

32. Rutland, The Papers of George Mason, 2:69; Harrison, Landmarks, 663.

33. All six of the Cameron vestrymen who voted in the election selected Ellzey. Four of them gave their second vote to West, two of them voted for Fairfax. Only one of the nine Truro vestrymen voted for Ellzey, while the only justice who lived in the Lower Parish to vote for him was his fa-

ther, Lewis. The three justices who resided in Cameron all supported William Ellzey.

34. There has been considerable confusion regarding the 1755 pollbook. Freeman claims to have viewed a copy entirely in Washington's hand, showing the totals as West 232, Fairfax 222, and Ellzey 220; see Freeman, *George Washington*, 2:147 n., 158. The editor of the most recent edition of Washington's papers (Abbot, *The Papers of George Washington, Colonial Series*, 2:227) concurs on these figures and the existence of this pollbook. In addition, Freeman claims that a later and incorrect copy of the pollbook showed West 252, Fairfax 232, and Ellzey 224. Finally, Griffith found only one pollbook in the Washington Papers, which showed West 252, Fairfax 222, and Ellzey 224; see Griffith, *The Virginia House of Burgesses*, 159. Similarly, the only pollbook I have found in the microfilm version of the Washington Papers is the same one Griffith located and the one Freeman believes to be incorrect. My totals are West 251, Fairfax 222, and Ellzey 224.

35. Adam Stephen to George Washington, Dec. 23, 1755, Abbot, *The Papers of George Washington, Colonial Series*, 2:226–28.

36. These calculations are based upon the voting records of only 188, or exactly 50 percent, of the total voters. The parish of residence is not known for the other half of the voters.

37. West and Fairfax received 36 and 38 percent, respectively, of their support from old voters, while Ellzey received only 25 percent from this group. Although Ellzey came in third, he polled a higher total (167) from the newer voters than either of the winners. Exactly 50 percent of those selecting West and Fairfax had voted previously, while only 25 percent of those selecting the other two combinations had voted in the 1740s. The Fairfax-Ellzey combination was the most popular choice in Cameron (Upper) Parish, while Fairfax-West was most often selected in Truro.

38. *JHB, 1752–1758*, 352, 425, 427, 432, 434, 446, 470, 492; Harrison, *Landmarks*, 326–27; Netherton et al., *Fairfax County*, 39; *EJC*, 6:78.

39. *EJC*, 6:100, 103.

40. *EJC*, 6:100; John Kirkpatrick to George Washington, July 6, 1758, Abbot, *The Papers of George Washington, Colonial Series*, 5:264–65.

41. *Minutes of the Vestry*; Sprouse, *A Surname and Subject Index*; Fairfax Rentals for 1761, Brock Collection; *EJC*, 5:231, 279; Jackson, *The Diaries of George Washington*, 1:218; John Kirkpatrick to George Washington, July 21, 1758, Abbot, *The Papers of George Washington, Colonial Series*, 5:315.

42. *EJC*, 6:177; Francis Fauquier to the Board of Trade, May 12, 1761, Reese, *The Official Papers of Francis Fauquier*, 2:524. The governor may have hoped that new elections would bring in a better assembly; the one just dissolved had refused to support a large regiment to fight the Indians. After the elections, however, he lamented that "God knows . . . what the

Dissposition of the new Assembly . . . may be." Fauquier to William Byrd, June 2, 1761, ibid., 535. The total number of voters in this election is taken from voter canvas, ca. July 1765, George Washington Papers, Library of Congress.

43. *JHB, 1761–1765,* 116, 118, 119, 136, 156, 157, 165.

44. *JHB, 1761–1765,* 23, 75, 117–18, 233, 236, 238–39, 273, 308. George Washington recorded the election results in his papers under the date of July 1765 (George Washington Papers, Library of Congress). This document is reprinted in Abbot, *The Papers of George Washington, Colonial Series,* 7:361–62.

45. Francis Fauquier to the Board of Trade, June 5, 1765, Reese, *The Official Papers of Francis Fauquier,* 3:250–52.

46. Parish taxes were no small matter and were in fact three times larger than county taxes. See Netherton et al., *Fairfax County,* 52.

47. *JHB, 1761–1765,* 337, 341, 346, 347, 348, 350, 363; Harrison, *Landmarks,* 290–91; Slaughter, *The History of Truro Parish,* 36–43. The adjusted parish boundaries produced another set of vestry elections in July. In Truro, George Mason now led the field, with George Washington in third place and John Posey in fourth. In Fairfax Parish, John West again won, but county burgess George Johnston dropped from seventh to sixteenth place and left the vestry, while Charles Broadwater moved from sixth to seventh and retained his place. See George Washington Papers, Library of Congress.

48. Johnston's declining health may have been the reason for his withdrawal from politics; he died the next year. See Freeman, *George Washington,* 3:141.

49. Fairfax Rentals for 1761, Brock Collection; Jackson, *The Diaries of George Washington,* 1:211; George Washington Papers, Library of Congress.

50. Thirty justices and vestrymen voted in the 1765 election: Washington received twenty-eight votes, Posey sixteen, and West fifteen. The Washington-Posey combination obtained fifteen votes, the Washington-West thirteen, while one person voted for West only, and another selected West and Posey.

51. Parish of residence is known for 186 (72%) of the 257 voters.

52. The levy per poll, or tithable, for Truro Parish doubled following the division in 1765 and remained at the higher level for about six years. See *Minutes of the Vestry;* Slaughter, *The History of Truro Parish,* 49.

53. Reese, *The Official Papers of Francis Fauquier,* 1:xxxviii; *EJC,* 6:301, 304, 617

54. *EJC,* 6:304, 616–17; Jackson, *The Diaries of George Washington,* 2:100–113.

55. The pollbook for this election is filed in the George Washington Pa-

pers, Library of Congress, with the 1765 election material, and therefore a good deal of confusion has arisen regarding the document. The 1765 pollbook is an alphabetized version in Washington's hand; the 1768 pollbook is undated, with the freeholders listed in the order in which they voted. A number of Washington scholars have reported the wrong totals for the 1768 election, including Freeman, *George Washington*, 3:208–10; Jackson, *The Diaries of George Washington*, 2:114. On the other hand, Sydnor seems to have assigned the pollbook to the proper year and come relatively close to establishing the number of persons who voted (*Gentlemen Freeholders*, 122). The pollbook is assigned to the correct year and reprinted also in Abbot, *The Papers of George Washington, Colonial Series*, 8:114–49. The inclement weather is described in Jackson, *The Diaries of George Washington*, 2:116. The courthouse moved to Alexandria in 1752 (*EJC*, 5:379, 387). Parish of residence is known for 67 percent of the voters.

56. Jackson, *The Diaries of George Washington*, 1:211; ibid., 2:30, 158; Abbot, *The Papers of George Washington, Colonial Series*, 8:1–4, 34–37, 51, 53. For an illuminating discussion of the Posey-Washington "etiquette of debt," see T. H. Breen, *Tobacco Culture: The Mentality of the Great Tidewater Planters on the Eve of the Revolution* (Princeton: Princeton University Press, 1985), 97–101.

57. Jackson, *The Diaries of George Washington*, 2:153–80; *EJC*, 6:326.

58. Dunmore to Earl Hillsborough, Nov. 1, 1771, PRO C.O. 5/1349 ff. 195–96 (copy courtesy Colonial Williamsburg); *EJC*, 6:432; Jackson, *The Diaries of George Washington*, 3:74.

59. George Washington to George William Fairfax, June 10, 1774, Abbot, *The Papers of George Washington, Colonial Series*, 10:94–101; *EJC*, 6:578; Council of Virginia to Dunmore, June 18, 1774, PRO C.O. 5/1352 ff. 139–40; and Dunmore to Earl of Dartmouth, June 20, 1774, PRO C.O. 5/1352 ff. 143–44.

60. George Washington to George William Fairfax, June 10, 1774, Abbot, *The Papers of George Washington, Colonial Series*, 10:94–101; Jackson, *The Diaries of George Washington*, 3:256.

61. R. H. Lee to Arthur Lee, June 26, 1774, *Lee Papers, 1754–1811* (New York, 1872), Collections of the New York Historical Society, 1:117.

62. George Washington to Bryan Fairfax, July 4, 1774, Abbot, *The Papers of George Washington, Colonial Series*, 10:109–11; Jackson, *The Diaries of George Washington*, 3:257.

63. Bryan Fairfax to George Washington, July 3, 1774, Abbot, *The Papers of George Washington, Colonial Series*, 10:106–9; Jackson, *The Diaries of George Washington*, 3:259. John West Jr. served with George Mason in the Fifth Revolutionary Convention held in Williamsburg from May 6 to July 5, 1776, and in the General Assembly, which served later that year. See *GAV*, 119, 122. West died in 1777.

64. Jackson, *The Diaries of George Washington*, 3:261; *The Journal of Nicholas Cresswell*, 27–28.

65. Pole, *Political Representation in England*, 150–51.

Chapter 7: Halifax County

1. *JHB, 1766–1769*, 230–31, 242–45; *JHB, 1770–1772*, 21–28; Abraham Maury to Col. Theodrick Bland Sr., July 17, 1758, Campbell, *The Bland Papers*, 1:12.

2. *GAV*, 88–130; Wirt J. Carrington, *A History of Halifax County* (Richmond: Appeals Press, 1924), 248.

3. Hubbell and Adair, "Robert Munford's *The Candidates*."

4. Ibid.; Beeman, "Robert Munford."

5. Beeman, "Robert Munford," 179–80, 183.

6. In addition to controversies brought before the House concerning Halifax, see *JHB, 1752–1758*, 339, 344, 420–21; *JHB, 1758–1761*, 8, 14–15, 60–61, 82–83, 85; *JHB, 1761–1765*, 9, 15, 73–74, 348, 358–59; *JHB, 1770–1772*, 158, 163, 251–52, 254, 263–64, 286–89.

7. Pollbooks do survive for several other Southside counties, but they are either incomplete or too far apart to appropriately show changes in voting behavior in this region of colonial Virginia. These include Amelia: 1752 (partial), 1755 (partial), 1761 (partial), and 1768; Brunswick: 1748 and 1768; Prince Edward: 1754 (partial), 1755 (partial), and 1758.

8. Hening, 6:252. Halifax County was four times the size of the original Fairfax County and twenty times that of Lancaster County. A two- or two-and-one-half day trip on horseback would have been required to travel from one end of the county to the other.

9. Beeman, *The Evolution of the Southern Backcountry*, 12–13, 22–23, 29–30.

10. Population estimates here, in table 7.1, and throughout the chapter are based on a data file containing information on 3,043 adult males who resided in Halifax County between 1750 and 1773. This file has been assembled from the following sources: A List of Tithables Taken by Cornelius Cargill for the Year 1750, reprinted in Landon C. Bell, comp., *Sunlight on the Southside: Lists of Tithes, Lunenburg County, Virginia, 1748–1783* (Philadelphia: George S. Ferguson Co., 1931), 129–34 (which covers that section of Lunenburg County that became Halifax); A List of Land Tax and Negro Returned by Robert King for the Year 1755, VSL (which appears to cover the eastern one-quarter of the county, most of the slaveholders, and about one-third of the households); William A. Crozier, ed., "Index to Land Grants 1753–1767," *Virginia County Records* 6 (1909): 136–38, 271–76; William A. Crozier, ed., "Index to Land Grants, 1753–1767," *Virginia County Records* 9 (1911): 103–9; 1764, 1765, 1768, and 1769 pollbooks, Halifax County Deed

Book 3, 389–411, VSL; Pittsylvania County Tithables, 1767, VSL (a complete transcript of the names from this list but without tithable and land data is found in Maud C. Clement, *The History of Pittsylvania County Virginia* [Baltimore: Regional Publishing, 1981; original ed., 1929], 276–86; a partial transcription of the list with tithable and land data is found in "First List of Tithables of Pittsylvania County, Year 1767," *Virginia Magazine of History and Biography* 23 [1915]: 79–80, 303–4; "First List of Tithables of Pittsylvania County, Year 1767," *Virginia Magazine of History and Biography* 24 [1916]: 180–92, 271–74); List of Tithables, 1771, VSL (partial list containing perhaps 15% of the households); A General List of Fees Due to Paul Carrington, Clerk of Halifax County, for the year 1773, January 1774, in Account Book of Paul Carrington, 1773–79, VHS. Additional aggregate population data are compiled from List of Tithables in the Dominion of Virginia, 1755, PRO CO5, 1338:364; List of Tithables in Va. Taken 1773, reprinted in *Virginia Magazine of History and Biography* 27 (1920): 81–82; U.S. Bureau of the Census, *Heads of Families at the First Census of the United States Taken in the Year 1790: Virginia* (Washington, D.C.: U.S. Government Printing Office, 1907), 9–10.

11. Lack of appropriate data makes it impossible to know whether all these adult white males owned or leased enough land to qualify to vote. Information from the 1755 tax list suggests that 9 percent of the male heads of household may not have been qualified (see A List of Land Tax and Negro Returned by Robert King). The full adult white male population estimate is used here to calculate turnout rates; it may, therefore, underestimate actual participation. During the Revolution, the white population remained nearly constant, while the black population increased slowly. In the decade following the war, both the white and black populations increased by nearly 60 percent.

12. Hubbell and Adair, "Robert Munford's *The Candidates*," 231.

13. Terry's name does not appear in either of the surviving land-ownership records of 1750s. See A List of Tithables Taken by Cornelius Cargill for the Year 1750; A List of Land Tax and Negro Returned by Robert King.

14. Information on the county economic elite and the leadership comes from a variety of sources, including A List of Tithables Taken by Cornelius Cargill; A List of Land Tax and Negro Returned by Robert King; Halifax County Pleas 1–6, VSL; Halifax Deed Books 1, 4, 5, VSL; *EJC*, 5:386, 423; *EJC*, 6:51, 410, 504, 547, 682; "Justices of the Peace of Colonial Virginia," 59, 81–82, 102, 108, 116, 123; Carrington, *A History of Halifax*, 24–32, 515; Meade, *Old Churches*, 2:9–13; "Extracts from First Vestry Book of Antrim Parish," *William and Mary Quarterly*, 2d ser., 7 (1927): 61–63.

15. A List of Tithables Taken by Cornelius Cargill; A List of Land Tax and Negro Returned by Robert King; *EJC*, 5:205, 275–76; Landon C. Bell,

Cumberland Parish: Lunenburg County, Virginia, 1746–1816, and Vestry Book, 1746–1816 (Richmond: Byrd Press, 1930), 26–29. The tithable lists record sixty-one slaves in 1750 and twenty in 1755 for Byrd.

16. A List of Tithables Taken by Cornelius Cargill; A List of Land Tax and Negro Returned by Robert King. For comparison, justices in frontier Augusta County held on average 554, 450, and 355 acres each in 1749, 1765, and 1773, while the median for burgesses was just under 1,000 acres. See Albert H. Tillson Jr., *Gentry and Common Folk: Political Culture on a Virginia Frontier, 1740–1789* (Lexington: University of Kentucky Press, 1991), 20–21.

17. The House of Burgesses journals list a William Samuel Harris as one of the representatives from Halifax during the assembly of 1752–55 and a Samuel Harris as a representative in the assembly of 1756–58 (*JHB, 1752–1758*, vii, ix). I assume these both refer to Samuel Harris, who was a Halifax justice, vestryman, militia officer, and landowner, and not to William Harris, who was an obscure landowner in that portion of Lunenburg County that did not become part of Halifax. See W. B. Hackley, "Sidelights on Samuel Harris," *Virginia Baptist Historical Register* 10 (1971): 456–66.

18. Carrington, *A History of Halifax*, 49; Bell, *Sunlight on the Southside*, 66, 70, 111, 115, 117, 133–34, 189, 236, 246 ; Bell, *Cumberland Parish*, 326, 329; Beeman, *The Evolution of the Southern Backcountry*, 105–6, 116.

19. *JHB, 1752–1758*, 153, 160; *EJC*, 5:223, 250, 281.

20. *JHB, 1752–1758*, 160; *EJC*, 5:457.

21. Robert Baylor Semple, *History of the Baptists in Virginia*, rev. ed. (Philadelphia, 1894), 17–19; Beeman, *The Evolution of the Southern Backcountry*, 105–6, 116; Hackley, "Sidelights on Samuel Harris."

22. *JHB, 1752–1758*, 350; *JHB, 1770–1772*, 27; Semple, *History of the Baptists*, 18.

23. *EJC*, 6:91; Marion Tinlind, ed., *The Correspondence of the Three Willliam Byrds of Westover, Virginia, 1684–1776* (Charlottesville: University Press of Virginia, 1977), 2:655. Captain Wade may have been overzealous in the execution of his duties, as he was accused later in the year of murdering several Cherokee (*EJC*, 6:120, 124).

24. Abraham Maury to Col. Theodrick Bland Sr., July 17, 1758, Campbell, *The Bland Papers*, 1:12.

25. Halifax County Deed Books 2, 3, 4, VSL; *JHB, 1752–1758*, 432; Carrington, *A History of Halifax*, 19, 113, 268. Robert Wade made out his will in January 1764.

26. Twelve county leaders voted in this election: eight supported Booker and four supported Wade.

27. Halifax County Deed Book 3, 389–92, VSL.

28. *JHB, 1761–1765*, 288, 290–91, 326.

29. *EJC*, 5:364; *EJC*, 6:682.

30. *GAV*, 92; Francis Fauquier to the Board of Trade, June 5, 1765, Reese, *The Official Papers of Francis Fauquier*, 3:1250–52.

31. Carrington, *A History of Halifax*, 341; *EJC*, 6:323, 534. Eighteen leaders voted in the 1765 election. For Donelson's activities a few years later in the new county of Pittsylvania, see *EJC*, 6:361, 381. He later moved to Tennessee, where he died in 1785; his daughter Rachael married Andrew Jackson in 1791. See James C. Curtis, *Andrew Jackson* (New York: Harper-Collins, 1976), 19–20, 26–28.

32. Green concentrated his major landholdings and political activities in Lunenburg County, not Halifax, although he was active in the county militia in 1758. See Bell, *Sunlight on the Southside*, 264; Bell, *Cumberland Parish*, 511, 544. James Bates may have been a son of candidate and burgess John Bates, who was active in the period 1753–58. Young Bates joined the county court in 1764, served as sheriff in 1769, and owned at least 350 acres in the eastern section of the county. See *EJC*, 6:332, 472.

33. Morris Cammel also received one vote. See Halifax County Deed Book 3, 392–401, VSL.

34. *JHB, 1758–1761*, 92; *JHB, 1766–1769*, 35, 44, 47, 58, 67, 70.

35. Carrington, *A History of Halifax*, 515; Meade, *Old Churches*, 2:13.

36. Halifax County Deed Book 3, 401–7, VSL. Biographical data on Robert Wooding is found in Carrington, *A History of Halifax*, 352, 515; *EJC*, 6:55, 192, 532. Information on John Lewis is found in Carrington, *A History of Halifax*, 515; *EJC*, 6:410; Bell, *Sunlight on the Southside*, 275.

37. Carrington, *A History of Halifax*, 248; *EJC*, 5:386, 430, 451; *EJC*, 6:225, 293; Abraham Maury to Col. Theodrick Bland Sr., July 17, 1758, Campbell, *The Bland Papers*, 1:12; *JHB, 1770–1772*, 27.

38. *JHB, 1770–1772*, 21–28.

39. *JHB, 1766–1769*, 231.

40. *JHB, 1766–1769*, 206, 209, 212–14.

41. *EJC*, 6:326; *JHB, 1766–1769*, 230–31. Isaac probably held a vestry seat at this point; he would not become a justice for another year.

42. *JHB, 1766–1769*, 230–31, 242–45.

43. *JHB, 1766–1769*, 242–45.

44. The weather apparently did not dampen turnout a year earlier at the December 2, 1768, election.

45. *JHB, 1766–1769*, 347, 351–52.

46. *JHB, 1770–1772*, 159–60.

47. Walter Coles was still active in county politics a few months later, when he tried to get the courthouse moved to a new site, but his activities beyond that point are uncertain. See *EJC*, 6:461.

48. "Extracts from First Vestry Book of Antrim Parish"; *EJC*, 6:547.

49. By way of comparison, sixty-eight men served in Fairfax County dur-

ing its thirty-three-year colonial period.

50. Hubbell and Adair, "Robert Munford's *The Candidates*," 231.

Conclusion

1. The desire for consensual politics may have been widespread. According to Mark A. Kishlansky, the electoral instinct—often assumed by scholars of the Anglo-American past—may not have been a natural one, at least in the early modern English world. To the contrary, the election process was regarded not as an opportunity for expression of the public will but rather as a divisive measure, likely to tear the community apart. A more harmonious selection process, sidestepping an actual vote, was preferred by both those being selected and those doing the selecting. See Kishlansky, *Parliamentary Selection: Social and Political Choice in Early Modern England* (Cambridge: Cambridge University Press, 1986), ix–x, 9–21. Not all agree with Kishlansky; see Edmund S. Morgan, *Inventing the People.*

2. For a discussion of the role of the disfranchised, especially women, see Kolp and Snyder, "Gender, Property, and Voting Rights."

3. Billings, Selby, and Tate, *Colonial Virginia*, 251–83.

4. Letter, "My Dear Countrymen," signed "No Party Man."

5. Ibid.; Theodorick Bland Sr., July 27, 1765, Campbell, *The Bland Papers*, 1:27.

6. Although no systematic study of Virginia elections during the Revolution has been attempted, limited evidence indicates fewer contests and lower turnout levels than elections of the late colonial period. See Dinkin, *Voting in Revolutionary America, 1776–1789* (1982), 12–13, 104, 124–27.

7. Richard Beeman, *The Old Dominion in the New Nation: 1788–1801* (Lexington: University of Kentucky Press, 1972); Norman K. Risjord, "How the 'Common Man' Voted in Jefferson's Virginia," in *America: The Middle Period, Essays in Honor of Bernard Mayo*, ed. John B. Boles (Charlottesville: University Press of Virginia, 1973), 36–64.

Note on Sources

The most significant secondary literature in the long historiographical debate over Virginia's eighteenth-century political culture appear in the notes to the introduction and will not be repeated here. Instead, this bibliographic essay reviews the most important archival and printed primary sources used to fashion the electoral history of the Old Dominion during the last fifty years of the colonial period. Primary sources contribute to the construction of distinct data bases, which elucidate, first, the provincial political culture and, second, the detailed workings of local political communities.

The provincial data base includes information on all 882 constituency-level elections held in the counties and boroughs of Virginia from the general election of January 1728 to the last by-election in 1775. *The Executive Journals of the Council of Colonial Virginia* (Richmond: Virginia State Library, 1930–67) include the governor-in-council orders for most general election writs and occasionally explain the reasons behind such actions. *The General Assembly of Virginia, July 30, 1619–January 11, 1978: A Bicentennial Register of Members*, compiled by Cynthia Miller Leonard (Richmond: Virginia State Library, 1978), provides a modern compilation of basic election dates and gives the names of all winners. This material should be checked against *The Journals of the House of Burgesses of Virginia*, edited by H. R. McIlwaine and John Kennedy (Richmond: Colonial Press, 1905–15), which gives greater detail on the dates and circumstances of by-elections. Reports of controverted elections appear here as well, often identifying losers and including detailed descriptions of campaign activities and election-day procedures.

Surviving letters, diaries, and newspapers of the period fill in some gaps. The most useful include *The Papers of George Washington, Colonial Series,* 10 volumes, edited by W. W. Abbot (Charlottesville: University Press of Virginia, 1983–95); *The Diaries of George Washington,* 4 volumes, edited by Donald Jackson (Charlottesville: University of Virginia Press, 1976–78); Diary of William Cabell Sr. (Virginia State Library); and Robert Wormeley Carter Diary (College of William and Mary Library). Personal account and commonplace books sometimes report election expenditures and results; see, for example, William Cabell Commonplace Books, 1769–70, 1771 (Virginia Historical Society); and Thomas Jefferson Accounts, 1764–79 (Huntington Library). Reports in the *Virginia Gazette* (Williamsburg, 1736–75) often pinpoint the timing of elections in specific communities and occasionally give other details.

Although the election writ required the local sheriff to report only the names (and not the total votes) of winning candidates, officials used various methods to validate the results of contested elections. In some cases, sheriffs simply divided the assembled freeholders into partisan groups and took a rough head count; in other cases, either local tradition or a candidate's prerogative dictated the use of pollbooks. Privately hired clerks kept the polls for individual candidates, but following the election the county clerk usually transferred these lists to the county deed, record, will, or order books. Pollbooks survive from one hundred, or approximately one-third, of the contested elections of the period and may be found today in microfilm or photostat copies in the county records collections of the Virginia State Library. Local politicians sometimes made their own copies, presumably for future reference; three for Frederick County and five for Fairfax County survive in the George Washington Papers (Library of Congress), for example. These documents provide the most detailed statistical information for comparing elections: the number of candidates running, the total votes received by each, and the number of freeholders participating.

The four community case studies rely on these pollbooks and a host of other local records in which the individual freeholder is the focus of the analysis. The attributes of the economic and political elite for each community can be constructed from county records and parish vestry books as well as from *The Executive Journals of the Council of Colonial Virginia; The Statutes at Large; Being a Collection of All the Laws of Virginia, from the First Session of the Legislature, in the Year 1619,* edited by William W. Hening (Richmond,

1809–23); "Justices of the Peace of Colonial Virginia, 1757–1775," *Bulletin of the Virginia State Library* 14 (1921); *Virginia Colonial Militia, 1651–1776* (Baltimore: Genealogical Publishing Company, 1965); and "Public Officers in Virginia, 1702, 1714," *Virginia Magazine of History and Biography* (1894), 1:368, 375; 2:7–8. Tithable, rental, quitrent, and other documents listing size of landholdings or number of slaves establish the economic elite for each community. The Brock Collection at the Huntington Library contains a significant number of quitrent lists for counties in the Northern Neck.

Each case study also entailed the construction of a data base containing all surviving information on every adult white male resident for the relevant time period. This includes, for example, a data file of 2,084 persons for Fairfax and one of 3,043 persons for Halifax. Pollbooks form the core of each community database and are collated with all available landholding, tax, tithable, militia, and parish listings. Since one of the primary goals of the project is an investigation of the political workings of subcounty units such as parishes, precincts, and neighborhoods, documents with geographic identifiers were critical.

For Accomack, Ralph T. Whitelaw, *Virginia's Eastern Shore: A History of Northampton and Accomack Counties*, 2 volumes (Richmond: Virginia Historical Society, 1951; reprint, Gloucester, Mass.: Peter Smith, 1968), links nearly every land transaction of the colonial period to the original 192 patents and thus provides extremely accurate information on the location of freeholds. For Lancaster County, parish or precinct of residence appears in "Tithables in Lancaster Co., 1716," *William and Mary Quarterly*, 1st ser., 21 (1912): 106–12; Lancaster County Rentals 1748 and 1750 (Brock Collection, Huntington Library); Christ Church Vestry Book 1739–86 (Virginia State Library); and Lancaster County Rental for 1773 (Virginia Historical Society).

Within Fairfax, parish of residence can be identified or surmised from Fairfax County Lists of Tithables for 1749 (Miscellaneous Manuscript Collection, Manuscript Division, Library of Congress); *Minutes of the Vestry, Truro Parish, Virginia, 1732–1785* (Lorton, Va.: Pohick Church, 1974); Fairfax Rentals for 1761, 1764, and 1770, and Loudoun Rentals for 1761 (Brock Collection, Huntington Library); and an untitled but probable 1761 listing by parish in George Washington Papers (Library of Congress). Subparish areas identified in Donald M. Sweig, "The Virginia Nonimportation Association of

1770 and Fairfax County: A Study in Local Participation," *Virginia Magazine of History and Biography* 87 (1979): 316–25, can be applied to actual listings in *The Papers of Thomas Jefferson*, volume 1, edited by Julian P. Boyd (Chapel Hill: University of North Carolina Press, 1950), 43–48.

The location of adult males within the large frontier county of Halifax can be partially determined through listings from its parent county, Lunenburg, and from counties subsequently created from it: A List of Tithables Taken by Cornelius Cargill for the Year 1750, reprinted in *Sunlight on the Southside: Lists of Tithes, Lunenburg County, Virginia, 1748–1783*, compiled by Landon C. Bell (Philadelphia: George S. Ferguson Co., 1931), 129–34; A List of Land Tax and Negro Returned by Robert King for the Year 1755; Pittsylvania County Tithables, 1767; the incomplete List of Tithables, 1771 (Virginia State Library); and A General List of Fees Due to Paul Carrington, Clerk of Halifax County, for the year 1773, January 1774, in Account Book of Paul Carrington, 1773–79 (Virginia Historical Society).

Index

trends in, competition, 62–66
Truro Parish, 133, 144, 147, 154, 159;
  divided, 149, 155; division petition, 155; vestry dissolution petition, 155; vestry elections, 155,
  156
Tucker, Robert, Jr., 72
Tunstall, Thomas, 175, 177, 178
turnout, 37, 49–58, 66, 102, 104, 127,
  159, 163, 178, 185, 186, 188, 196,
  197, 198; community involvement
  and, 55; geographical factors and,
  55; landowners, 51; for multiple
  election, 53, 55, 180, 184, 185; and
  tenants, 51, 210n. 43; trends, 52;
  wealth and, 56, 57, 196
Two-Penny Act, 7

Veal, Bond, 141, 145, 146
Veale, George, 72
vestries, 178, 194; bill to dissolve,
  89, 91; bill to require elections of,
  100; church construction, 118;
  defined, 86; elections, 86, 108, 155,
  169; inoperative, 214n. 3; membership controversy, 84; petition to
  dissolve, 94, 118
vestrymen, 142, 144, 154, 155, 191,
  192, 193; turnout, 56; wealth of,
  119, 139, 223n. 7
Virginia law code revision, and Board
  of Trade, 3
Virginia Gazette, 27, 78, 83, 108, 114
voters: choice at elections, 5, 9;
  consistency over time, 176, 185,
  197; crucial to political process, 6;
  Fairfax County, 136, 164; frequent,
  53, 54, 153, 163, 180, 184, 189;
  Halifax County, 168; irregular, 53,
  176, 177, 180, 184, 188; Lancaster
  County, 127; nonresident, 34;
  parish loyalties, 152, 157, 158,
  159; participation and wealth,
  56; perceptions, 146, 197, 198;
  plumpers, 158, 176, 177, 180, 183;
  precinct loyalties, 128, 129, 131,
  132; qualifications, 33, 70, 175;

wealth and voting behavior, 131,
  132. See also turnout
voting procedures, 36, 179, 182, 236

Wade, Hampton, 174, 175, 177, 178
Wade, Robert, Jr., 174
Wade, Robert, Sr., 170
Wager, William, 70
Wallace, James, 71
Waller, William, 71
Wallop, John, 98, 99
Warwick County, competition in, 72
Washington, Augustine, 34, 67
Washington, Edward, 159
Washington, George, 19, 27, 51, 133,
  151, 155, 156, 157, 158, 160, 161,
  162, 189; gentry support for, 26;
  and treating, 31; uncontested elec-
  tion of, 66
Washington, Lawrence, 141, 144,
  145, 146, 147, 148, 149
Watkins, George, 176, 177, 178, 187
Watkins, Micajah, 187
wealth: average farm size, 126; pre-
  cinct voting and, 132. See also
  candidates; gentry; officeholders;
  voters
weather, 159, 186
West, Charles, 103, 104, 105
West, Hugh, 147, 149, 150
West, John, 19, 27, 150, 151, 153–57,
  159, 160–62
West, John, Jr., 151, 162
Westmoreland County, 35, 133;
  competition in, 67; interest, 28;
  sheriff, 34
Westwood, William, 70
Westwood, Worlich, 71
William and Mary, College of, 60,
  119; competition in, 77; franchise,
  38
Williamsburg, 15, 158, 161, 181, 191;
  as center of provincial politics,
  192, 195; competition in, 77; electorate, 39; franchise, 38
Wilson, John, 68, 72
winners: career path, 143; divided

Library of Congress Cataloging-in-Publication Data

Kolp, John Gilman, 1943–
    Gentlemen and freeholders : electoral politics in colonial
Virginia / John Gilman Kolp.
        p.   cm. — (Early America)
    Includes bibliographical references and index.
    ISBN 0-8018-5843-7 (alk. paper)
    1. Virginia—Politics and government—To 1775.   2. Political
culture—Virginia—History—18th century.   3. Elections—Virginia—
History—18th century.   I. Title   II. Series.
F229.K75   1998
324.9755'02—dc21   97-49956
                                                                  CIP